Excel Macro Library

Mary V. Campbell

Que™ Corporation
Indianapolis, Indiana

Library of Congress Catalog No.: 85-638-78
ISBN 0-88022-225-5

90 89 88 87 86   8 7 6 5 4 3 2 1

Interpretation of the printing code: the rightmost double-digit number is the year of the book's printing; the rightmost single-digit number, the number of the book's printing. For example, a printing code
of 87-4 shows that the fourth printing of the book occurred in 1987.

Dedication

To David and Keith

Product Director
David P. Ewing

Editorial Director
David F. Noble, Ph.D.

Managing Editor
Gregory Croy

Editors
Kathie-Jo Arnoff
Jeannine Freudenberger, M.A.
Pamela Fullerton
Virginia Noble, M.L.S.

Technical Editor
Rebecca Kenyon, Ph.D.

About the Author

Mary V. Campbell

Mary V. Campbell is president of Campbell & Associates, a consulting firm in Grand Rapids, Michigan. The firm serves Fortune 1000 companies by providing training and custom templates for microcomputer software products. A frequent speaker at seminars and conferences, Ms. Campbell has more than 20 years of experience in the computer field. She held senior management positions in several corporations before starting her own firm. She earned her B.S. and M.B.A. degrees from Indiana University. Ms. Campbell, author of Que's *Using Excel*, has written articles for a number of major computer magazines including *Absolute Reference*, the *CPA Journal*, *LOTUS* magazine, and *IBM PC Update*.

Composed by Que Corporation in
Garamond

Cover designed by
Listenberger Design Associates

Table of Contents

6 Creating Macros for the Chart Environment 231

7 Automating Applications 265

Glossary of Macro Functions

Trademark
Acknowledgments

Que Corporation has made every effort to supply trademark information about company names, products, and services mentioned in this book. Trademarks indicated below were derived from various sources. Que Corporation cannot attest to the accuracy of this information.

1-2-3, Lotus, and Symphony, are registered trademarks of Lotus Development Corporation.

dBASE III is a registered trademark of Ashton-Tate Company.

IBM is a registered trademark of International Business Machines Corporation.

ImageWriter and LaserWriter are trademarks of Apple Computer, Inc.

Macintosh is a trademark of McIntosh Laboratory, Inc., licensed to Apple Computer, Inc., and is used with its express permission.

Microsoft is a registered trademark of Microsoft Corporation.

Paradox is a trademark of Ansa Corporation.

WordPerfect is a trademark of Satellite Software International.

Conventions Used in This Book

A number of conventions are used in *Excel Macro Library* to help you better understand the book.

1. When you are not working in macro mode, Excel's menu options appear with an initial capital letter followed by lowercase letters. For example, you could select Define Name from the Formula menu.

2. The names of Excel's macro functions appear in all capital letters both in the text and in the screen illustrations. For example, DEFINE.NAME( ) AND SELECT( ) appear in all capital letters.

3. When the arguments of Excel's macro functions are referred to, they appear in italic. For example, when the syntax of a function is discussed, such as OPEN(document,update), subsequent references to *document* and *update* are shown in italic.

4. Within screen illustrations, certain elements appear in upper- and lowercase letters. In general, these include names of macros, macro sheet names, subroutine labels, worksheet names, prompts, alert messages, user-created menus, and comments.

5. Some keyboard commands are issued by pressing one or more of the special keys (Command [⌘], Shift, or Option) and a letter or symbol key such as m or =. For example, Option-Command-m means that you press and hold down the Option and Command keys then press m. Pressing the special key(s) first is important; if you press the letter key first, the letter or other character is entered in the active cell of the worksheet.

Introduction

Excel Macro Library is designed to help Microsoft® Excel users start using macros in a minimum amount of time. No matter what your level of expertise with Excel, you can benefit from the ready-to-use macros presented in this book. Moreover, the tips and techniques described here can help you create macros quickly and efficiently.

If you are an experienced Excel user, you probably have developed some sophisticated applications, and with Excel macros, you can make those applications easier to use. In fact, you may be able to use macros to delegate tasks such as data entry to other operators.

If you are a new Excel user, you may feel intimidated by what you have heard about macros. Although macros *can* be as complicated as computer programs, you do not have to build complex macros in order to tap the power of Excel's Macro Command Language. Simple macros can handle many tasks. *Excel Macro Library* will show you that Excel's macros are easier to understand and use than those in other software packages. With the Recorder function, you even can make Excel enter macros for you. By using the macros in this book, you can ensure that your first attempts at using macros are successful.

The Library of Excel Macros

Excel Macro Library contains a collection of macros that can help you, in turn, build a library of your own. This collection of macros, accumulated during the author's work as a consultant, supports tasks in each of the Excel environments. Each macro was created originally either with Excel or another macro language in order to solve a specific business need. Although many of the macros are presented as solutions to a specific business problem, the macros are not oriented toward a particular industry segment.

The basic steps involved in creating macros are described early in the book. These early chapters provide a framework for creating the specific types of macros (function and command macros) presented in subsequent chapters. Because Excel's function macro capability is unique, an entire chapter is devoted to a wide range of function macros. In later chapters, you will find macro applications that apply specifically to Excel's data management and chart environments, as well as some more complex applications.

Who Should Use This Book?

Excel Macro Library is designed for all Excel users. Whether you are experienced or not, you will find that this book enables you to extend Excel's capabilities by using macro commands. You will find the information you need in order to start using macros immediately in your work.

If you are an experienced user, you can expand your own macro library significantly with the collection of macros in this book. You also can improve your own macros by using the tips and techniques for constructing macros. In addition, you probably will be interested in learning about such sophisticated models as menu macros.

If you are a beginning user, you will find that this book contains all the basics. *Excel Macro Library* defines Excel macros and describes each of Excel's macro commands. You will learn each of the steps necessary to create and access your own macros. By starting with solid groundwork on the essentials, you will find yourself quickly moving on to building more complex macros.

About This Book

Chapter 1 defines macros and describes the "building blocks" needed to create them. You will learn about Excel's different macro options and the contribution each can make to your use of the package. You also will learn what macro sheets are and how to organize them for maximum efficiency.

Chapter 2 focuses on the importance of planning. You will learn how building shells and using straight-line code can help you make your macros work correctly. Function macros and command macros are described separately, and clear guidelines for creating each type of macro are provided.

Chapter 3 describes a variety of function macros. You will examine a step-by-step approach to creating macros. You can use this approach either to duplicate the macros presented or to build similar macros.

Chapter 4 presents numerous command macros that automate simple worksheet tasks such as formatting. Also presented are more sophisticated macros for applications such as creating menus.

Chapter 5 concentrates on data management applications for macros. The information in this chapter can help you automate menu-driven tasks such as sorting records. The chapter also goes beyond the use of menu commands. For example, you will learn techniques for adding a record to an existing file and making Excel adjust the database range for you automatically.

Chapter 6 explains how to use macros to create charts. You will learn to automate commonly used chart features as well as perform more complex tasks such as creating a timed slide show.

Chapter 7 takes a look at the use of macros in integrated, complex applications. You will see how to use macros to automate four systems, including personnel and budget consolidation systems. After mastering the concepts in this chapter, you will be able to develop full-scale applications that even novice Excel users can use successfully.

The appendix contains a comprehensive list of Excel's macro commands along with descriptions of each command. As you create your own macros, you can refer to this valuable reference source.

What This Book Can Do For You

Excel Macro Library presents a timesaving approach to mastering macros. Rather than create macros with a trial-and-error-based method, you can use this book to learn all the important rules and procedures for the efficient creation of macros.

In addition to saving you time, this book helps you exploit the full power of Excel. Macros are a strong feature of the software package, and you are not getting all you can out of Excel until you master macros.

The macros in this volume have been tested, so you do not have to worry about whether they work. (All you have to do is enter them correctly.) After you enter a macro, you can use it immediately.

How To Use This Book

For new users, the first two chapters in *Excel Macro Library* are essential because they explain the basics involved in creating and using macros. After studying these first chapters, novices will want to read the rest of the chapters in sequence, moving from simpler to more complex macros.

Experienced users also may want to read the first two chapters in order to pick up a few pointers on creating successful macros quickly. If you are an experienced user and you are anxious to solve an immediate problem, you may want to browse through the macros in the various chapters. However, even if you initially use this book to obtain an immediate solution to a problem, you should return for a close-up look at each chapter. A careful reading will help ensure that you expand your macro expertise to its fullest potential.

As you review the macros, you may want to copy some of them onto a macro sheet immediately. Other macros you may want to revise slightly. No matter what you choose to do, you will find this macro library to be a valuable resource as you explore Excel's macro capability.

1

Macro Basics

If you have never created an Excel macro, you are not using the full power of Excel. Whether you are working with data management, charts, or worksheets, macros can make your tasks much easier. This chapter puts Excel's macro capabilities into perspective by explaining what macros are, what they can do, and what macro support other software packages provide.

Then the chapter takes a closer look at the two kinds of Excel macros: command macros and function macros. You will learn about the Recorder, which makes creating macros easy, and some of the logical structures that you can borrow from programming techniques to organize your macro instructions. The last section of this chapter focuses on macro sheets and the role they play in macro storage and execution.

If you already are creating your own macros, you might want to review the "Macro Structure" section. Then you can move directly to Chapter 2, which covers macro success strategies.

What Are Macros?

Macros are sequences of commands that you store, then execute whenever you want. Because macros are stored instructions, they are very useful for tasks that you perform frequently. For example, you can create a simple macro that formats a column of numbers as currency. To execute the macro, all you have to do is press one key. Without the macro, you have to drag down the Format menu to select the appropriate number, then scroll through the Format options until you find the one you want.

You also can create more sophisticated macros—for instance, one that requests the operator to enter a Social Security number. The macro can check the number's validity as well as request the operator to enter other fields (such as employee name and address) and check their validity. Moreover, you can execute this macro with one keystroke sequence.

Macros are also ideal for automating complete applications. All users have to know is what keys to press in order to execute the macros.

The level of sophistication in a macro depends on your specific needs and the time you are willing to spend developing the macro. You can start with simple macros and work up to more complex models. Before you begin building them, however, you must learn the rules and procedures involved in the creation process.

The History of Macros

Because you are about to spend a considerable amount of time working with Excel macros, you may be interested in knowing a little bit about their history. Macros have been around for a long time. In the early seventies, mainframe programmers, using the CICS package from IBM® to design on-line systems, used macro-level code in programming in order to speed up the system implementation process. The macros in these CICS programs expanded into a series of instructions that were executed every time a program was run.

The use of macro instructions shortened development time for new applications. CICS programmers wrote macro code for tasks that had to be performed repeatedly and used it whenever necessary. For example, programmers may have used a macro to read or write information to a file rather than use the detailed program lines that the task would have required.

The use of macros on microcomputers is much more recent. 1-2-3® was one of the first packages to support macros. In the early releases (1 and 1A) of 1-2-3, that support was somewhat limited. The primary function of macros was to duplicate menu options, thereby saving keystrokes. Some of the instructions required to build sophisticated programs were available, but experienced programmers found the macro language commands lacking in several areas.

When Lotus® introduced Symphony® and 1-2-3 Release 2, these deficiencies had been eliminated. The new macro commands enabled programmers to duplicate keystrokes and also to construct all the logical structures found in the programming environment. Users now can write complete programs in Symphony's and 1-2-3's macro command languages.

Macro commands are not unique to spreadsheets and are now available in some database packages and with other software. Ashton-Tate's dBASE III® and Ansa's Paradox™ are but two examples of packages with sophisticated macro command languages. Even word-processing packages are beginning to provide macro capabilities—for example, Release 4.1 of WordPerfect™.

Part of the rush to add macro features has to do with the realization on the part of software developers that people with various levels of expertise use the packages. Experienced users can develop macros to expedite their work and also create macros that increase the productivity of other less experienced users.

Macros are becoming increasingly flexible and sophisticated. Each new macro command language surpasses its predecessors in terms of capabilities. You will see that Excel follows this trend, providing options not available at this time in any other spreadsheet package.

The Unique Features of Excel Macros

Excel macros have the same general capabilities as macros in other software packages—and then some. With Excel's Macro Command Language, users can duplicate menu options and programming structures. In this sense, Excel's macro capability is similar to that of other packages.

However, Excel's comprehensive set of macro commands has an edge over others because, frequently, you can choose from among several solutions. For example, suppose that you want to format a range of cells. You can use a defined option like DATE; you can offer the operator unlimited choices by using the question-mark (?) option, as with FORMAT.NUMBER?( ); or you can build a menu that offers a limited set of choices. Excel's macro commands are also much easier to remember because they are complete English words that, in many cases, are identical to menu options.

Excel also has other impressive features. For example, the built-in macro generator eliminates much of the drudgery involved in creating macros, reducing the time required to create sophisticated macros. And function macros, a new kind of macro not available in other spreadsheet packages, enable users to create their own functions in order to perform complex calculations.

With Excel, you can design macros that create windows, open files on a disk, create charts, and automate entire applications. Macro instructions can duplicate Excel's menu selections or carry out special commands, such as accepting keyboard input.

Excel has two kinds of macros—command macros and function macros—each of which has its own unique set of features and capabilities. The following sections take a brief look at the differences between these macros and their applications. Chapters 3 through 7 contain many examples of macros that can make you more productive. In Chapter 3, you will find a variety of applications for function macros; they also are scattered throughout other chapters. The primary focus of Chapters 4 through 7 is on applications for command macros.

Command Macros:
What They Can Do

Command macros are a series of instructions. They can be keyboard alternatives—that is, duplicate menu options—or act as a programming language, with iterative processing, logical condition checks, self-created menu options, and other capabilities of languages such as BASIC and COBOL. In both cases, you store functions within cells in a macro sheet, then you execute those functions whenever you want.

To write command macros, you use the Macro Command Language. This special set of macro commands is unlike the formula capabilities you have encountered up to this point. In one sense, many of the commands will be somewhat familiar to you because they access menu commands; but they do so from within the macro.

You can enter macro instructions from the keyboard, or, if you are duplicating menu commands, you can use the Recorder to make Excel enter the macro instructions for you.

After you begin to get an idea of the things you want to do with Excel, you will discover that using macros to perform certain tasks can save you a great deal of time. For example, you can use command macros to do the following:

1. Perform repetitive functions such as formatting

2. Correct errors. People tend to be frustrated by errors and therefore become prone to making additional mistakes. The error can be as simple as incorrect alignment of a column of labels or as complicated as names out of order in a column (where you need to invert first and last names for sorting records). In any case, corrections should be as easy to make as the mistakes were.

3. Automate selections in applications designed for people who aren't Excel experts and who may have minimal knowledge of the package. For example, you can create a macro that references information in an external worksheet and creates a consolidated budget report. To produce an accurate report, the operator needs neither a knowledge of Excel nor budgeting; all the operator has to do is press two keys.

Command Macros as Keyboard Alternatives

Formatting cells as currency, sorting a database, opening a new worksheet file, and creating a window are all tasks that you can handle easily with keyboard commands. If you perform these tasks repeatedly, however, using a macro can be a shortcut. All you have to do is take a little time to enter the keystrokes in the macro. The result is a routine that you can execute hundreds of times simply by pressing a few keys. For example, figure 1.1 shows a command macro that could be used as a keyboard alternative for formatting cells as currency.

Keyboard alternative macros can save experienced users significant amounts of time. But these macros can help inexperienced users even more because the macros "remember" and execute sequences of instructions that novices may not have mastered. For example, with keyboard macros, worksheet designers can delegate worksheet update tasks to individuals who are less familiar with Excel. Worksheet designers will be interrupted with fewer questions and will feel more comfortable about the integrity of the updated worksheet, because macros allow a more controlled access to data than use of menu options.

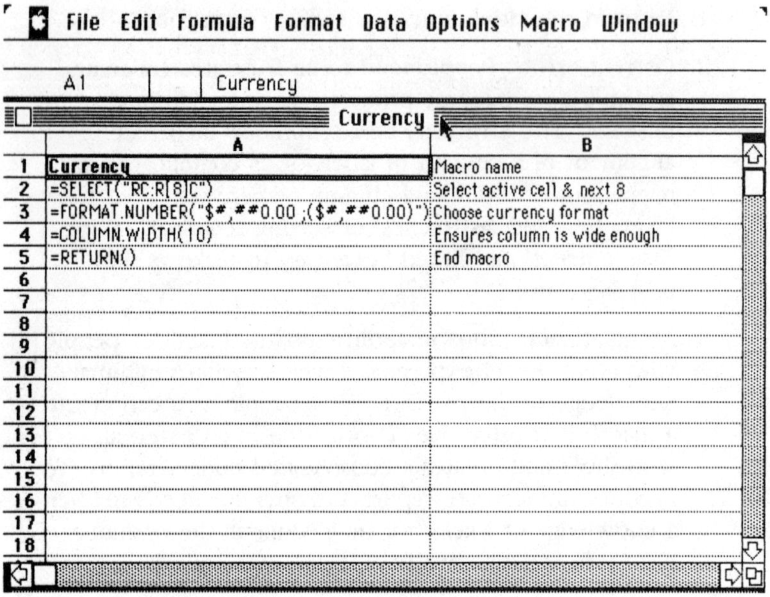

Fig. 1.1. A command macro used as a keyboard alternative.

Command Macros as a Programming Language

In addition to duplicating menu options, a macro can loop, perform logical condition tests, and branch to subroutines. These are all options that programmers take for granted when automating business applications, and you will want to have these capabilities at your disposal when you build sophisticated macros. What if you want to change the width of every third column on your worksheet? Or what if you want a series of commands to be executed only in the presence of an exception condition? With the menu commands, you cannot specify these options. To provide a truly flexible and full-function macro language, Microsoft added commands that handle these tasks to Excel's Macro Command Language.

Excel's Macro Command Language goes well beyond duplication of menu commands. The Macro Command Language has all the components of a programming language, including conditional statements, looping, and branching instructions (see fig. 1.2). Some of the earlier spreadsheet macro functions did not provide the full range of programming constructs needed to develop these automated applications. Excel's commands are sophisticated enough to require some experience before you realize their full functionality. With a little practice, you will begin thinking of macros as an integral part of Excel's command structure and using them in all kinds of situations.

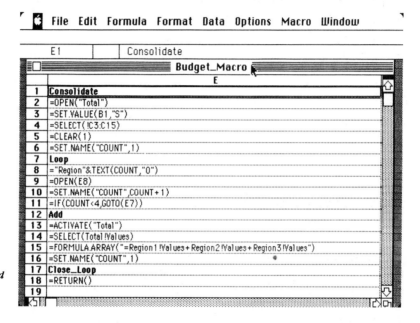

Fig. 1.2. A command macro used as a programming language alternative.

Function Macros: What They Can Do

Function macros, which are similar to Excel's built-in functions, are an exciting new Excel feature. A *function macro* works like a subroutine or instruction set that takes data, manipulates it according to a preestablished formula, and returns the result of the formula's calculations. Function macro instructions will look familiar to you because they are similar to worksheet formulas (see fig. 1.3).

You use function macros to create your own functions. The functions you create have capabilities similar to Excel's built-in functions, such as SUM, AVERAGE, and NPV. You know that to use Excel's built-in functions, you enter the function and its arguments in a worksheet cell—for example, =SUM(R4:R16). Then Excel executes the function.

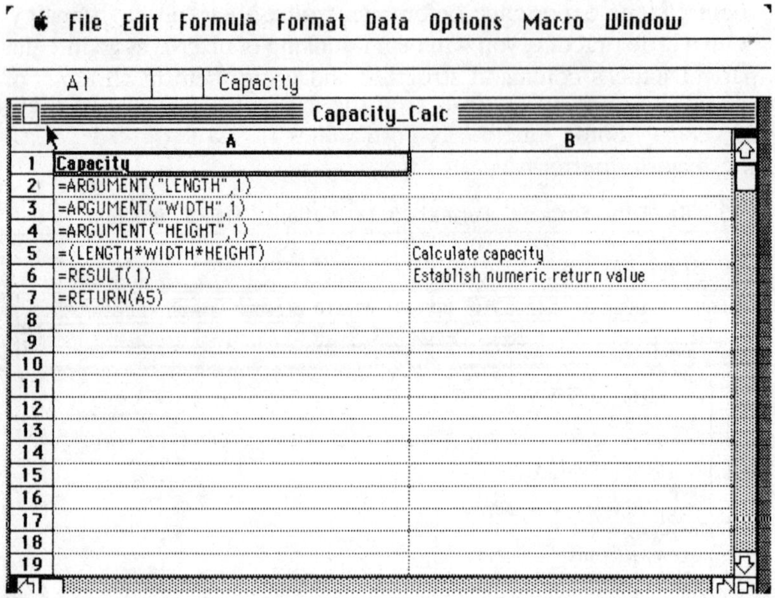

 File Edit Formula Format Data Options Macro Window

| A1 | | Capacity | |

Capacity_Calc

	A	B
1	**Capacity**	
2	=ARGUMENT("LENGTH",1)	
3	=ARGUMENT("WIDTH",1)	
4	=ARGUMENT("HEIGHT",1)	
5	=(LENGTH*WIDTH*HEIGHT)	Calculate capacity
6	=RESULT(1)	Establish numeric return value
7	=RETURN(A5)	
8		
9		
10		
11		
12		
13		
14		
15		
16		
17		
18		
19		

Fig. 1.3. A function macro.

You use function macros in this same way. For instance, suppose that you create a function called PURCHASE, which computes purchase discounts, and you put the function and its arguments in a cell. If you assume that the arguments are the total purchase (stored in A11) and the customer type (stored in B11), you might find the following entry in cell D11:

=PURCHASE(A11,B11)

You can call any of your custom functions from formulas, just as you do with Excel's built-in functions. You use formulas to enter function macros in a macro sheet, just like you do with command macros. You can't use the Recorder to type the entries because you can't use keyboard commands to make the entries.

The Building Blocks

To build macros, you have to follow Excel's established syntax. This section takes a look at the basic structure of command macros and function macros.

Excel's Macro Command Language

Excel's Macro Command Language is a special set of functions designed for creating macros. (See the appendix for a list of these functions.) Some functions return values to the macro sheet, but the majority perform actions that you have been using the menus to accomplish: copying, pasting, defining names, formatting, and so forth.

By nesting functions, you can develop sophisticated structured macros that are complete applications. These activities can be as extensive as consolidating a budget for five company divisions and printing the reports, or as simple as updating monthly interest-rate figures and printing a new table. Such macros let inexperienced Excel users accomplish sophisticated tasks without having to remember Excel commands.

The Basic Components of Function Macros

Excel's function macros can perform a variety of calculations, but you must follow specific syntax rules when you create the macros. For example, you precede each formula in a macro with an equal sign.

Function macros have ARGUMENT functions, RETURN functions, formulas, and RESULT functions (if you want to specify the type of value to be returned). Formulas in function macros can use special macro functions such as SET.VALUE. The following sections take a look at each component of function macros.

The ARGUMENT Statement

The ARGUMENT statement defines a name for a value that is passed to a function macro. Each value passed to the macro must be represented by an ARGUMENT statement in the macro. The ARGUMENT statement takes one of the following formats:

    =ARGUMENT(name,type)

    =ARGUMENT(name,type,ref)

In the first format, *name* specifies a name for the value being passed to the macro, and *type* indicates the kind of data that Excel will accept for the value. For *type*, the number 1 specifies numeric data; 2, text; 4, logical; 8, reference; 16, error; and 64, array. If the correct type of value is not passed to the function, and Excel cannot convert the value, #VALUE! is returned, and the macro does not execute.

In the second format, the value stored in the cell that *ref* specifies is the value of the argument passed to the macro. Using the *ref* argument enables you to refer by name to variables in other formulas in the macro.

The *name* in the ARGUMENT statement refers to the cell address included in the function. For example, in the following ARGUMENT statement, the value passed to the function is stored in cell B18 and referenced by the name SALES. SALES is the variable name that refers to the contents of B18. The *type* is 1, so only numeric data is acceptable. The statement would be entered exactly as shown here:

    =ARGUMENT("SALES",1,B18)

Specifying a *name* actually is optional. However, even though the ARGUMENT function will operate properly without this argument, its use is recommended. If you *do* use names, make sure that each ARGUMENT function in a macro has a unique name. If you use a name more than once, the second occurrence will wipe out the *type* and *ref* for the first occurrence.

To make your macros self-documenting, choose names that "point" to the data that the macros refer to. For instance, argument names such as SALES, DISCOUNT, and INTEREST are more meaningful than S, D, and N.

Default Arguments

Some functions have optional arguments, and this can cause problems. If an argument value is missing, Excel uses #N/A, which causes all the formulas using this value to take on the error value #N/A rather than the results you would like to see.

To solve this problem, you can spend a little time setting up default values for one or more arguments. You can build into your macros a check for the value #N/A; if it occurs, you can have the macro convert that variable's value to the default setting. For instance, the macro in figure 1.4 establishes a default value of 1 if a value is not provided.

```
        File   Edit   Formula   Format   Data   Options   Macro   Window
```

	A1	Area	

Areamacro

	A	B
1	**Area**	
2	=ARGUMENT("LENGTH",1)	
3	=ARGUMENT("WIDTH",1)	
4	=IF(NOT(LENGTH=0),GOTO(A6))	Check to see whether entry has been made
5	=SET.NAME("LENGTH",1)	Set default to 1
6	=IF(NOT(WIDTH=0),GOTO(A8))	Check to see whether entry has been made
7	=SET.NAME("WIDTH",1)	Set default to 1
8	=(LENGTH*WIDTH)	Calculate area
9	=RETURN(A8)	
10		
11		
12		
13		
14		
15		
16		
17		
18		
19		
20		

Fig. 1.4. A default value established for a macro argument.

The RESULT Statement

The RESULT statement can screen result types for variables returned by a function macro. The syntax for RESULT is

=RESULT(type)

To specify the function's *type*, you use the same argument values described in the section on the ARGUMENT statement. For instance, to specify a numeric result, you enter

=RESULT(1)

If the result is not the correct type, and Excel cannot convert the result, the macro returns #VALUE!. Specifying a *type* with the RESULT statement ensures that you have valid numeric data to use in other calculations. Or if you need a cell address to complete a range, specifying the correct *type* can ensure that you have a cell reference.

If you don't want to restrict the type of result returned, don't use a RESULT statement in your macro. By not using RESULT, you are specifying that a number, text, or logical value is an acceptable result.

The RETURN Statement

Every function macro must include a RETURN statement. This state-ment returns the calculated value to the worksheet that contains the reference to the function. The RETURN function has three forms of syntax:

=RETURN(cell address)

=RETURN(range)

=RETURN(condition,cell address 1,cell address 2)

The first format is typical because most function macros compute the results for a single cell. The values calculated for the return value take into account all the conditions pertaining to the calcu-lation and calculate one final result.

You use the second format to send an array of values back to the worksheet that included a reference to the function. Because a single worksheet cell can store only one result, you must select, in advance, a range of cells in the original worksheet to store the array of results. You also need to include a RESULT function that specifies a *type* of 64 (arrays).

You use the last format to test the value of a condition and return a value. Depending on the outcome of the condition test, the func-tion returns one of two values stored in two different cell addresses.

If you include a RESULT statement in a function macro, you must ensure that the value stored in the cell address being returned meets the criteria for a valid RETURN value, as established in the RESULT statement. For a macro to return a cell reference, error value, or array, the macro must contain a RESULT statement that specifies the correct *type*. If you do not use a RESULT statement in a function macro, the result *type* is assumed to be 7. That is, the macro can return a number, text, or logical value.

A Sample Macro Stored in a Worksheet

Figure 1.5 shows a typical function macro stored in a macro sheet. Although entering macro functions hasn't been discussed, for now, assume that the macro instructions were typed as shown and that the macro was named appropriately so that it could be executed. First, you will examine the instructions in this macro, then you will learn how to access it from a worksheet.

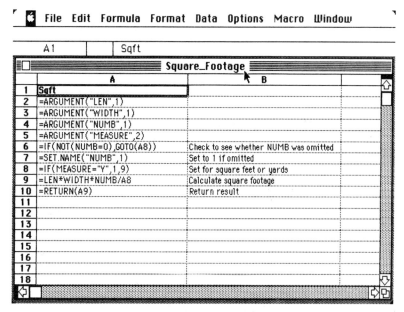

File Edit Formula Format Data Options Macro Window

| A1 | | Sqft |

Square_Footage

	A	B
1	**Sqft**	
2	=ARGUMENT("LEN",1)	
3	=ARGUMENT("WIDTH",1)	
4	=ARGUMENT("NUMB",1)	
5	=ARGUMENT("MEASURE",2)	
6	=IF(NOT(NUMB=0),GOTO(A8))	Check to see whether NUMB was omitted
7	=SET.NAME("NUMB",1)	Set to 1 if omitted
8	=IF(MEASURE="Y",1,9)	Set for square feet or yards
9	=LEN*WIDTH*NUMB/A8	Calculate square footage
10	=RETURN(A9)	Return result
11		
12		
13		
14		
15		
16		
17		
18		

Fig. 1.5. A function macro that calculates square footage.

This macro processes a flooring order, using the room dimensions you enter. The macro, which calculates square feet, can process calculations for one room or many. You can modify this sample macro for many kinds of applications, such as calculating shipping costs, purchase discounts, or project costs.

The first three macro instructions set up the length, width, and number of rooms. These instructions specify that the variables should be numeric (a *type* of 1). The variable NUMB indicates the number of rooms. If NUMB is blank, the instruction in A7 substitutes a 1. A fourth variable, MEASURE, is a text variable that indicates whether the final dimensions are in feet or yards. A value of Y indicates yards, and any other value is assumed to be feet. If the unit of measure is yards, the primary calculation in A9 is divided by nine because one square yard contains nine square feet.

You do not execute a function macro from a macro sheet. Function macros are given names, and these names are used in worksheet formulas just like built-in functions are. Excel will calculate the macro and return the result to the worksheet.

For a built-in function, you type an equal sign, the function name, and (in parentheses) the function arguments. For example, you could store SUM in a cell as

=SUM(B2:B10)

You use the same format when you enter a function macro, except that you type the name of the macro sheet before the function name—for instance

=Square_Footage!Sqft(B2,C2,D2,E2)

Figure 1.6 shows a worksheet cell that contains a reference to the macro shown in figure 1.5. Notice the calculated result displayed in cell F2, where the function macro reference was entered.

You can recreate this example by entering the constants shown in columns A through E. After you enter the label in column F, you enter an equal sign and the macro sheet and function macro names followed by an opening parenthesis. Next, you use the mouse to select cells B2, C2, D2, and E2. Finally, you close the parentheses and press Return. You can copy this formula down column F for the other entries.

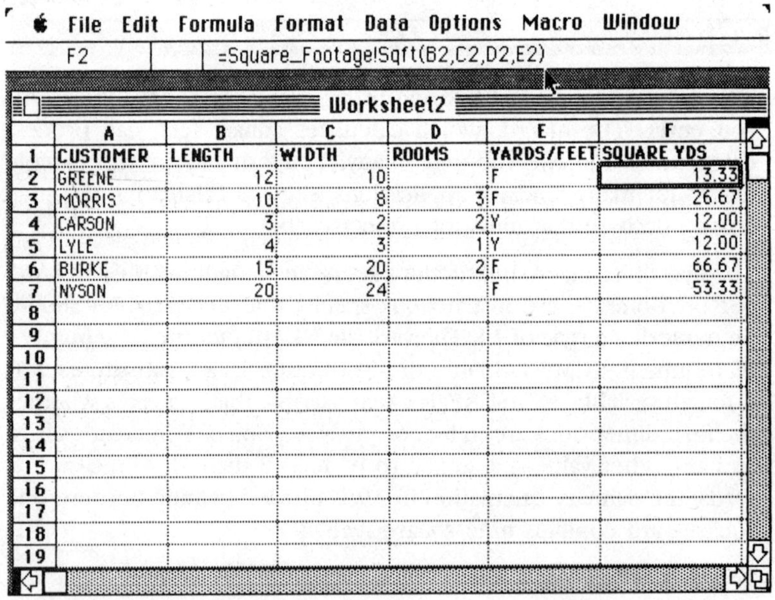

	A	B	C	D	E	F
	CUSTOMER	LENGTH	WIDTH	ROOMS	YARDS/FEET	SQUARE YDS
2	GREENE	12	10		F	13.33
3	MORRIS	10	8	3	F	26.67
4	CARSON	3	2	2	Y	12.00
5	LYLE	4	3	1	Y	12.00
6	BURKE	15	20	2	F	66.67
7	NYSON	20	24		F	53.33

Cell reference: F2 = Square_Footage!Sqft(B2,C2,D2,E2)

Menu: File Edit Formula Format Data Options Macro Window

Window: Worksheet2

Fig. 1.6. A worksheet that uses a function macro.

The Basic Components of Command Macros

Command macros are more free-form in their construction than function macros. Basically, command macros consist of functions that you want to perform. A RETURN( ) statement at the end of a macro indicates its end.

As you do with function macros, you place the command macro's name in the first cell. To ensure that Excel treats the name as a comment, do not precede the name with an equal sign. The name you enter on your macro sheet serves to document the macro. However, you still must use Define Name from the Formula menu to name the macro before you execute it.

Functions

Following the macro's name, you list the macro's main components: the Excel functions. (See the appendix for a list of them, including built-in functions such as the logical IF.) When you enter a function in a cell, you always precede the function with an equal sign. In other words, you enter each function as a formula, which is evaluated when the macro runs.

Arguments

Many of Excel's functions have corresponding menu commands. With most of these functions, you can enter *arguments*—specific values for the responses that would have been requested in a dialog box if you had issued the same command from a menu. By putting these values in the macro, you can automate an operation completely without requesting any operator response.

The disadvantage to this approach is that the macro is not flexible and works only with the values established in the macro. If you use the macro function with the syntax that follows, you must specify values for each of the arguments.

   =DEFINE.NAME(name,refers to,type,key)

You can use an alternate form of the DEFINE.NAME function:

   =DEFINE.NAME?( )

In this format, a question mark (?) precedes the parenthesis following the function name. The question mark causes the dialog box for the command's menu to appear on the screen and enables the operator to type responses in the box. You can use this option only with functions that parallel menu options. The result of this approach is increased flexibility for the operator, but diminished control on the part of the macro creator. (The macro creator cannot control which options are offered to the operator; all of Excel's menu options appear in the dialog box.)

Suggestions for Using Command Macros

Sometimes you will want to format a row, column, or range of cells as currency, percentages, or some other format. You can create a command macro to handle formatting. For example, the macro at the bottom of figure 1.7 formats a column of nine cells as currency. The SELECT statement in cell A2 specifies the cells to be formatted, and the formula in cell A3 formats them.

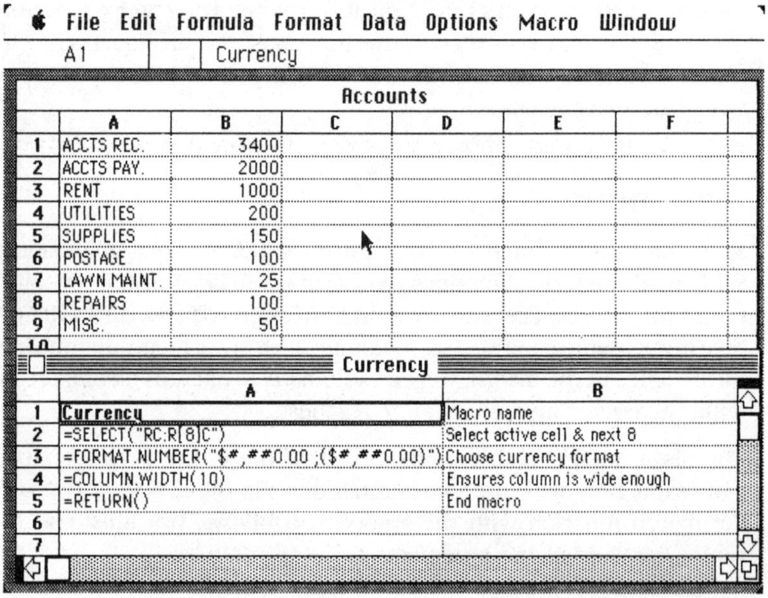

Fig. 1.7. Original worksheet cells and formatting macro.

This macro works on a column of numbers, as shown in figure 1.8. Specialized macros like this one are called *closed macros* because their execution follows a closed, unchanging path. If you create this particular closed macro, the next time you have to format a row of 10 cells or a rectangle of 8 cells, you must create new macros.

You can make the macro more versatile by making it *open-ended*. To do so, you have to modify the macro so that, whenever you execute it, you can change the cells you want to format. You ac-

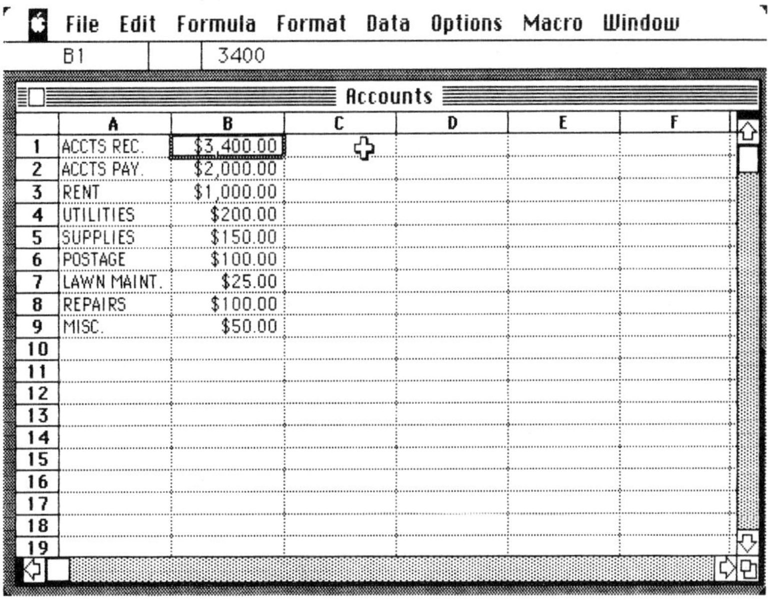

Fig. 1.8. Worksheet cells formatted as currency.

complish this task by adding an INPUT statement to the macro. When you execute the macro, the beginning of the range is the active cell. Each time you run the macro, the INPUT statement lets you specify the end of the range.

Figure 1.9 shows the modified macro. Cell A2 uses the active cell as the beginning of the range and creates an Input box that prompts the operator for the end of the range (see fig. 1.10). Notice that the INPUT statement specifies a *type* of 8, indicating that only a cell reference will be accepted in response to the prompt. You need to specify INPUT types in your macros to ensure that you get the type of data you want. With the Input box displayed, the operator selects the last cell to be formatted. Sometimes, the Input box may cover the cell you want to select; in this case, you can drag the Input box off to the side in the same way that you move any window. Figure 1.11 shows the results of macro execution.

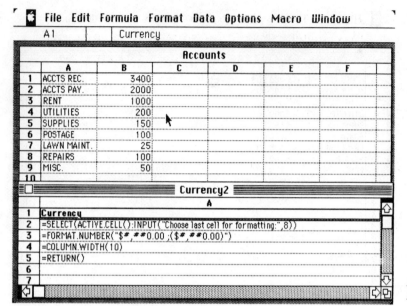

Fig. 1.9. Macro modified with INPUT statement.

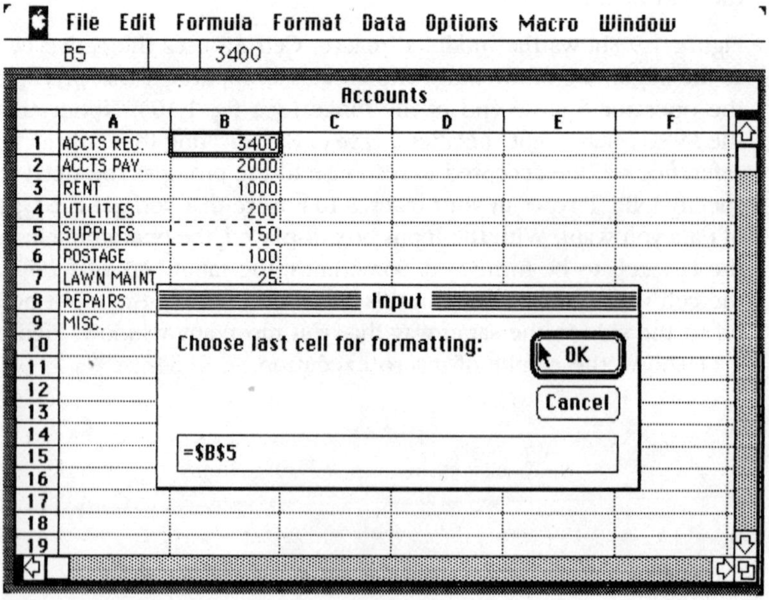

Fig. 1.10. Input box for operator selection.

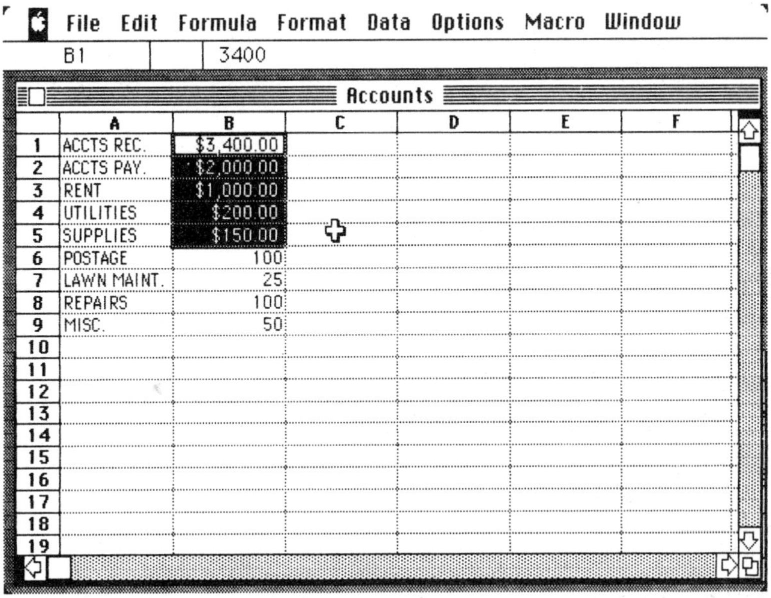

Fig. 1.11. Macro results.

Macro Structure

The suggestions in this section relate to macro design—that is, how you combine macro instructions to build a cohesive, useful macro. All the recommendations focus on the command macros that act as a programming language, but you should read this section even if you plan to create only function macros or keyboard alternatives. You will learn valuable tips as well as gain some insight into logical methods of macro construction.

Straight-Line Code

Straight-line code, whether in a BASIC program or an Excel macro, is code that is executed consecutively from top to bottom. The code does not contain branching instructions and flows smoothly from beginning to end. The logic for this code is easy to follow; it always progresses downward.

Straight-line code is not appropriate for all applications. For example, to execute a particular set of instructions repeatedly, you should set up the macro instructions in a loop. This is preferable to duplicating instructions the required number of times in order to avoid branching.

You should not use straight-line code if the instructions take up several pages. Using subroutines, which perform some of the detail work, is better. Subroutines enable you to contain the main logic in a manageable section of code and relegate the detail to other routines. This strategy is used commonly in programming.

Changing the Execution Flow

Usually, macros are executed in the order in which instructions appear in columns of cells. Sometimes, however, altering execution flow is necessary. This approach is also most practical in situations that require looping or lengthy detailed code.

Avoid making unnecessary changes in the execution flow; they make the logic of your macro much more difficult to follow. The examples in figure 1.12 illustrate this fact. The macros in column A and column B achieve the same results. The macro in column B, however, is much more obscure because it contains six unnecessary GOTO statements (in cells B2, B4, B6, B8, B10, and B12). Not one of these GOTO instructions adds anything but confusion to the macro's logic.

	File Edit Formula Format Data Options Macro Window

B1		Unnecessary_Branching

	Macro4	
	A	**B**
1	Straight_Line	Unnecessary_Branching
2	=SELECT("RC:R[2]C[1]")	=GOTO(B5)
3	=FORMAT.NUMBER("$#,##0_);($#,##0)")	=FORMAT.NUMBER("$#,##0_);($#,##0)")
4	=COLUMN.WIDTH(13)	=GOTO(B7)
5	=SELECT("R[2]:R[2]C[2]")	=SELECT("RC:R[2]C[1]")
6	=PRECISION(FALSE)	=GOTO(B3)
7	=RETURN()	=COLUMN.WIDTH(13)
8		=GOTO(B11)
9		=PRECISION(FALSE)
10		=GOTO(B13)
11		=SELECT("R[2]:R[2]C[2]")
12		=GOTO(B9)
13		=RETURN()
14		
15		
16		
17		
18		

Fig. 1.12. Straight-line code versus branching.

You can alter top-to-bottom execution flow by using GOTO or another macro call. GOTO and ref( ) are branching instructions that continue execution but change its flow. GOTO(ref) branches to the cell range that *ref* specifies. When you use GOTO, control does not return to the point of the GOTO instruction. To call another macro, you use ref( ), in which *ref* is the name of the macro you are calling. When you use a macro call, control returns to the calling macro.

Using GOTO Statements

Look at the example in figure 1.13. The command macro, called Correct, corrects incorrect entries in a column of worksheet cells. The macro is designed to work regardless of the length of the column of cells containing the mistakes. The macro uses a GOTO statement to change the flow of execution (A16).

 File   Edit   Formula   Format   Data   Options   Macro   Window

A1		Reverse

Macro25

	A	B
1	Reverse	
2	=ARGUMENT("STRING",2)	Text type argument
3	=LEN(STRING)	Determine length
4	=SEARCH(" ",STRING,1)	Look for a space
5	=MID(STRING,A4+1,A3-A4)&", "&MID(STRING,1,A4-1)	Formula to reverse
6	=RETURN(A5)	Return reversed string
7		
8		
9	Correct	
10	=ROWS(SELECTION())	Determine number of rows
11	=SELECT("RC[4]")	Select cell 4 cols to right
12	=SET.VALUE(A15,1)	Initialize counter to 1
13	=FORMULA("=Macro1!Reverse(RC[-4])")	Create formula
14	=SELECT("R[1]C")	Select cell same col down 1 row
15	=A15+1	Increment counter
16	=IF(A15>A10,GOTO(A17),GOTO(A13))	Counter > # Rows
17	=RETURN()	End Macro
18		
19		

Fig. 1.13. GOTO used to change execution flow.

The macro must first check the length of the column of cells containing the errors, then initialize a counter. Cell A10 determines the length of the column of cells and holds the value. Execution continues from top to bottom until Excel reaches cell A16. The instruction in that cell has the potential to alter execution flow and keep the macro in the execution loop. Because of this loop, the macro continues making corrections instead of moving down to cell A17, which ends the macro.

The formula in cell A16 checks the value of the loop counter in A15. If the value of the counter exceeds the number of rows requiring correction, GOTO transfers execution control to A17, which ends the macro. If the value of the counter is not greater than the number of rows, the second GOTO causes the instruction in A13 to be the next one executed.

Using a Subroutine Call

Macros containing references to subroutines (other macros) are *calling macros*. To call another macro, you use either of the following syntax formats:

   ref( )

   ref(argument-1,argument-2,...)

ref specifies the first cell in the macro to which you are branching. For instance, if you are branching to a macro called Sales, and you are passing two arguments or values, you type

   =Sales(3,6)

The arguments represent values for variables used by the macro. Suppose that you are calling a macro to process sales records. The 3 indicates that you want only the records for Division 3, and the 6 means that you want only the first six entries.

If Sales is in another macro sheet, you type the name of the macro sheet before the name of the macro:

   Sheet2!Sales(3,6)

The calling macro can pass as many as 13 arguments or values to a second macro. With these arguments, you can design flexible macros and tailor the execution of each. For each argument passed to the second macro, the calling macro must contain an ARGUMENT statement.

The called macro is executed until a RETURN is encountered. Control then returns to the calling macro, to the cell immediately following the *ref* instruction that called the second macro. If you do not want to return, you can end the second macro by using the HALT command.

The macros that you specify in the call instructions are *nested macros*. Nesting can be several layers deep. In other words, macro A can call macro B, macro B can call macros C and D, and so forth.

The number of nesting levels that you use in a macro is up to you. Many people have difficulty handling macros that are nested more than three levels deep.

Figure 1.14 shows examples of calling and nested (called) macros. Although this sample macro serves little purpose, a macro like this one can be created for testing the logic flow in a complicated macro. You test the logic before adding additional commands.

File Edit Formula Format Data Options Macro Window

Returned from Called macro

| A1 | | Call | |

Macro30	
	A	B
1	**Call**	
2	=Called( )	
3	=MESSAGE(TRUE,"Returned from Called macro")	
4	=RETURN( )	
5		
6	**Called**	
7	=MESSAGE(TRUE,"Called macro")	
8	=RETURN( )	
9		
10	*** Note message above formula bar	
11		
12		
13		
14		
15		
16		
17		
18		
19		

Fig. 1.14. A calling macro and a called macro.

The calling macro is in cells A1 through A4. Cell A1 contains the macro's name: Call. Cell A2 calls the macro named Called, which is in cells A6 through A8. The empty parentheses in the CALLED( ) statement indicate that no arguments are being passed to the macro being called. At this point, execution passes to the called macro, which executes the instruction in A7. This instruction causes the message *Called macro* to appear, indicating that the instruction has been executed.

Then execution flows to A8, which returns control to the calling macro, specifically to the cell following the call instruction. The instruction in A3 is executed, and a message indicating the return from the called macro is displayed. Execution stops after the instruction in A4 is carried out.

Condition Tests

In addition to using Excel's special macro functions, you can use the program's built-in functions in your macros. One of the most frequently used built-in functions is the logical IF. It enables you to test for a particular condition and take one of two different actions, depending on the results of the condition test. IF's syntax is

IF(logical,value-if-true,value-if-false)

The *logical* is the condition to be tested. If the condition is true, the function returns the first value; if the condition is false, the second value is returned. If you don't list a *value-if-false* in the function, FALSE is returned when the condition is false. The action to be taken when the condition is false is not part of the function but is stored in the cell below the IF statement. An example is

=IF(A10=2,GOTO(End))

This statement checks the value of cell A10 during the execution of the macro. If A10 contains a 2, the macro branches immediately to the macro named *End*. If cell A10 contains anything other than 2, the condition is false and the macro executes the instruction in the cell following the IF statement. If you assume that the IF statement is stored in A15, then the instruction in cell A16 is executed next.

As in the example, the condition test frequently is combined with a branching instruction. In the presence of a certain condition or set of conditions, that instruction alters the execution flow within the macro.

Looping Instructions

Iteration is the repeated execution of a series of instructions. Whether you are writing a program or creating an Excel macro, using this technique can speed up the creation and testing of your final product. To use the technique, you establish a loop and specify the number of times that the instructions within the loop should be executed. Or, you can specify that the instructions be executed whenever a certain condition is true. Programmers refer to these logical constructs as FOR. . .NEXT and DO. . .WHILE loops.

Excel has specific FOR. . .NEXT and DO. . .WHILE instructions, just as many programming languages do. In addition, Excel has instructions you can use to create your own loops. An example of each is provided in the sections that follow.

Using a FOR. . .NEXT Loop

A FOR. . .NEXT loop performs a set of instructions a specific number of times. The loop has three components. First, a counter must be initialized at a given value. Next, the counter must be incremented a fixed amount with each execution of the instructions. Finally, before each subsequent execution of the instructions, a logical IF checks to see whether the counter has reached the maximum allowable value. The following shows the structure of this looping condition.

```
=SET.VALUE(B2,10)
toploop
instruction 1
instruction 2
=B2+10
=IF(B2<100,GOTO(toploop))
```

This macro outline shows a loop counter that has an initial value of 10. Each time the loop is executed, the counter in B2 is incremented by 10. At the bottom of the loop is a logical IF statement that determines whether the conditions necessary to continue looping are still in effect. The condition established is that the value in B2 is less than 100. The loop executes 9 times before control passes to the instruction following the IF statement.

Using a DO. . .WHILE Loop

In a DO. . .WHILE loop, the IF statement is at the top of the loop, and the condition test is based on a negative condition test. A counter is not required. The macro, which checks for the absence of a condition, continues looping until the condition is no longer true. The following shows the DO. . .WHILE loop's basic structure:

```
toploop
IF(NOT(X=10),GOTO(afterloop))
instruction 1
instruction 2
=GOTO(toploop)
afterloop
```

This loop tests the condition that X is not equal to 10. As long as this condition is not true, the loop continues executing.

Operator Input

Any argument in an Excel macro function can be entered as input from the keyboard during the macro's execution. To provide for a keyboard entry of an argument value, you need to include an INPUT statement in the macro instructions. The INPUT statement asks the operator to supply the value for the function's argument. In this way, the operator can interact with the macro, supplying new values each time the macro runs. The INPUT statement includes a prompt message for the operator (see fig. 1.15). During the macro's execution, the prompt message appears at the top of the screen.

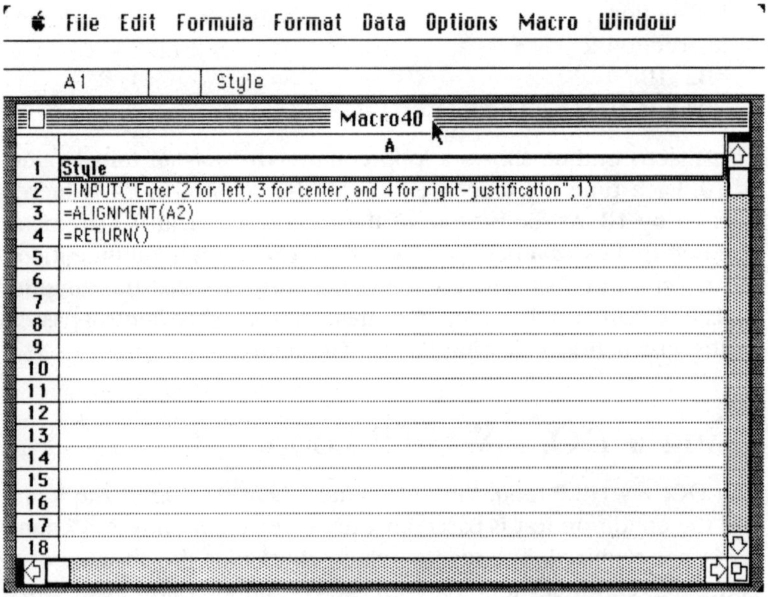

```
 * File  Edit  Formula  Format  Data  Options  Macro  Window

   A1              Style

===================== Macro40 =====================
                              A
 1 | Style
 2 | =INPUT("Enter 2 for left, 3 for center, and 4 for right-justification",1)
 3 | =ALIGNMENT(A2)
 4 | =RETURN()
 5 |
 6 |
 7 |
 8 |
 9 |
10 |
11 |
12 |
13 |
14 |
15 |
16 |
17 |
18 |
```

Fig. 1.15. A macro that interacts with the operator.

This sample macro is interactive; the operator's entry determines the alignment of the active cell. The INPUT statement in cell A2 contains the prompt message. The ALIGNMENT statement in A3 uses the number entered by the operator, which is stored in A2, to determine the alignment type.

Macro Sheets

Macro sheets are documents that contain only macro instructions. With macro sheets, which are the storage vehicles for both command and function macros, you can create a library of macros for all your applications. If you have special needs in some of your applications, you can create specialized macro sheets for those applications. You can access a macro sheet from any other worksheet or chart document.

A macro sheet can contain one or many macros. As you begin creating macro sheets to store a library of macros, you will see the importance of the programming techniques presented in the preceding sections. Consistently using these techniques will ensure that your entire library of macro functions is well-organized and readable.

Although macro sheets are similar to worksheets, major differences between the two exist. For example, macro sheets are not evaluated in the same manner as other worksheets. In a worksheet, unless you turn off the automatic recalculation capability, the worksheet is re-evaluated when cell entries are changed. Macro sheets, on the other hand, are evaluated only when you execute the macro and only on a line-by-line basis as the flow of execution moves down the sheet from one macro command to the next.

With many other spreadsheet packages, you enter macros right in the worksheet. This procedure is not a good one, for two reasons. First, the macros are not easily accessible for a number of applications. Before you can use the macros, you have to duplicate them in each of your worksheets. And, second, if you start storing macros in out-of-the-way locations in the worksheet itself, the macros can take up a significant amount of memory. Isolating macro instructions on a sheet of their own has significant advantages over these other approaches.

Creating Macro Sheets

To create a macro sheet, you give the File New command and click the Macro Sheet option. Although you can record macros anywhere in a macro sheet, storing them in scattered locations all over the sheet is an inefficient use of memory. To record information in macro sheets, you should use the same method you use with worksheets—that is, leave only as much blank space as is required for readability. Figure 1.16 illustrates a macro sheet that contains scat-

tered entries. Figure 1.17 presents a more efficient method for recording macros. In the latter figure, large pockets of blank space
are not left between the macros.

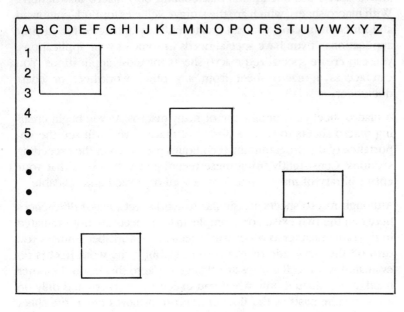

Fig. 1.16. Inefficient macro
placement.

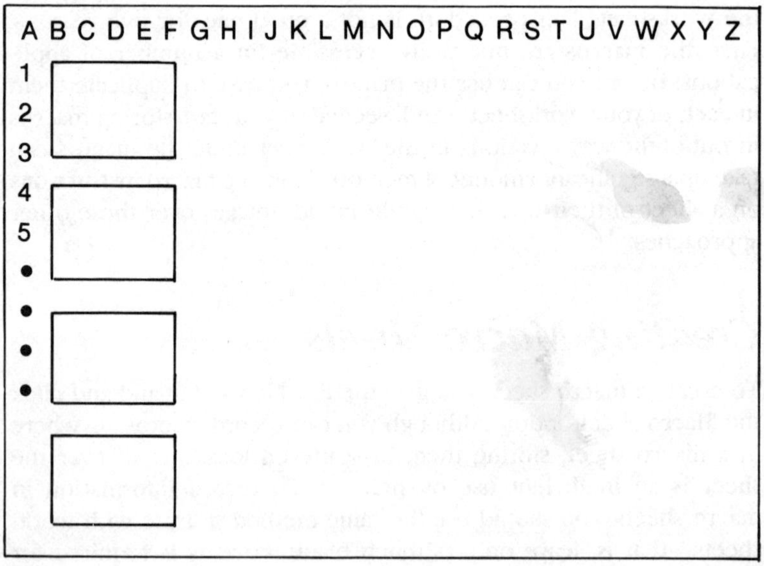

Fig. 1.17. Macros placed
efficiently to conserve memory.

When you record information in a macro sheet, you may want to group similar macros together. For example, if you have four related print macros, you can store them in one area of the macro sheet. Or if several subroutines service a calling macro, you can group them near the main macro on the macro sheet. Such arrangements make locating potential problems easier.

Before you make any entries in a macro sheet, take time to review the Macro menu options. These are described in the section that follows.

Using the Macro Menu

The Macro menu is the list of commands that appears at the top of the macro sheet (see fig. 1.18). The menu selections for a macro sheet do not differ much from those for a worksheet menu. Several commands, such as Formula Define Name, have additional options and commands in the macro window. These additional options are tailored to the needs you have when working with a macro sheet. For example, the Formula Define Name command enables you to select either Function or Command when you name a macro.

The options on the Macro menu are the same whether you are working in the worksheet or chart environment. No matter what kind of document you are working on, you can use the commands from the Macro menu to help you build macros. You can use these commands to set the Recorder, start storing Recorder menu entries in the location specified, stop the Recorder, run the macro, and use either absolute or relative record references. The procedures for using each menu option for command and function macros are described in the sections that follow.

Entering Command Macros

You can enter command macros in two different ways. You can type all the instructions into a macro sheet from the keyboard, or, in some situations, you can use Excel's Recorder to make the program enter the instructions for you. With either approach, your first step is to create a macro sheet by using the File New Macro Sheet command.

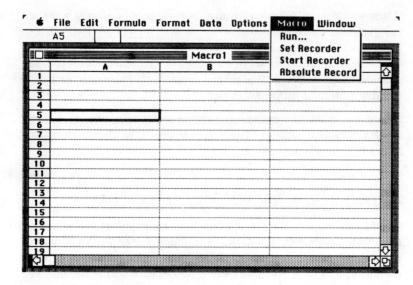

Fig. 1.18. The Macro menu.

Using the Keyboard

To create a macro from the keyboard, you first type the name of the macro in the top cell of the macro sheet. Then, in a column of cells, you type the action-taking formulas that you want the macro to execute.

You use Excel's Macro Command Language to write the formulas, and you precede each one with an equal sign (=). For instance, if you want the macro to change the column width, you use the COLUMN.WIDTH function. To specify a column width of 14, you type

   =COLUMN.WIDTH(14)

You can use the keyboard to type this entry, or you can copy COLUMN.WIDTH( ) into the entry cell with the Paste Function command from the Formula menu. Regardless of the method you choose, you can enter only one command in a cell. The Paste Function command works in the same way on a macro sheet as it does on a worksheet. The only difference is that the function names on the macro sheet correspond to the options in the Macro Command Language.

To make your next entry, you move to the cell below without skipping any blank lines. After you finish typing the macro, you name it with the Define Name command. Only then can you execute the macro.

Using the Recorder

You can make Excel do your entry work by using the Recorder. The Recorder can handle most of the work involved in creating command macros.

First, you either create or open a macro sheet by selecting File New or File Open. When the macro sheet is on the screen, you can select a cell or range of cells that Excel can use to record the instructions you select from menus and type from the keyboard. If you select a single cell, Excel stores the macro instructions in that cell and the cells directly below it. If you select a range of cells, it should be in a single column. Excel uses only the cells you specify and tells you when they are full by displaying an error message.

To tell Excel what cells you want to use for storage, you select Set Recorder from within the macro sheet. After you do this, you can leave the macro sheet and move to the worksheet or chart environment to start recording the instruction sequence.

When you are ready to start recording your actions in the selected cells, you use the Start Recorder command. Enter as much as you like, but after you finish, remember to use Stop Recorder. Your most difficult task probably will be to remember to turn off the Recorder so that you can try running the macro. You can switch back to the macro sheet by clicking it or choosing its name on the Window menu. Then you can view or edit the recorded instructions.

While you are recording macro instructions, you can use the last option on the Macro menu. This option allows you to toggle between Absolute Record and Relative Record. Relative Record enters all references in a macro relative to the active cell at the time the selection is made. When you run a macro recorded with the Relative Record option, the macro uses the same relative directions, although the active cell may be different. Absolute Record causes the macro to record absolute references. When you run the macro, the same cells always are selected. If you want, you can toggle between Relative Record and Absolute Record while recording a macro.

You have to do one more thing before you can execute the macro: name it. That procedure is discussed in this chapter's "Naming Command Macros" section.

Editing a Command Macro

Suppose that you want to make changes to a command macro you just entered with the Recorder. Do you have to record all the commands again and run the risk of making a mistake? No. You can change the individual macro sheet cells in the same way you change worksheet cells. You choose the cell you want to change, select the formula bar, and alter it by using various Edit menu options. When you are finished, click Enter. You can add and delete instructions and make any modifications you want.

Entering Function Macros

You enter a function macro from the keyboard only. You cannot use the Recorder because it captures only menu selections, and the formulas in function macros are not made up of menu selections.

You type the macro's name and, in the following cell, the formulas for results and arguments. Then you enter the formulas for your calculation. You end the macro with a RETURN statement, which returns the result of the calculation.

Figure 1.19 shows an example of a function macro stored in a macro sheet. Although this macro sheet may look similar to a worksheet because of the table in columns B through E, it is not a worksheet. The macro uses the VLOOKUP function and its associated table, which is stored in the macro sheet. The macro should calculate shipping costs when an invoice is processed. These calculations could have been placed right in your worksheet file. However, if they were, they could not have been used in other applications requiring the same calculations. The function macro shown in the figure can be used from any worksheet in order to look up the shipping weight in a table, using TYPE to determine the column of values.

Naming Command Macros

To assign a name to a range of cells that make up a command macro, you use the Define Name command. You use this command every time you create a command macro. You must perform this step before trying to run a macro.

You placed the macro name in the first cell, so select that cell in the macro sheet. Select Define Name from the Formula menu. Be-

 File Edit Formula Format Data Options Macro Window

| A1 | | Shipping | | | | |

Shipping_Macro

	A	B	C	D	E	F
1	**Shipping**		1	2	3	
2	=ARGUMENT("LBS",1)	1	1.65	0.85	1.1	
3	=ARGUMENT("TYPE",1)	2	1.6	0.85	1	
4	=VLOOKUP(LBS,B2:E15,TYPE+1)	3	1.55	0.85	0.85	
5	=(A4*LBS)+0.75	4	1.25	0.85	0.8	
6	=IF(A5<2,2,A5)	5	1.25	0.85	0.8	
7	=IF(A6>50,50,A6)	6	1.25	0.85	0.75	
8	=RETURN(A7)	7	1	0.85	0.75	
9		8	1	0.85	0.7	
10		10	0.95	0.85	0.6	
11		12	0.9	0.85	0.6	
12		15	0.8	0.85	0.6	
13		20	0.75	0.85	0.5	
14		30	0.6	0.85	0.45	
15		50	0.55	0.85	0.45	
16						
17						
18						
19						

Fig. 1.19. A function macro that calculates shipping costs.

cause some macro sheets are named, you will notice some extra options in the Define Name dialog box (see fig. 1.20). Just like in the worksheet environment, the Define Name dialog box in the macro environment displays the list of existing names, in this case the names of the macro sheets. In the dialog box, you type the macro name in the box under the word *Name:*. Follow the same rules for naming macros as you use for naming other ranges.

The box under *Refers to:* displays the location of the macro's first cell, just as a range name's first cell is displayed in the worksheet environment. The Macro box at the bottom of the dialog box is a feature specific to Define Name in the macro environment. You use this box to indicate whether you are creating a command macro or a function macro. Click Command if you are entering a command macro; Function, if you are entering a function macro.

If you want to be able to execute the macro with an Option-Command-key sequence, you must type the appropriate letter for the key. Uppercase and lowercase entries are not considered equivalent. You cannot use the lowercase letters *e, i, n,* or *u*; these are reserved for Excel's needs. Click OK when you are finished with the Define Name options.

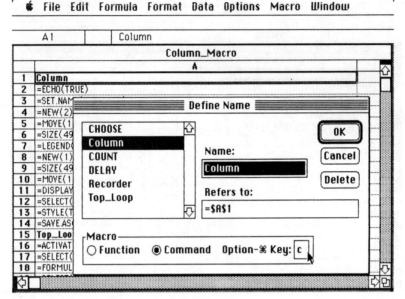

Fig. 1.20. The Define Name
dialog box with extra macro
options.

Naming Function Macros

Naming function macros is a little different than naming command macros because you assign only one name. A command macro can have a name and a special Option-Command-key sequence. Function macros have only a name. In other ways, the process is the same. The first step is to select the first cell in the macro.

For example, look at figure 1.21. This macro calculates the number of cubic inches a container can hold. The first three ARGUMENT statements define the container's length, width, and height values. The formula in cell A5 calculates the cubic inches the container can hold, and the RESULT function in cell A6 indicates that a numeric value will be returned.

To name this macro, you select the first cell of the macro. Then you choose Define Name on the Formula menu. You can use the default name in the first cell for the name of the macro, or you can type another name in the box under *Name:*. Then click Function and OK. You cannot use Option-Command-key for function macros because you do not execute them directly from the keyboard. They are called from other function or command macros or referred to by name from within a worksheet cell, just like a built-in function.

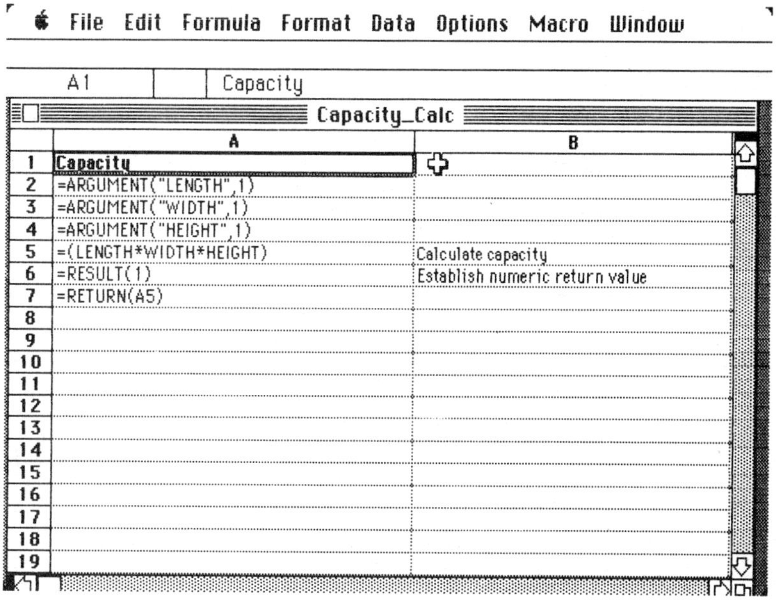

Fig. 1.21. A function macro named Capacity.

Executing Command Macros

To run your macro, you have two choices. Both require that the sheet from which you want to run the macro be active.

Your first choice is to use the Run command on the Macro menu. The dialog box displays all your named macros. Notice the structure of the list in figure 1.22. Each entry contains the Option-Command-key code (if one has been assigned), the macro sheet's name, and the macro's name. Click the macro you want to run; then click OK.

The second way to run the macro is by using an Option-Command-key sequence, if you have assigned one to the macro. You hold down the Option and Command keys while pressing the appropriate key.

No matter which method you use, Excel goes to the first cell in the macro and begins executing the formulas. Execution continues from top to bottom until a branching instruction or RETURN alters the downward flow. A branch changes the logic flow, and a RETURN ends the macro.

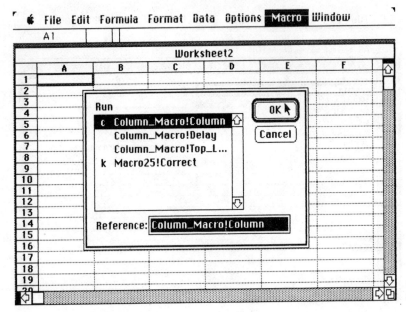

Fig. 1.22. The dialog box for Macro Run.

Executing Function Macros

Function macros are executed from a formula in a worksheet or from within another macro in a macro sheet. They are executed in the same way as built-in functions. You type the macro's name, then the arguments; the arguments are separated by commas and enclosed in parentheses. As with the built-in functions, you can use Paste Function to copy the function name into the entry cell rather than type it.

Figure 1.23 shows an example of a function macro used in a worksheet to calculate the cubic storage capacity of containers. Figure 1.24 shows an example of the Paste Function. When the operator selects the macro's name from the Paste Function list, Excel enters in the active cell the macro's name followed by a pair of parentheses. The macro positions the cursor between the parentheses so that you can enter arguments if necessary.

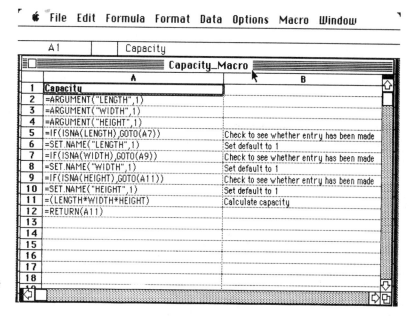

Fig. 1.23. A function macro that calculates capacity.

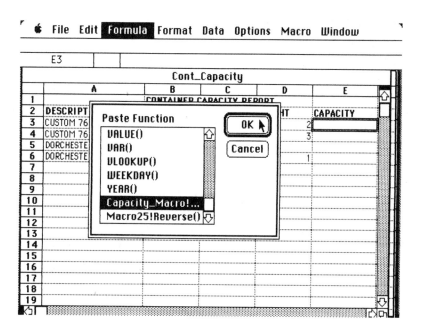

Fig. 1.24. A function macro's name selected in the Paste Function dialog box.

Evaluating the Macro Sheet

After you enter macros in a macro sheet, you execute them by selecting the macro name from the Macro Run menu. You also can
assign to a command macro a letter code that enables you to start
the macro with one keystroke sequence. Neither method causes
Excel to recalculate the entire macro sheet. With both methods,
Excel begins executing the macro instructions in the macro's top
cell and continues downward through all the cells until encoun-
tering either a HALT or RETURN.

Excel skips over cells that contain constants, whether they are text
or values. You can use this feature to your advantage to label sections
of the macro without affecting the results or execution flow.

In cells that contain formulas rather than constants, Excel executes
the instructions the formulas contain. Formulas that produce values
are calculated, and the resulting values are placed in the cell. In
formulas that take actions, Excel carries out the actions immediately.
Examples of such actions are selecting cells, printing a range of cells,
and reading a file.

Macro Return Values

Macro sheet formulas that take actions return values, even though
the focus is on the actions the formulas take. Logical values (TRUE
and FALSE) and error values (such as #N/A) are the most common
kinds of values that these formulas return. The formulas actually are
not calculated, but changed when the action in the called macro is
successfully taken. The change from FALSE to TRUE takes place
automatically.

Invalid arguments and requests for illegal actions can cause the action specified in a macro to fail, leaving the value at FALSE or changing the value to an error value such as #REF! or #VALUE!. A value
of FALSE indicates that the action has not been executed. Examples
include setting a column width to -5, creating a cell address outside
the range of the worksheet, and copying or cutting cells and at-
tempting to paste them to a range of cells that is invalid because
of its size or shape. In such situations, Excel displays a dialog box
that indicates the cell in which the error occurred; this can help
you in your debugging efforts.

Reference Styles

Excel supports both absolute and relative references, and both types are used throughout this book. The distinction between absolute and relative references is the addition of the dollar sign ($) to indicate an absolute cell address. The characters A1 in a formula represent a relative reference to A1, so the reference is altered when the formula is copied. On the other hand, the characters $A$1 in a formula constitute an absolute reference to cell A1. This reference remains the same even if copied to another cell.

In the original formula, the use of absolute and relative references makes no difference in the result of the calculation. The use of relative and absolute references is distinctly different, however, when a formula is copied.

Including both relative and absolute references, most of the macros in this book have been built using the A1 style of reference. The columns are referenced with alphabetic characters beginning with the letter A for the column to the far left. The rows are referenced with numbers beginning with 1 for the top row. A cell reference consists of the column reference followed by the row reference (A1).

Excel also supports a second reference style: the R1C1 style. With the R1C1 reference style, both rows and columns have numeric references. The top row is row 1 and the left column is column 1.

To change from A1 to R1C1, you choose R1C1 from the Options menu. This option is replaced with A1 on the Options menu as soon as you select it because this menu choice functions as a toggle switch between the two styles.

Absolute and relative references look different in R1C1 style. A relative reference to the current cell is RC. A relative reference to a cell in the same column but six rows below is R[6]C. The relative direction is enclosed in brackets. A cell below the current cell is a positive increment, and the one above is negative, for example, R[-2]. The same approach is used for references to the right C[3] and left C[-2].

An absolute reference to a row specifies the row and column number without brackets. The reference R1C3 always refers to the cell in the first row and third column.

A Recap of the Macro-Creation Steps

In upcoming chapters, you will practice creating function and command macros. You can use the steps in the following sections as checklists for the macros you create.

Steps for Creating a Command Macro

Here is a brief outline of the steps for creating a command macro:

1. Request a new macro sheet or open an existing one.

2. In the macro sheet, type the macro's name in the top line of the macro storage area.

3. Code the functions that will perform the required processing and type them in the macro sheet. If you prefer, you can use the Recorder. To do so, select a range of cells and choose Macro Set Recorder. Then, to get ready to begin recording, move back to the worksheet environment (or wherever you want to start recording commands) and select Macro Start Recorder. After you finish recording, choose Macro Stop Recorder.

4. Put a RETURN statement at the end of the macro.

5. Use Define Name to assign a name to the macro and specify in the dialog box that the macro is a command macro. If you want to execute the macro from the keyboard, supply in the dialog box the letter you will use to execute the macro.

6. Try executing the macro either by giving the Macro Run command or pressing both the Option and Command keys with the letter assigned to the macro.

Steps for Creating a Function Macro

Here is a brief outline of the steps for creating a function macro:

1. Request a new macro sheet or open an existing one.

2. In the macro sheet, type the macro's name in the top line of the macro storage area.

3. Consider whether you want to restrict the results returned to a specific type, such as text, a cell reference, or an array. If you do, put a RESULT function in the line under the macro's name.

4. Use an ARGUMENT statement for each value passed to the macro.

5. Code the formula that will make the calculations you need and enter it in the macro.

6. Use a RETURN statement at the end of the macro.

7. Use Define Name to assign a name to the macro and specify in the dialog box that the macro is a function macro.

8. Try executing the macro by putting in a worksheet a reference to the macro and its associated arguments.

2
Macro Success Strategies

With sufficient perseverance, you can make even the most badly planned macro work properly. A planned approach to creating macros, however, ensures that they work correctly with a minimum investment of time. You will find, in the long run, that the time you spend planning your macros *saves* you time during the implementation and testing stages.

By borrowing a few guidelines from programmers' strategies, you can save significant development time and ensure that your macros work correctly. Macros, just like computer programs, are stored sets of instructions that are executed at a later time. Because macros and computer programs fit this same definition, borrowing from what has been learned about computer programming over the years is appropriate. This chapter describes how you can adapt such strategies to the process of creating command and function macros.

This chapter discusses four topics:

- Macro planning
- Guidelines for successful function macros
- Guidelines for successful command macros
- Testing procedures

The first section, on planning macros, applies to both command and function macros. Two methods are described; you can choose the one you like best.

Macro Planning

Before beginning to create a program, a programmer establishes a plan of attack—a mental or written map of the program's logic. That plan enables the programmer to view the entire problem from an overview level, never getting so caught up in details that the program's main purpose is forgotten. The map also serves as a checklist, helping the programmer make sure that all aspects of the problem have been examined.

Another advantage of the map—and perhaps the most important one for novices—is that it prevents programmers from confusing logic problems with syntax problems. Trying to discover whether a problem is the result of faulty logic or is a misuse of the software's commands can be very frustrating. Using the "road map" approach, programmers can establish a strong logic base for their solution before dealing with a software package's particular syntax.

Flowcharts

Programmers often use flowcharts to record their maps. A *flowchart* uses a standard set of symbols to provide a pictorial representation of the logic flow in a program (see fig. 2.1). For example, a rectangle is used to represent a calculation or to assign a value to a variable. A parallelogram represents input or output, and a circle represents a label for a location in the logic flow. A diamond represents a decision or condition test, and the points of the diamond represent different paths determined by the evaluation of the condition inside the diamond.

In the diamond in the flowchart in figure 2.1, the condition checked is whether the counter is equal to the number of records to add. If the answer is No, execution moves along the path to the right and back up to the point indicated. If the answer is Yes, execution moves down to the end of the program.

Pseudocode

Another method that programmers use to record program maps is pseudocode. *Pseudocode* is English-language shorthand for what a program will do. The objective is to present the steps in a program clearly, using a minimum of words.

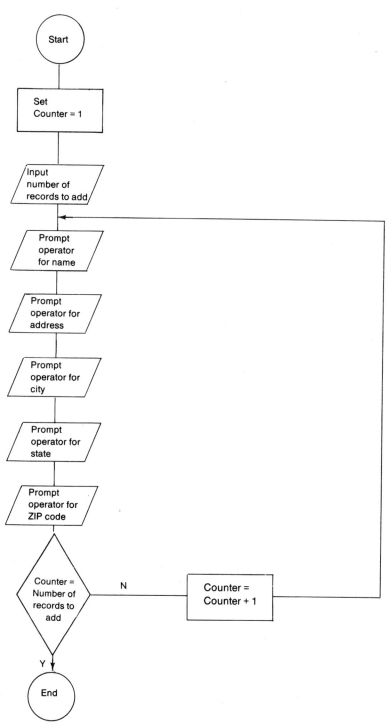

Fig. 2.1. A flowchart to map out logic.

You can use pseudocode to map out macro instructions. You should strive for brevity, but you also should convey a clear picture of what the macro will do. When you write pseudocode, grammar and standard abbreviations are not important. Pseudocode of the logic in figure 2.1 follows:

> Establish a counter
> Determine number of records to add

Top Loop   Prompt for name
> Prompt for address
> Prompt for city
> Prompt for state
> Prompt for ZIP

> If number of records is not correct,
>   add to counter and go to Top Loop
> Else end

For complicated macros, you should consider using either a flow-chart or pseudocode to plan the macro's logic flow. The choice is yours; both can be equally effective.

Guidelines for Successful Function Macros

The purpose of function macros is to perform calculations that are needed repeatedly. Function macros, which complete a single calculated result, usually have fewer instructions than command macros, which contain elaborate logical constructs.

Because the number of instructions required is limited, you may think that one approach for creating function macros works just as well as any other. But this is not the case. Good planning and a consistent, logical approach to creating function macros can save you time during the initial creation period and even more time if the macros are modified later. By adopting the guidelines in this section as standards, you can ensure that your approach is consistent.

Using the ARGUMENT Function

The ARGUMENT function is used to define the *names* for the values that function macros use. The ARGUMENT function also can specify the *type* of value that a specific argument can use. When you create self-documenting macros, you may find these two features of the ARGUMENT function useful. For example, look at the macros in figures 2.2 and 2.3. The figures show the ARGUMENT function used in the two ways described. Both macros are called Interest_Calc, and both compute an interest calculation.

In the first macro, the *names* of the values are single letters: X, Y, and Z. Because no *types* are specified, the statements can contain numbers, text, or logical values. The formula in A5 multiplies X times Y times Z, but what the letters represent is unclear.

The macro in figure 2.3 performs the same calculation as the macro in figure 2.2, but is much clearer. The *names*—PRINCIPAL, RATE, and TIME—are indicative of the values they contain. Each ARGUMENT statement contains a *type* of 1, which specifies numeric values. The formula in A5, PRINCIPAL*RATE*TIME, calculates the final result. Although you have to use a few more keystrokes to enter a *name* for each statement, you save time in the long run by avoiding confusion. Including *names* also makes modifying the macro in the future easier.

Specifying a *type* has two benefits. First, the *type* makes clear what kind of data is expected. This feature can be useful to individuals

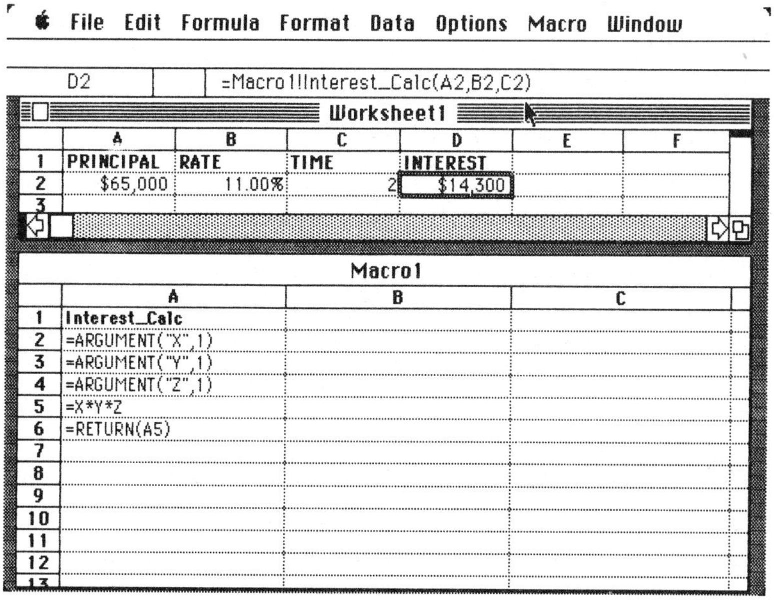

Fig. 2.2. Single-letter variable names in a macro.

 ⊞ File Edit Formula Format Data Options Macro Window

| D2 | =Macro1!Interest_Calc(A2,B2,C2) |

Worksheet1

	A	B	C	D	E	F
1	PRINCIPAL	RATE	TIME	INTEREST		
2	$65,000	11.00%	2	$14,300		
3						

Macro1

	A	B	C
1	Interest_Calc		
2	=ARGUMENT("PRINCIPAL",1)		
3	=ARGUMENT("RATE",1)		
4	=ARGUMENT("TIME",1)		
5	=PRINCIPAL*RATE*TIME		
6	=RETURN(A5)		
7			
8			
9			
10			
11			
12			
13			

Fig. 2.3. Meaningful variable names that enhance readability.

unfamiliar with the way macros work and can prevent mistakes. Second, the *type* checks the data passed to a macro. For example, in the macro in figure 2.3, if *Saturday* were passed as the PRINCIPAL, an error message would appear, because a *type* of 1 specifies only numeric data. If no *type* were used, the error would not occur until later in the macro, when the cause of the problem would be more difficult to detect.

Using the RESULT Function

Using the RESULT function is an extra step, but one that can provide a better understanding of the way macros work as well as eliminate future problems. RESULT, like ARGUMENT, uses a *type* to ensure that a macro returns only a particular kind of result. Unlike ARGUMENT, however, RESULT cannot specify a *name*.

If you do not use a RESULT function, a *type* of 7 is assumed—that is, the result can be a number, text, or logical value. Not using a RESULT function can cause misinterpretation of the kind of result expected and potentially can lead to incorrect modifications to the macro.

Figure 2.4 uses the RESULT function with a *type* of 64 specified, which means that an array will be returned. The function must return an array because the purpose of the macro is to return three separate commission values: the commission paid in the current month, the commission paid in the following month, and the commission paid in the second month following the sale.

 File Edit Formula Format Data Options Macro Window

A1	Commission

Commission

	A
1	**Commission**
2	=RESULT(64)
3	=ARGUMENT("SALES",1)
4	=IF(SALES<5000,SALES*0.1,5000*0.1)
5	=IF(AND(SALES>5000,SALES<10000),(SALES-5000)*0.12,IF(SALES>10000,5000*0.12))
6	=IF(SALES>10000,(SALES-10000)*0.15)
7	=A4+A5+A6
8	=SET.VALUE(A12,A7*0.7)
9	=SET.VALUE(B12,A7*0.2)
10	=SET.VALUE(C12,A7*0.1)
11	=RETURN(A12:C12)
12	4445
13	
14	
15	
16	
17	
18	
19	

Fig. 2.4. A macro that uses the RESULT function to return an array.

Using Formulas

Formulas are the "heart" of function macros. When you construct formulas, your two most important considerations are readability and accuracy.

If you have a choice of several calculation methods, select the most commonly accepted one. Using a common method will help other people who may use the macro to understand it. Simple mathematical formulas that use addition, subtraction, and multiplication are preferable to trigonometric and other more complex functions, unless the latter are required to perform the calculation.

Formulas must allow for the typical calculation and also for any exceptions that can occur. To "intercept" the exceptions, you can use the logical IF as well as error routines. Exception conditions might include salaries that exceed a specific level, interest rates that fall outside an allowable range, or a principal amount that is negative or beyond the lending limits of the financial institution.

If a formula is very long, you can divide it into shorter formulas and use several intermediate results to calculate the final result. For instance, suppose that you enter a formula that is 240 characters long. Two problems arise in this situation. First, the formula is so long that it extends beyond the screen's boundaries. (Printing the formula presents a similar problem.) Second, if the formula does not produce the correct result, you must examine the entire formula in order to find the source of the problem.

You can create a series of shorter formulas to solve both of these problems. First, each shorter formula can be displayed within screen limits. Second, if the formula returns an incorrect result, you can find the origin of the problem more easily.

The macro in figure 2.5 contains a long formula in cell A5. The macro shown in figure 2.6 performs the same calculation as the macro in figure 2.5, but uses four shorter formulas. In figure 2.6, cells A6, A8, and A10 return results that then are added together in cell A12 to return the salary result.

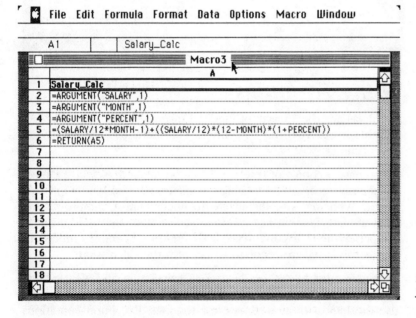

Fig. 2.5. A macro with a long formula in A5.

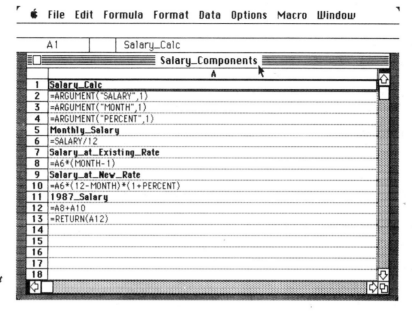

Fig. 2.6. Short formulas that simplify a long formula.

Documenting Function Macros

When you are creating a macro, you might not realize the importance of the comments that document the macro. You enter the instructions, so of course you know what they represent. A month later, however, you are unlikely to remember any details about that macro. As you modify the macro, you might misinterpret it, and the erroneous results could require a significant amount of time to correct. Documentation can prevent many problems. In function macros, two kinds of documentation are helpful: section labels and instruction descriptions.

Section labels act as divisions in a macro (like paragraph headings in a document). These labels group sets of instructions into logical units. For instance, suppose that you create a macro with several sections. The first section calculates total sales; the next section, commission; and the last section, take-home pay for an individual salesperson.

By inserting the words *Total Sales, Commission*, and *Pay Amount* on the appropriate lines, you document each section. To specify that the words are labels or comments, you enter them without an equal sign (=) preceding them. As long as they are on separate lines and are not preceded by equal signs, the words are interpreted as comments (see fig. 2.7).

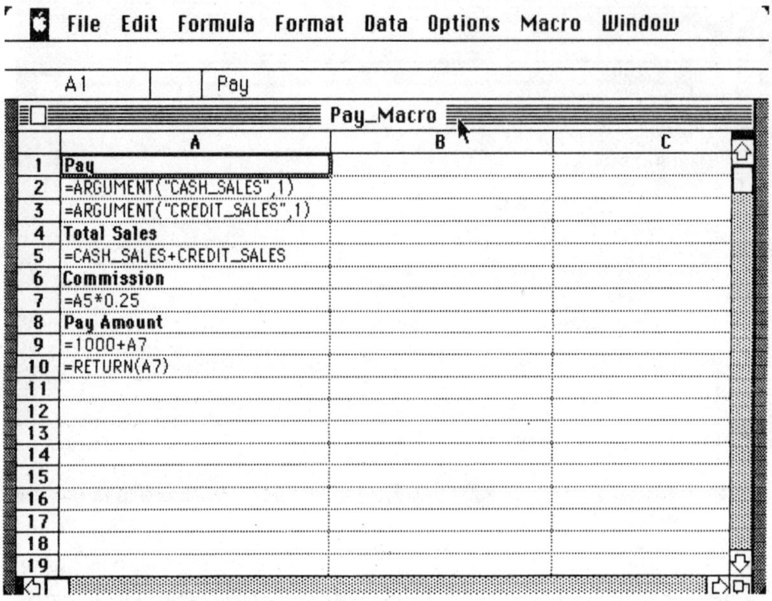

Fig. 2.7. *A function macro documented by section labels.*

Instruction descriptions, which explain the purpose of each line in the macro, should be placed in a column to the right of the macro instructions. Figure 2.8 shows macro instructions in column E and instruction descriptions in column F. The instructions are especially important when more than one calculation method could have been used. For instance, suppose that you use the Rule of 78s method in a macro to perform loan calculations. Specifying the method in the rightmost column enables anyone looking at the macro to see which method you used.

Building and Testing Shells

If a macro is especially long, you can test parts of it to make sure that they work correctly. You test a macro by building a *shell* that contains simple "dummy" constants rather than the complex functions needed for the application. If the shell runs correctly, you insert the "real" formulas.

Look at the sample shell in figure 2.9. This macro, which calculates total project costs, requires formulas to determine (1) labor costs

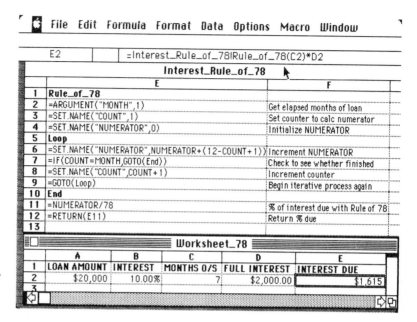

File Edit Formula Format Data Options Macro Window

| E2 | | =Interest_Rule_of_78!Rule_of_78(C2)*D2 |

Interest_Rule_of_78

	E	F
1	Rule_of_78	
2	=ARGUMENT("MONTH",1)	Get elapsed months of loan
3	=SET.NAME("COUNT",1)	Set counter to calc numerator
4	=SET.NAME("NUMERATOR",0)	Initialize NUMERATOR
5	Loop	
6	=SET.NAME("NUMERATOR",NUMERATOR+(12-COUNT+1))	Increment NUMERATOR
7	=IF(COUNT=MONTH,GOTO(End))	Check to see whether finished
8	=SET.NAME("COUNT",COUNT+1)	Increment counter
9	=GOTO(Loop)	Begin iterative process again
10	End	
11	=NUMERATOR/78	% of interest due with Rule of 78
12	=RETURN(E11)	Return % due
13		

Worksheet_78

	A	B	C	D	E
1	LOAN AMOUNT	INTEREST	MONTHS O/S	FULL INTEREST	INTEREST DUE
2	$20,000	10.00%	7	$2,000.00	$1,615
3					

Fig. 2.8. Comments in column F that enhance the macro's readability.

per hour based on the type of labor and (2) material costs based on the part number and shipping location. To calculate both costs, the final macro must use the CHOOSE and LOOKUP functions. But instead of including the CHOOSE and LOOKUP functions in the macro now, you can write a shell, use simple constants to test it, and add the real functions later.

To write the shell in figure 2.9, you use the constant $10 as the labor cost per hour, the constant $5 as the material cost based on the part number, and the constant $10 as the shipping cost. If the macro works correctly with these "dummy" constants, you can substitute the CHOOSE and LOOKUP functions that actually perform the calculations (see fig. 2.10). You will find this method of creating and testing a shell very useful in macros that perform more complex calculations than those used in this example.

Guidelines for Successful Command Macros

Because function macros are used mainly for performing calculations, most of the macros you create will be command macros. These

File   Edit   Formula   Format   Data   Options   Macro   Window

A1 | Project_Costs

	Macro4	
	A	**B**
1	**Project_Costs**	
2	=ARGUMENT("TYPE",1)	
3	=ARGUMENT("HOURS",1)	
4	=ARGUMENT("NUMB",1)	
5	=ARGUMENT("PART_NO",1)	
6	**Cost_Per_Hour**	
7	=10	
8	**Cost_Part_No**	
9	=5	
10	**Shipping**	
11	=10	
12	**Project**	
13	=HOURS*A7+(A9*NUMB)+A11	
14	=RETURN(A13)	
15		
16		
17		
18		
19		

Fig. 2.9. A shell built for a function macro.

File   Edit   Formula   Format   Data   Options   Macro   Window

A1 | Project_Costs

	Proj_Costs			
	A	**B**	**C**	**D**
1	**Project_Costs**	1902	10	1
2	=ARGUMENT("TYPE",1)	2180	12	2
3	=ARGUMENT("HOURS",1)	2345	5	2
4	=ARGUMENT("NUMB",1)	3419	6.5	1
5	=ARGUMENT("PART_NO",1)	3560	70	2
6	**Cost_Per_Hour**	3899	100	3
7	=CHOOSE(TYPE,5,10,15,20,50,100)	3941	5	3
8	**Cost_Part_No**	4562	66	1
9	=VLOOKUP(PART_NO,B1:D10,2)	6650	72	3
10	**Shipping**	8888	150	4
11	=VLOOKUP(PART_NO,B1:D10,3)			
12	=CHOOSE(A11,10,20,30,40)			
13	**Project**			
14	=HOURS*A7+(A9*NUMB)+A12			
15	=RETURN(A14)			
16				
17				
18				
19				

Fig. 2.10. A shell with the remaining instructions filled in.

can vary from the simple duplication of a menu sequence to a completely automated application. As you begin creating more sophisticated macros, using strategies that ensure that your macros will work becomes essential.

Using the Recorder

When you are creating a command macro that duplicates menu options, you should not overlook the Recorder. You might be tempted to bypass the Recorder, especially if your macro has only a few steps. However, because you easily could make a typographical error or forget a step, you should use this capability for command macros with even the simplest menu selections.

You also should not overlook the Recorder when you create command macros that incorporate both menu options and logical constructs such as iteration. (*Iteration* is a loop that causes macro instructions to be executed a repeated number of times.) You can use the Recorder to handle the portions of the macro that contain menu commands. Then, to complete your macro, you can insert blank lines in the macro sheet where you can add the commands for iterative or other nonmenu options.

To supply the nonmenu options that cannot be entered with the Recorder, you can use the Paste function sequence on the Formula menu. This procedure not only will save time, but will ensure that your syntax is accurate.

Figure 2.11 shows an example of a macro created with the Recorder. After the Recorder is used to enter the menu instructions, the macro is modified as shown in figure 2.12. A blank line is inserted at the top for the macro name, Format. In addition, the SELECT statement has been modified. The original version is restrictive because it uses an absolute reference to a range of cells. The new statement prompts the operator to specify the range from the keyboard. If desired, several blank lines can be inserted for additional instructions. Instructions can be added to the end of the macro to specify the number of iterations for processing the menu commands.

Because you visually can verify macro instructions as they are entered with the Recorder, this approach minimizes the time required to debug the macro. For the most part, the only sections of the macro that you need to check are the instructions that involve the iteration process.

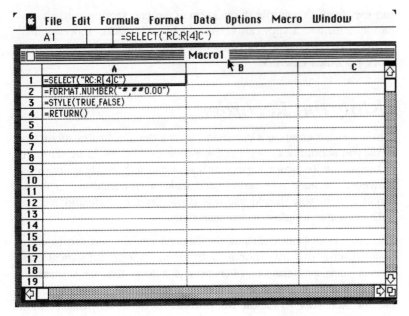

Fig. 2.11. Initial instructions entered with the Recorder.

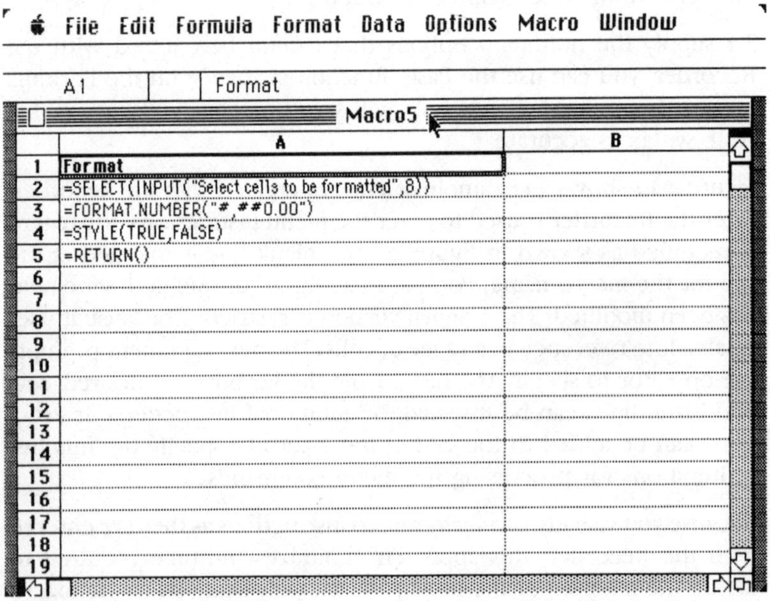

Fig. 2.12. The revised macro with the macro name and some macro instructions added.

Building Complex Macros

As your macro skills improve, you will want to develop more complex macros. For example, you may want to create a macro that automates an application for users less familiar with Excel, thereby freeing them from having to master the command sequences. To create this kind of macro, you can take advantage of many techniques developed by programmers over the last 20 years.

Separating Logic and Syntax

A section at the beginning of this chapter described plans of attack. Nowhere is such a plan more important than in a complex command macro. When you create a complex command macro, having a clear understanding of the exact, complete task to be accomplished and the methodology to be used is essential.

If you start entering macro instructions before you establish a plan, you probably will end up with a hopeless, tangled mess. Moreover, when the macro fails, you will not be sure whether the problem is an error in syntax or faulty logic. Because you will not have a written guide to follow, you will have to patch instructions in place and, in many cases, you may make the problem worse. This approach could increase the amount of time required to complete the macro by three- or fourfold. Therefore, if you follow only one of the suggestions presented in this chapter, let that suggestion be the following: Before you write an Excel macro, map out its logic.

Keeping Code Manageable

Good programmers keep their main logic within a page of code. Restricting a macro's main logic to 50 or 60 lines of instructions is a good idea. If you were given a choice between reading either 400 or 50 lines of macro code to determine what a macro's principal tasks are, you probably would choose the 50 lines. Although your main logic should be kept short, you still can have many more lines of code. You should separate these additional lines from the main logic by placing them within a subroutine.

Figure 2.13 is an example of good code management. Suppose that you have three subroutines: one creates additional windows, another establishes specific column widths and formats, and the third handles printing. By reviewing the various subroutine calls, you easily can see the macro's main logic. In some macros, the main logic instructions are nothing more than a series of subroutine calls.

| | File | Edit | Formula | Format | Data | Options | Macro | Window |

| | A1 | | Main_Logic |

Macro7

	A	B	C
1	Main_Logic		
2	=Window_routine()	Call window subroutine	
3	=Width_routine()	Call width subroutine	
4	=Print_routine()	Call print subroutine	
5	=RETURN()		
6			
7			
8			
9			
10			
11			
12			
13			
14			
15			
16			
17			
18			
19			

Fig. 2.13. An example of good code management.

Building a Shell

You already have learned about shells for function macros. Shells are even more important for command macros because they are usually more complex.

When a macro has several subroutines, shells can be particularly useful. By constructing a shell for each subroutine, you can speed up the testing stage. To create a shell, you omit the real subroutine code, and instead you enter a dummy INPUT statement or indicate in some other fashion that the subroutine was enacted. The purpose of using a dummy INPUT statement is to make the macro display a prompt message that indicates that the subroutine was reached. You can enter anything in response to the prompt; the input is not the important part of the statement.

You can use other methods, aside from an INPUT statement, to indicate that a subroutine has been executed. You can use a BEEP statement to sound the bell or you can use an ALERT statement to display an Alert box. Figure 2.14 demonstrates several shells. The first uses an Alert box to let the user know that the routine has been executed. The second uses three BEEP statements, and the third uses an INPUT statement.

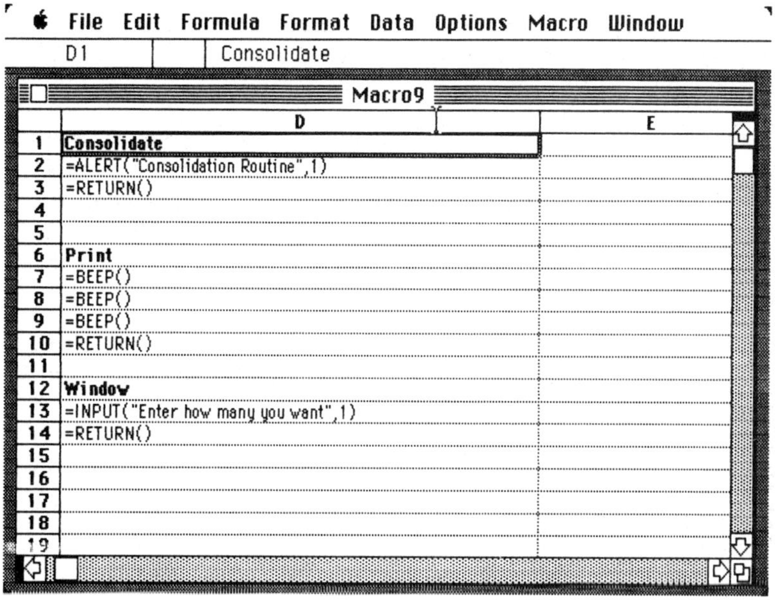

```
 File  Edit  Formula  Format  Data  Options  Macro  Window

     D1                  Consolidate

                              Macro9
                    D                              E
  1  Consolidate
  2  =ALERT("Consolidation Routine",1)
  3  =RETURN()
  4
  5
  6  Print
  7  =BEEP()
  8  =BEEP()
  9  =BEEP()
 10  =RETURN()
 11
 12  Window
 13  =INPUT("Enter how many you want",1)
 14  =RETURN()
 15
 16
 17
 18
 19
```

Fig. 2.14. Three ways to indicate that a subroutine has been executed.

Using this approach, you can check the overall logic flow without having to create all the detailed instructions for accomplishing your task. You add the detailed instructions after you are sure that the overall logic flow is working correctly at this level. Creating a shell before you create your final macro is a proven timesaver in macro development.

Using Straight-Line Code

Straight-line code (as explained in Chapter 1) is code that is executed from top to bottom, without unnecessary branching. In complex command macros, straight-line code is essential. Without it, you end up with what programmers affectionately call "spaghetti bowl" programs. In these programs, as changes are made to the logic, many branches are created. It all but takes a genius to keep up with the interwoven logic. This kind of twisted coding has been the bane of programmers for years.

Documenting Command Macros

Many command macros are as complex as computer programs, and therefore these macros require documentation. The documentation describes the process used to arrive at the results and explains program steps that may not be clear. The same concepts that are applied in programming departments of large organizations are useful for documenting macros.

To minimize the time required to document a macro, you can assign meaningful variable names. Then, just by looking at the variable names referenced, the user can understand what the statements do. For instance, most people would understand that the name Sales_Cost_Goods relates to profit. Using such names minimizes the need for supplemental documentation.

You should document any statement that is not intuitively clear. Enter the comments in the cell to the statement's immediate right. You also should explain menu selections in your documentation. If the macro instruction creates a new window, for example, you could use the comment *Create new window*. Comments do not have to be elaborate or even complete sentences. Comments are just quick reminders of the purpose of each statement in the macro.

The material on function macros (earlier in this chapter) suggested that you include section names in your macros. This advice is even more important for command macros, because the average command macro is longer and more complex than most function macros. Again, just as with variable names, the names of these sections should be meaningful and should remind the user of the purpose of the instructions that follow. To add a section name to a macro, you type a label in the appropriate macro cell. Remember that you do not precede the label with an equal sign. The absence of an equal sign causes the macro to regard the entry as a comment and skip to the next line. Figure 2.15 shows an example of section names added to a command macro to improve its readability.

Testing Procedures

After you create a macro, you must test it to ensure that it works correctly in the application you designed the macro for. You can test the macro by using simple data. For example, if the macro will be used to perform a task a specific number of times, make the

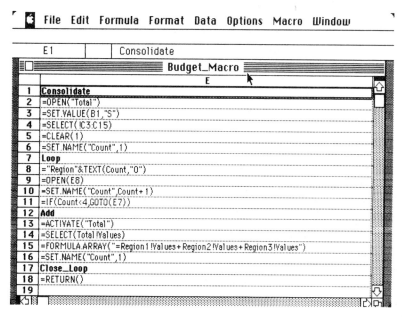

Fig. 2.15. A command macro with section names.

```
 File  Edit  Formula  Format  Data  Options  Macro  Window

        E1              Consolidate
                              Budget_Macro
                                    E
 1  Consolidate
 2  =OPEN("Total")
 3  =SET.VALUE(B1,"S")
 4  =SELECT(!C3:C15)
 5  =CLEAR(1)
 6  =SET.NAME("Count",1)
 7  Loop
 8  ="Region"&TEXT(Count,"0")
 9  =OPEN(E8)
10  =SET.NAME("Count",Count+1)
11  =IF(Count<4,GOTO(E7))
12  Add
13  =ACTIVATE("Total")
14  =SELECT(Total!Values)
15  =FORMULA.ARRAY("=Region1!Values+Region2!Values+Region3!Values")
16  =SET.NAME("Count",1)
17  Close_Loop
18  =RETURN()
19
```

macro perform the task two or three times. You then should be able to determine whether the macro is producing the desired results. (Using 200 iterations would take too long; using -50 iterations would cause an error.)

To test macros that are not iterative, you can supply some simple data such as price and discount rate. For example, for your first test, you could use easy-to-compute numbers such as a price of $100 and a discount of 10 percent.

If a macro fails this first test, you should change the macro display format so that cell values rather than the macro formulas are displayed. You can do this by selecting Options Display and clicking Formulas. By eliminating the formulas display, you can see the values stored in macro cells, error messages, and logical TRUE and FALSE values that result from the execution of the macro's functions. This procedure can give you a clue as to why the macro failed.

If your macro will be used under varying conditions, you should add another step to your testing procedure: You should check for all potential exception conditions. These conditions might be negative numbers, variables that exceed an acceptable range, or alphabetic data where numeric data is expected. You should make a list of the conditions that you want to check so that you are sure not to overlook any.

If you create a macro for someone else, make sure that person tests it. A user test of a macro is a critical step. The user can tell you whether you have misinterpreted specific requirements—for example, expecting numeric data where alphabetic data will be provided.

Conclusion

When you are anxious to write a macro and to get it working, you may not want to take the time to do anything that could delay the process. Following some of the suggestions in this chapter *will* cause slight delays. Experience, however, has proved that the time these procedures save during the final testing and implementation stages far outweighs such delays. You also will find modifying macros easier because of these guidelines. The suggestions provided here tend to improve the success rate of your macros and thus reduce the frustration level caused by macros that do not work correctly.

3

Creating Function Macros

For many people, entering spreadsheet formulas is a tedious task. Formula arguments and operators must be entered carefully and tested to ensure accurate model results. To help users, spreadsheet developers have provided many built-in functions, including those for determining sums, averages, and net present value.

Excel, like other spreadsheet programs, provides a comprehensive set of functions to reduce your work and ensure the accuracy of your model results. But unlike some other spreadsheet programs, Excel, through its function macro capability (described in Chapter 2), enables you to create your own functions. This chapter provides many examples of function macros that will help you learn how to create your own functions. You can use the macros just as they appear or modify them for your needs.

As indicated in previous chapters, a function macro performs a calculation and returns a result. Function macros enable you to create your own built-in functions, which you can use over and over simply by storing the macro in your macro sheet and entering the function macro keyword into your worksheet whenever you need to use the macro. You can store on a macro sheet as many macros as you like, as long as you leave at least one blank cell between macros.

You use the function macro keyword the same way you use the names of functions (such as SUM or MIN) already provided in Excel. In other words, whenever you use a function macro, you enter the keyword and complete the function with arguments contained within parentheses, just as you would use any other function included in Excel's set. For example, suppose that you created a function macro that calculates a purchase discount. The form of this function would appear as

DISCOUNT(PURCHASES,DISCOUNT_RATE)

To use this function in a worksheet, you would enter

=DISCOUNT(B2:B10,.05)

In this chapter, you will learn how to create and use many function macros similar to the purchase discount macro. Included in the chapter are the following types of macros:

- Date and time macros

- Numeric conversion macros

- Financial macros

- Depreciation macros

- Permutation and probability macros

- Customized function macros

Date and Time Macros

Date computations have a wide range of applications in business, from scheduling meetings to scheduling payments due. Excel has a full complement of built-in functions to date-stamp a worksheet, extract the day or month from a date, and determine the day of the week. Although these built-in functions are useful, they won't determine the next month or year, set an appointment on a weekday, or return a word representing a day of the week. With Excel's function macro capability, you can create macros that will accomplish these tasks.

In the next sections, the following date and time macros are described:

- A macro that looks one month into the future

- A macro that determines the next year

- A macro that determines weekdays

- A macro that returns a word for a day of the week

Macros like these enable you to move beyond Excel's built-in date and time functions. By adapting the macro concepts used in these examples, you can develop similar macros to meet your own date-manipulation needs. For instance, the macro that determines a day of the week can be used to determine a loan due date or a closing date for a real estate transaction.

Instead of placing each macro on a separate macro sheet (which is the method followed for convenience in other sections of the chapter), you will include all four macros on one macro sheet. This method of developing macros is the one you should use in building your own macro library.

A Macro That Looks One Month into the Future

This first macro examines a date and then returns a date one month into the future. The task may seem easy if you think that all the macro has to do is add 1 to the month number. With this method, though, month 12 would become month 13. Nor can the macro add a fixed number of days to each month. That method will eventually result in an error because all months don't have the same number of days. The best solution is to create a function macro flexible enough to handle these potential problems.

Begin with a fresh macro sheet on your screen. Select New Macro Sheet from the File menu and click OK. Although you can begin your entry anywhere, cell A1 is a good place to start. Type the macro name *Next_Month* into cell A1 and then press the Return key (see fig. 3.1). Excel will move the cursor to A2, where you will enter the first instruction in the macro.

This macro requires a single argument for the potential variable: the date. ARGUMENT statements correspond in number and order to the arguments the function macro will pass to the macro sheet.

In this example, the name of the argument is DATE. To provide the argument name and to specify that only numeric data is acceptable, enter the following statement into A2:

    =ARGUMENT("DATE",1)

Notice that you must enclose the name of the argument in double quotation marks. You also must use a comma delimiter after the argument name (as for any macro variable argument), separating the argument name from the data *type* (or types). The number 1 indicates that only numeric values are acceptable.

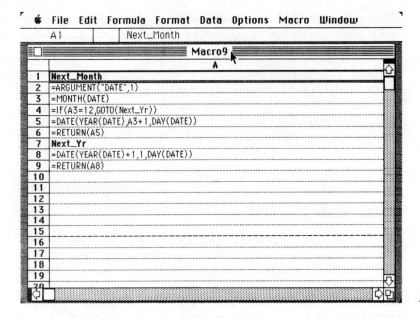

Fig. 3.1. The Next—Month macro.

The next step is to use Excel's MONTH function to extract the month from the date. To provide this calculation in the macro, enter the following statement into the next available cell, A3:

    =MONTH(DATE)

Now you must check for the exception—any instance in which adding 1 to the month number won't work. If the month number is 12, you must do two things: (1) set the month number to 1 and (2) increment the year number by 1. To check for the exception condition, you enter the IF and GOTO functions into A4:

    =IF(A3=12,GOTO(Next_Yr))

This statement means that if the value in A3 or the MONTH(DATE) equals 12, the program will branch to a new location. If A3 is any other number, the statement in A5 will be executed next. The instruction you place in A5 must compute the new date for months other than December, for that is the only month to which 1 cannot be added.

You use Excel's DATE function to construct the new date. The year and day will be the same as for the original date. The month number will be incremented by 1. Because the month number is currently stored in A3, A3+1 will represent the month. You enter the DATE function into the next blank cell, A5:

=DATE(YEAR(DATE),A3+1,DAY(DATE))

A RETURN function will return the date value. You enter the following statement into A6:

=RETURN(A5)

The macro is now complete for the non-December path, but you still have to provide a statement for Next_Yr.

At the beginning of the next section, A7, you type the label *Next_Yr*. Again, you need the DATE function, which will be used only when the original date has a month of 12. For this path, you want to increment the year by 1, use 1 for the first month (January), and retain the day of the original date. You can accomplish all this by typing the following statement into A8:

=DATE(YEAR(DATE)+1,1,DAY(DATE))

Finally, you type into A9 the last statement for this path:

=RETURN(A8)

This statement will return the date calculated in A8.

You are now ready to name the macro. First, make A1 the active cell by moving your mouse pointer to that location and clicking the mouse button. Then select the Define Name command from the Formula menu at the top of your screen. A dialog box will appear (see fig. 3.2). The dialog box for Define Name has a special appearance on a macro sheet. In addition to displaying the name for the range of cells and the cell reference, the dialog box (at the bottom) contains the new information for the macro sheet. Because the macro you are naming is a function macro, you click Function (by placing the mouse pointer on the Function circle) and then click OK. Next, move to A7 and again use Formula Define Name. This time, you click just OK because A7 is only part of the function macro and does not contain the function macro name. Your new macro is now ready for action.

To try running the macro, move to a blank worksheet by selecting Window and choosing a worksheet name. If you don't have a blank worksheet open at this time, select File New Worksheet. In either case, you type the macro sheet name and the function macro name.

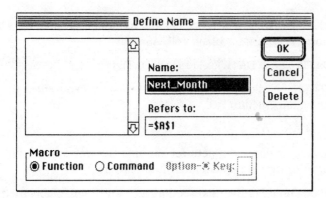

Fig. 3.2. The Define Name dialog box.

To operate the macro, you place the date between the parentheses for the function. As an example, you might enter

=Macro9!Next_Month("4/15/86")

This entry consists of the macro sheet name followed by an exclamation point and then the function macro name, Next_Month, and an opening parenthesis. The argument expected is either a date enclosed in quotation marks ("4/15/86") or a reference to a cell containing a date. A closing parenthesis follows the argument. The macro will return the answer, 5/15/86.

Figure 3.3 shows how this function macro is used to convert the dates on a worksheet. Rather than type each reference to the function macro, you can use Paste Function and then Copy to expedite the task.

The first step is to use File New Worksheet to obtain a new worksheet. Then you enter *DATE* in A1 as the column heading. In A2 through A6, you enter the dates as shown in those cells in figure 3.3: 3/15/86, 12/7/85, 1/2/82, 11/30/84, and 12/3/86. Quotation marks are not required in this example because you are not entering the dates directly into the macro as you did in the preceding example.

The next step is to complete the results column. You enter the heading *NEXT MONTH* in B1. Now you are ready to use Paste Function and Copy.

First, move the cursor to B2 so that it is the active cell. Then drag the mouse down the Formula menu to the Paste Function command. Scroll through the entries until you find Macro9!Next_Month. Remember that the function macros for the active macro sheets always are listed after Excel's built-in functions (see fig. 3.4).

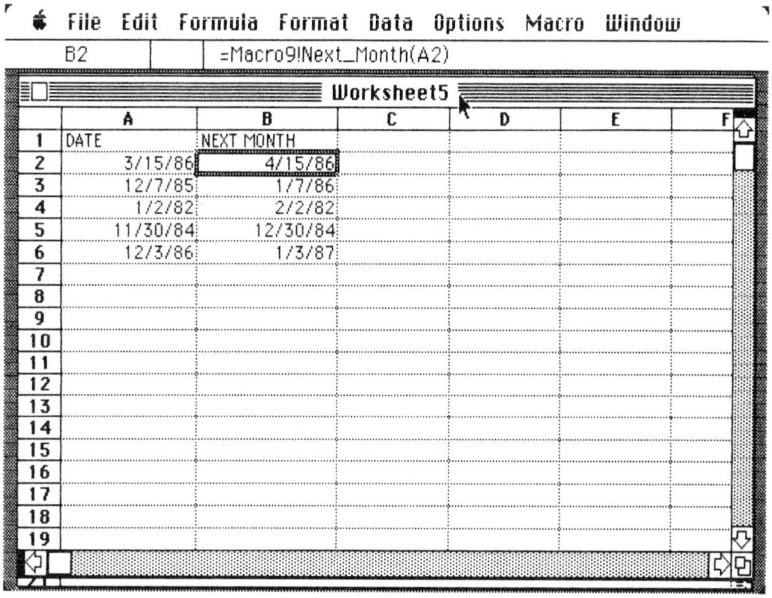

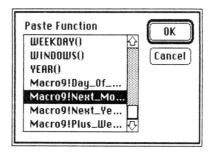

Fig. 3.3. The Next – Month macro used on a worksheet.

Fig. 3.4. The Paste Function dialog box.

Place the cursor on the entry that reads Macro9!Next_Mo. . . . (Excel cannot display the entire macro name in the allotted space, so the name is abbreviated.) Click the mouse button with the cursor on this entry, and it will be selected. When you click OK, this function will be placed in B2 and preceded by an equal sign.

The edit line will display =Macro9!Next_Month( ), and the cursor will be positioned between the parentheses. You can add arguments within the parentheses by typing them or by pointing and clicking the mouse. Point to A2, click the mouse button, and then press Return. All you need to do now is format the cell as a date with Format Number and copy the contents to cells B3 through B6.

For creating other macros, you also need to know how Excel handles arguments with missing values. If the missing argument is numeric, Excel substitutes a zero. For example, suppose that you have an interest rate and you want to check for a missing value. You then want the function to branch to A8 if RATE equals zero. You use the following statement:

=IF(RATE=0,A8)

Nonnumeric arguments are assigned an error value of #N/A. You can check for a missing value in one of these with

=IF(ISNA(ADDRESS),A17)

In a later section of this chapter, "Customized Function Macros," you will see the instructions for performing these checks in a working macro such as the Sqft macro.

A Macro That Determines the Next Year

This macro is similar to the Next_Month macro except that this one determines the next year. You create this macro on the original macro sheet, the one containing the Next_Month macro. If the worksheet window is still visible, you should reactivate the macro window by selecting the macro sheet name from the Window menu. Be sure to leave at least one cell blank in order to separate the Next_Month macro from this new macro.

First, you move the cursor to A11 and type the label *Next_Year* (see fig. 3.5). Like the previous macro, this macro has only one argument, DATE. You enter the following ARGUMENT statement into A12:

=ARGUMENT("DATE",1)

The reshaped date is created in A13 with the DATE function. The year for the new date will be the original date plus 1, and the month and day will remain the same. You enter the DATE function as

=DATE(YEAR(DATE)+1,MONTH(DATE),DAY(DATE))

Finally, you enter into A14 the following statement, which will return the date:

=RETURN(A13)

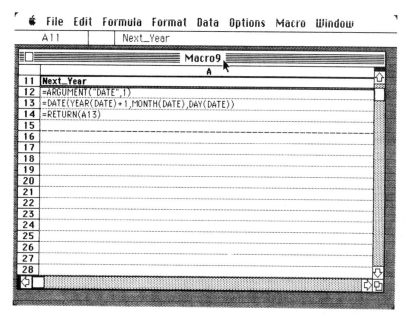

Fig. 3.5. The Next_Yr macro.

Now move your cursor to A11 and use the Define Name command from the Formula menu to establish the function macro name. Afterward, you can move to the worksheet environment and try the new macro.

A Macro That Determines Weekdays

This macro is more sophisticated than either of the previous macros. It is useful for scheduling appointments or due dates on weekdays only. Suppose, for example, that you work in a medical clinic, where follow-up appointments must be scheduled on the basis of doctors' instructions. Sometimes a doctor will ask that a patient be scheduled for suture removal or some other follow-up procedure in 5 or 10 days, and then complain if the patient is scheduled to return on a weekend when the staff is low. This macro can solve that problem. Both the current date and the doctor's follow-up instructions are recorded. The macro attempts to schedule the appointment by adding the follow-up days to the current date. The macro then checks whether the calculated date falls on a weekday or a weekend and whether the date is one of the clinic's few holidays.

Creating the Weekday Macro

Scheduling an appointment on a weekday can be handled in several ways. First, try the strategy described in this section and then create your own macro, if you like. To begin, type the label *Plus_Weekday* into cell A16 on the macro sheet you used for the previous macros, leaving a blank cell between the macros (see fig. 3.6).

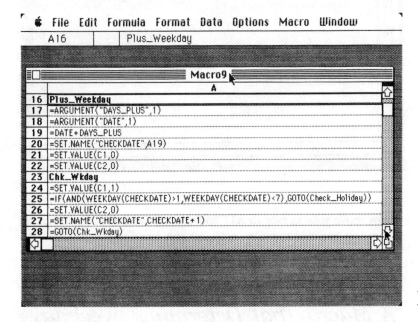

Fig. 3.6. The first section of the Plus_Weekday macro.

The weekday macro will have two arguments: DAYS_PLUS and DATE. The first argument represents the number of days to increment the date, which is the second argument. Enter the following ARGUMENT statements into A17 and A18, respectively:

    =ARGUMENT("DAYS_PLUS",1)

    =ARGUMENT("DATE",1)

Note that DAYS_PLUS is listed first. The following formula, which you enter into A19, calculates the incremented date:

    =DATE+DAYS_PLUS

The incremented date is saved in a variable called CHECKDATE. You can alter this variable if the original date falls on a weekend or holiday. CHECKDATE is initialized with the following statement, which you type into A20:

=SET.NAME("CHECKDATE",A19)

Here, the SET.NAME function assigns a value to the name specified.

This macro must check for two separate conditions: a weekday and a holiday. The initial weekday check might be okay, but the holiday check could cause the date to be incremented, and the resulting date for scheduling the appointment then might fall on a weekend. You need a method for ensuring that both the weekday and holiday checks have been passed before a date is returned for scheduling the appointment.

To check both these conditions, you can set up two flag cells to store the "okay" indicators for the weekday and holiday tests. Use cell C1 for the weekday flag. This cell will be initialized with a zero flag, indicating that the weekday check has not been satisfied. Enter the following statement into A21:

=SET.VALUE(C1,0)

Cell C2 provides a similar flag for the holiday check. A value of zero indicates that the holiday check has not been satisfied. Type into A22 the initializing statement for the flag in C2:

=SET.VALUE(C2,0)

The next step is to begin a loop that will handle the weekday check. A loop is needed because the initial date could fall on a Saturday or a Sunday. In other words, you won't want to pass through all the macro instructions the same number of times for each date. For this loop, use the label *Chk_Wkday*, which you enter into A23. Because the loop will find a weekday (that is, Monday through Friday), enter *1* into the flag cell for the weekday check by typing the following statement into A24:

=SET.VALUE(C1,1)

An IF statement, which comes next in the weekday loop, relies on Excel's WEEKDAY function. The WEEKDAY function returns 1 for Sunday, 2 for Monday, 3 for Tuesday, and so on. Thus, the numbers 1 and 7 are weekend days, and 2 through 5 are weekdays. If the number returned is greater than 1 but less than 7, you have a weekday. In that case, you can proceed to the holiday check (A29 in fig. 3.7). To provide this macro instruction, enter the following statement into A25:

```
=IF(AND(WEEKDAY(CHECKDATE)>1,WEEKDAY(CHECKDATE)<7),
   GOTO(Check_Holiday))
```

If the date returned is not a weekday, control will pass to A26. Here you set the flag for the holiday check to zero if this is your second pass through the weekday check after passing the holiday check. Even though the holiday check may have been passed once, if the date is incremented, the new date might be a holiday. You set the flag to zero by entering the following statement into A26:

```
=SET.VALUE(C2,0)
```

The date stored in CHECKDATE is incremented with the following statement, which you type into A27:

```
=SET.NAME("CHECKDATE",CHECKDATE+1)
```

After the date is incremented, all you need to do is supply a branch that returns to the beginning of the weekday loop. You can enter this instruction in the next available cell, A28, by typing

```
=GOTO(Chk_Wkday)
```

You still need a routine to check for a holiday (see fig. 3.7). Begin in A29 by typing the label *Check_Holiday*. (Remember that you never use an equal sign in front of a label.) For this routine, the first step will be to check the flags for 1's. This pass may be the second one through the holiday check. If the date passed the weekday check on the second trip, the weekday flag will still be set to 1, and the macro can return that number, for the 1 means that the date was not incremented. You will recall that if the date is incremented in the weekday check, the holiday flag is set to 0. In that case, the macro will have to check the new date to see whether it is a holiday. For these calculations, enter into A30 the following statement:

```
=IF(AND(C1=1,C2=1),GOTO(Return))
```

Your next task will be to set the holiday flag to 1. Enter into A31 the statement

```
=SET.VALUE(C2,1)
```

The medical clinic's holidays have been stored in B33 and B34 as 12/25/85 and 1/1/86, respectively. You should also make these entries in your macro sheet. Don't be surprised at the serial date numbers that appear when you type the entries. Cells A32 and A33 contain the instructions for checking CHECKDATE against these hol-

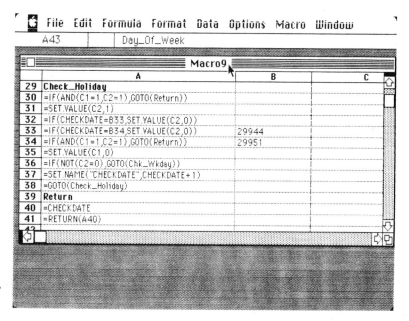

File Edit Formula Format Data Options Macro Window

A43	Day_Of_Week

Macro9

	A	B	C
29	Check_Holiday		
30	=IF(AND(C1=1,C2=1),GOTO(Return))		
31	=SET.VALUE(C2,1)		
32	=IF(CHECKDATE=B33,SET.VALUE(C2,0))		
33	=IF(CHECKDATE=B34,SET.VALUE(C2,0))	29944	
34	=IF(AND(C1=1,C2=1),GOTO(Return))	29951	
35	=SET.VALUE(C1,0)		
36	=IF(NOT(C2=0),GOTO(Chk_Wkday))		
37	=SET.NAME("CHECKDATE",CHECKDATE+1)		
38	=GOTO(Check_Holiday)		
39	Return		
40	=CHECKDATE		
41	=RETURN(A40)		

Fig. 3.7. The Check_Holiday routine.

idays. If a holiday is encountered, C2 will be set to 0. Enter into A32 and A33, respectively, the following statements:

=IF(CHECKDATE=B33,SET.VALUE(C2,0))

=IF(CHECKDATE=B34,SET.VALUE(C2,0))

Because the date already has been through the holiday check, C2 will be equal to 1 if CHECKDATE didn't match one of the holidays. At this point, the weekday flag still will be set to 1 because the date already passed the weekday check and hasn't been incremented. There has been no reason yet to turn off the weekday flag.

You will need to check whether both flags are 1 so that the date can be returned. Type into A34 the following statement:

=IF(AND(C1=1,C2=1),GOTO(Return))

This statement branches to the code that will return the date (A39:A41). If CHECKDATE is a holiday, this branch is not taken, and the date needs to be incremented.

You must set the weekday flag to zero when you are about to increment the date. Enter into A35 the following statement:

=SET.VALUE(C1,0)

The statement in A36 is necessary because the macro will stay in the holiday loop until you have a nonholiday date. Cell A34 checks for the holiday and weekday flags set to 1, indicating that the holiday loop did not need to increment the date and that it passed the check. If the macro does not take the branch in A34, you know the date has been incremented because of a holiday. The statement in A36 checks for a value in C2 other than zero, which indicates that the date has been incremented to a holiday and branches back to re-check the weekday.

Type the following into A36:

    =IF(NOT(C2=0),GOTO(Chk_Wkday))

Here, if C2 is not equal to zero, a branch to Chk_Wkday will be taken. If C2 is still equal to zero, the date must be incremented. You enter into A37 the following statement for incrementing the date:

    =SET.NAME("CHECKDATE",CHECKDATE+1)

Next, you need a branch for returning to the top of the holiday loop. Enter the following into A38:

    =GOTO(Check_Holiday)

The last part of the macro is the Return section. Enter the label *Return* into A39. Then set the value of cell A40 equal to the current value of CHECKDATE by placing the following instruction into A40:

    =CHECKDATE

The final instruction, which you type into A41, is

    =RETURN(A40)

You have one last task before you try running the macro. Name the macro and its various sections by using Define Name from the Formula menu. First, move the cursor to A16 and select Define Name. Click Function and then click OK. Next, move the cursor to A23 and select Define Name. Because this cell doesn't contain the macro name, you need to click just OK. Repeat this last step for cells A29 and A39. In both cases, click OK only. Neither the macro type nor the macro Option-key sequence is needed.

Using the Weekday Macro

To try the weekday macro, you need to request a new worksheet. Figure 3.8 shows a sample worksheet, containing data supplied to the macro. You may want to duplicate the entire worksheet or just make the essential entries shown in columns B, C, and D. The dates of each patient's initial visit are placed in column B. The doctor's follow-up instructions appear in column C. Column D shows the calculated results of the new macro. You type into D3 the macro sheet name and the macro name, or you can use the Paste Function command from the Formula menu and select the macro from the list displayed. As indicated previously, the two arguments required are DAYS_PLUS, for the follow-up days; and DATE, for the date of the initial visit. Remember that DAYS_PLUS must come first in the macro. To run the macro, you enter into D3 the following:

=Macro9!Plus_Weekday(C3,B3)

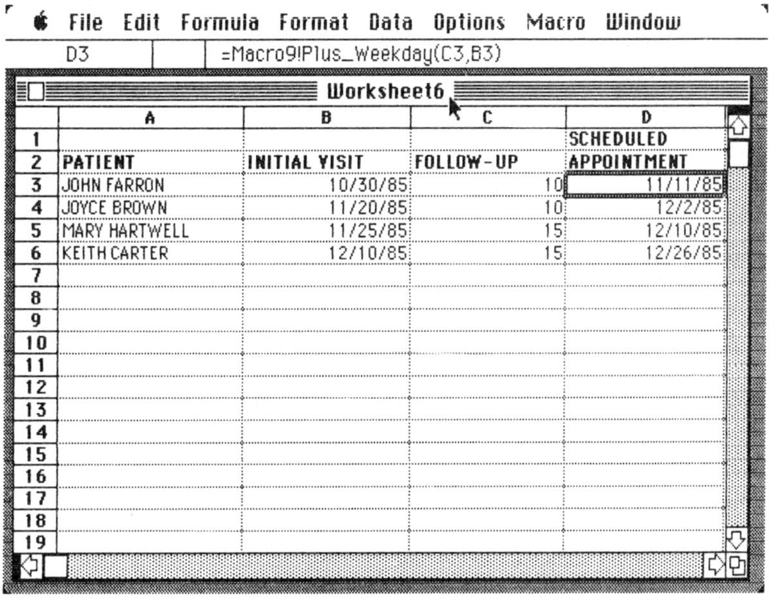

	A	B	C	D
1				SCHEDULED
2	PATIENT	INITIAL VISIT	FOLLOW-UP	APPOINTMENT
3	JOHN FARRON	10/30/85	10	11/11/85
4	JOYCE BROWN	11/20/85	10	12/2/85
5	MARY HARTWELL	11/25/85	15	12/10/85
6	KEITH CARTER	12/10/85	15	12/26/85

Fig. 3.8. The Plus_Weekday macro used in a worksheet.

To display the proper format, make sure that you have formatted the cell as a date. You then can use the Copy and Paste commands from the Edit menu to copy the formula to cells D4 through D6. Notice that in D4 the weekend days were skipped, and in D6 the Christmas holiday also was skipped for the scheduled appointment.

Modifying the Weekday Macro

The weekday macro can be modified to schedule certain kinds of appointments at set intervals. For example, you may want to schedule a follow-up visit in 5 days, 10 days, or 14 days. If patient information is stored in the system, the macro can suggest a follow-up date for the next checkup or inoculation. The function requires an argument for appointment type and a lookup table to determine how many days should elapse before the next visit.

A second modification is an expansion of the table for holiday dates. This table can be converted into a lookup table or expanded using the current approach. Using the current method, you type additional holiday dates following the serial date in B34. You can format the entries in B33 and B34 as dates or allow the serial dates to display, as in the example. You add additional IF statements after the two in A33 and A34 in order to compare CHECKDATE with the new entries.

If you have a long list of holidays, you may want to use the VLOOKUP function approach used in the next example (fig. 3.9). You can set a macro cell to a value and use the VLOOKUP result to change it if you find a match.

A Macro That Returns a Word for a Day of the Week

The day-of-the-week macro is much easier to create than the weekday macro (see fig. 3.9). All you need to accomplish with this macro is to convert a date into a word for a day of the week. You then can use that word in report headings. Place this macro on the same macro sheet you have been using for the previous macros. If this sheet is no longer visible on the screen, call it up with the Window menu.

Enter into A43 the label *Day_of_Week*, which you will use for the macro name. You enter the only argument, DATE, into A44 by typing the following ARGUMENT statement:

```
=ARGUMENT("DATE",1)
```

Next, you create a lookup table. Enter into B43 through B50, respectively, the following: *DAY #, 1, 2, 3, 4, 5, 6,* and *7.* Move to C43 and enter into C43 through C50, respectively, *DAY NAME, SUNDAY,*

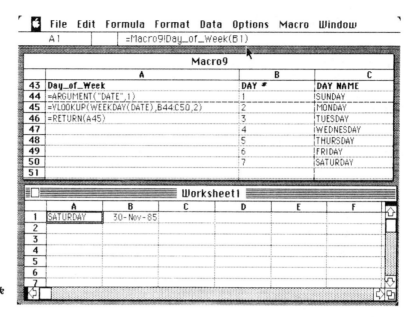

Fig. 3.9. The Day_of_Week macro.

MONDAY, TUESDAY, WEDNESDAY, THURSDAY, FRIDAY, and *SA-TURDAY*. Then move back to the next macro line, A45, and enter the statement

=VLOOKUP(WEEKDAY(DATE),B44:C50,2)

Here, Excel looks up the day-of-the-week number, which the WEEK-DAY function returns. Then Excel finds a match in the table and returns the word corresponding to the day of the week. To return this value to the worksheet cell that contains the function macro reference, you enter into A46 the following statement:

=RETURN(A45)

As you can see in figure 3.9, cells A43 through C43 were selected for labels, and Format Style Bold was used to highlight them. To name this macro sheet, you use Define Name for cell A43 and select Function. Also in this figure is a new worksheet, with the word *SATURDAY* returned in cell A1. The date for that day appears in B1, formatted with one of the date-formatting options to show how you might want such a heading to appear. You either can duplicate this example or create a similar one with your new function macro.

Numeric Conversion Macros

You will have many uses for numeric conversion macros. For instance, you can convert gallons and quarts to pints if pint is the only size container available. You can convert large-portion recipes to smaller portions for the weekend meal service. Other uses are for currency and metric conversions. Your options for this kind of macro are limited only by your needs and imagination.

Function macros provide an ideal solution when numeric values must be converted. The macros can be coded once and used whenever the conversion is needed.

The following macros are presented in this section:

- A macro that converts currency

- A macro that converts U.S. units to metric units

A Macro That Converts Currency

Currency conversion may be important to your business. For instance, you may need to consolidate the profits from foreign operations with the profits from your U.S. divisions. Or you may need to reimburse your employees for expenses incurred while visiting overseas operations. A function macro is ideal for automating such calculations because periodic updating of conversion rates is easy. If each model contained conversion calculations, each model would require revision whenever the rates fluctuated. With a function macro, you can update rates in just one location.

Suppose that you work for the Multilingual Company, whose foreign offices are in Canada, France, Germany, Great Britain, and Switzerland. You can create a macro that will convert these countries' currencies to U.S. dollars.

To create the macro, you begin by entering into A1 of a new macro sheet the label *Conversion* (see fig. 3.10). Two arguments are required: CURRENCY and AMOUNT. To define these arguments for Excel, you enter the following statements into A2 and A3, respectively:

=ARGUMENT("CURRENCY",2)

=ARGUMENT("AMOUNT",1)

Because the *type* for CURRENCY is 2, only text data will be acceptable. The *type* of 1 specified for AMOUNT means that only numeric data will be acceptable.

File Edit Formula Format Data Options Macro Window

| A1 | | Conversion | | |

Currency

	A	B	C	D
1	Conversion			
2	=ARGUMENT("CURRENCY",2)			
3	=ARGUMENT("AMOUNT",1)			
4	=VLOOKUP(CURRENCY,B11:C15,2)			
5	=A4*AMOUNT			
6	=RETURN(A5)			
7				
8				
9				
10		CODE	CONV. FACTOR	CURRENCY
11		B	1.46	BRITISH POUND
12		C	0.7375	CANADIAN DOLLAR
13		F	0.132	FRENCH FRANC
14		G	0.3906	GERMAN MARK
15		S	0.4785	SWISS FRANC
16				
17				
18				

Fig. 3.10. A currency conversion macro.

Your next step is to create a lookup table. First, move your cursor to B10 and select B10 through D15. Enter into B10 the column heading *CODE*. Next, enter the following codes into B11 through B15, respectively: *B, C, F, G,* and *S.* You enter into C10 the column heading *CONV. FACTOR.* And you enter into C11 through C15 the current conversion factors for British pounds, Canadian dollars, French francs, German marks, and Swiss francs. (For suggested conversion factors, refer to fig. 3.10.) Enter into D10 the column heading *CURRENCY.* Finally, enter into D11 through D15 the following: *BRITISH POUND, CANADIAN DOLLAR, FRENCH FRANC, GERMAN MARK,* and *SWISS FRANC.*

The statement in A4 will access this table. Move the cursor back to A4 and enter the following statement into that cell:

=VLOOKUP(CURRENCY,B11:C15,2)

The VLOOKUP function is used because the codes are stored vertically. Currency indicates which currency will be converted. The table entries are actually in B11 through C15, with B10 and C10 each containing a heading. The number 2 tells Excel to return the conversion factor from the second column of the table.

The actual conversion formula will be in A5. Type the formula as

=A4*AMOUNT

Finally, a RETURN function will return the result to the worksheet cell from which the macro is called. Enter the RETURN function into cell A6 by typing

=RETURN(A5)

Now all you have to do is name the macro. Because the function macro name is already in A1, the easiest method is to move your cursor to A1, select Define Name from the Formula menu, and and click OK.

To use the macro, open a new worksheet document and enter a reference to the macro sheet and the function macro name with the two arguments. Remember that function macros are not like command macros. You use function macros as you do Excel's built-in functions.

You easily can enhance this macro by including additional currencies and using the text functions. For example, you can use the MID function to extract the first letter of each currency description in a column of the worksheet and to substitute that letter for the current currency code. In fact, this macro can serve as a model for any kind of conversion you may need to make.

Setting up the worksheet is easy. You can follow the model in figure 3.11. Enter the labels *AMOUNT, CURRENCY,* and *CONVERTED AMOUNT* in A1 through C1. Enter *56, 30, 25, 100,* and *200,* respectively, in A2 through A6. Next enter *B, C, F, S,* and *G,* respectively, in B2 through B6. These letters stand for British pounds, Canadian dollars, French francs, Swiss francs, and German marks. You can add these descriptions in another column. They were left out in the practice example to save you some typing.

In C2 enter

=Currency!Conversion(B2,A2)

This statement says that you want to use the Conversion macro on the macro sheet called Currency. The first argument is the code for currency and the second is the amount of currency.

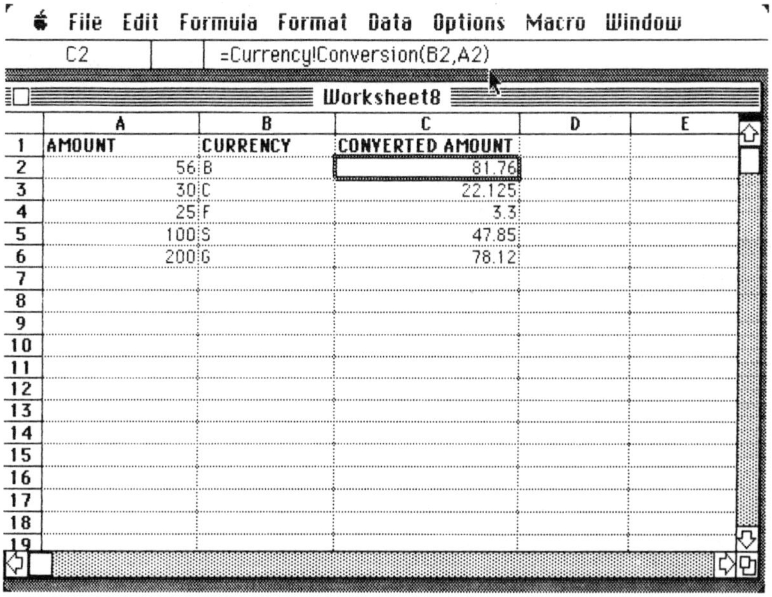

Fig. 3.11. The currency conversion macro used in a worksheet.

A Macro That Converts U.S. Units to Metric Units

If you deal with foreign customers, your product packaging may not present understandable quantity measures if you list only the U.S. values. A macro quickly can translate your U.S. values into their metric equivalents.

To create the macro, call up a new macro sheet and type the label *Metric* into cell A1 (see fig. 3.12). Then type into A2 the following statement:

=RESULT(2)

This statement specifies that only a text result is acceptable.

The macro has two arguments: NUMBER, for the number of units; and TYPE, for the unit of measure. Enter the following ARGUMENT statements into A3 and A4, respectively:

=ARGUMENT("NUMBER",1)

=ARGUMENT("TYPE",2)

🍎 File Edit Formula Format Data Options Macro Window

| | A8 | | =TEXT(A7,"0.00")&" "&VLOOKUP(A5,B2:D9,3) |

Macro21

	A	B	C	D
1	Metric	U.S. UNITS	FACTOR	CONVERSION UNITS
2	=RESULT(2)	F	30	CENTIMETERS
3	=ARGUMENT("NUMBER",1)	G	3.8	LITERS
4	=ARGUMENT("TYPE",2)	I	25	MILLIMETERS
5	=MID(TYPE,1,1)	M	1.6	KILOMETERS
6	=VLOOKUP(A5,B2:D9,2)	O	30	MILLILITERS
7	=NUMBER*A6	P	0.47	LITERS
8	=TEXT(A7,"0.00")&" "&VLOOKUP(A5,B3	Q	0.95	LITERS
9	=RETURN(A8)	Y	0.9	METERS
10				
11				
12				
13				
14				
15				
16				
17				
18				
19				

Fig. 3.12. A macro that converts U.S. units to metric units.

The first argument (number of units) will be numeric, and the second argument (unit of measure) will be text.

The MID function in A5 extracts the first character from the TYPE field and places that character in A5. Using that character, Excel will look up in the code field of a lookup table the conversion factor and conversion units. You create this lookup table on your macro sheet. First, select cells B1 through D9. Enter into the first cell the heading *U.S. UNITS*. Type into the remaining cells in column B the following lookup codes: *F, G, I, M, O, P, Q,* and *Y*. These codes for the U.S. units must be in ascending order. They represent feet, gallons, inches, miles, ounces, pints, quarts, and yards, respectively. Next, enter into column C the following: *FACTOR, 30, 3.8, 25, 1.6, 30, 0.47, 0.95,* and *0.9*. These conversion factors will be used with the U.S. unit numbers in calculating the conversions. Finally, type into column D the label *CONVERSION UNITS* and the following: *CENTIMETERS, LITERS, MILLIMETERS, KILOMETERS, LITERS, LITERS,* and *METERS.*

You then return to the macro statements and place in A6 the VLOOKUP statement to access this table. In A7, the NUMBER argument will be multiplied by the value obtained from VLOOKUP.

The last macro instruction is a creative use of the string capabilities of Excel. The TEXT function at the beginning of A8 converts the contents of A7 to text displayed in two decimal places of accuracy. The ampersand (&) joins this number to a blank space, and a second ampersand joins the space to the value returned by a second VLOOKUP function. Notice that this second VLOOKUP uses an offset of 3 rather than 2 to return the conversion unit.

Before you try the macro, you must complete one final step. You need to name the macro, using Define Name from the Formula menu.

You can try the new macro with a simple entry on your worksheet, or you can make several conversions like those shown in the worksheet in figure 3.13. For that worksheet, the U.S. units were placed in A3:A10, and the units of measure were placed in corresponding cells in column B. Column C was used for the function macro reference, and the macro was saved on a macro sheet called Macro21. To execute the macro, you either can type *Macro21!Metric(A3,B3)* or copy the macro reference by using the Paste Function command from the Formula menu. You will notice from the example that 5 inches automatically are converted to 125 millimeters, 10 yards are converted to 9 meters, and so forth.

File Edit Formula Format Data Options Macro Window

C3   =Macro21!Metric(A3,B3)

Worksheet9

	A	B	C	D	E	F
1		U.S. TO METRIC CONVERSION				
2		U.S. UNIT	METRIC EQUIVALENT			
3	5	INCHES	125.00 MILLIMETERS			
4	10	YARDS	9.00 METERS			
5	100	FEET	3000.00 CENTIMETERS			
6	2	MILES	3.20 KILOMETERS			
7	13	OUNCES	390.00 MILLILITERS			
8	4	PINTS	1.88 LITERS			
9	2	QUARTS	1.90 LITERS			
10	4	GALLONS	15.20 LITERS			
11						
12						
13						
14						
15						
16						
17						
18						
19						

Fig. 3.13. The Metric macro used to determine metric equivalents.

Financial Macros

Excel's function macros can help you work with financial ratios and perform other calculations. Financial ratios are simply comparisons of numbers on a company's income statement or balance sheet. Although most financial ratios require straightforward calculations, these are performed in the same way each time. This section contains two examples of macros for calculating financial ratios. Once you become experienced in building function macros with Excel, you can design similar macros for a variety of other financial uses. You can use macros to estimate receivables based on sales levels, compute rental income from a potential real estate investment, compute the tax effect of a purchase, or calculate standard financial ratios.

The following macros are presented in this section:

- A return-on-equity macro

- A current ratio macro

A Return-on-Equity Macro

Return on equity is one measure of a firm's performance. Investors often are interested in assessing the return on equity generated by a number of firms in the same industry. Although return on equity is not difficult to compute, making repeated calculations in order to look at many businesses can be time-consuming. Once created, a macro can handle this drudgery.

Your first step in creating this macro is to enter into A1 of a new macro sheet the label *Return_on_Equity*, which you will use as the macro name (see fig. 3.14).

This macro requires four arguments: (1) INC_BEFORE_TAXES, for income before taxes; (2) PREFERRED_DIV, for preferred dividends; (3) TAX_RATE, for the tax rate; and (4) COMMON_EQUITY, for common equity. You enter the following ARGUMENT statements into A2 through A5, respectively:

=ARGUMENT("INC_BEFORE_TAXES",1)

=ARGUMENT("PREFERRED_DIV",1)

=ARGUMENT("TAX_RATE",1)

=ARGUMENT("COMMON_EQUITY",1)

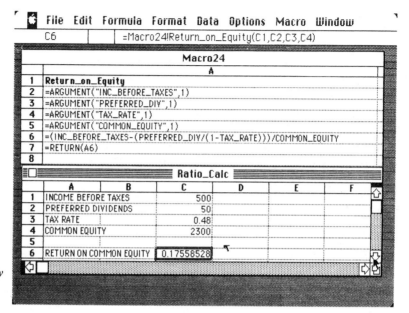

Fig. 3.14. The Return_on_Equity macro (top) and its result in a worksheet (bottom).

Notice that each of these argument statements has a *type* of 1, which restricts the argument to numeric data values.

Next, you enter the following formula into A6:

=(INC_BEFORE_TAXES-(PREFERRED_DIV/(1-
TAX_RATE)))/COMMON_EQUITY

In this calculation for determining the ratio, the preferred dividends divided by one minus the tax rate is subtracted from income before taxes. The result is then divided by common equity.

A RETURN function will return the final result. Type into A7 the following statement:

=RETURN(A6)

Now you name the macro by using Define Name from the Formula menu. In addition to showing the completed macro, figure 3.14 shows the result of the macro in calculating the return on equity with an income of $500, preferred dividends of $50, a tax rate of 48 percent, and common equity of $2,300.

A Current Ratio Macro

The current ratio function macro is even easier to calculate than the return-on-equity macro. Current ratio is simply a comparison of two income statement accounts: current assets and current liabilities.

To create this macro, you first type the label *Current_Ratio* into A9 of the same sheet you used for the return-on-equity macro (see fig. 3.15). Then you define the macro's two arguments by placing the following statements into A10 and A11, respectively:

=ARGUMENT("CURRENT_ASSETS",1)

=ARGUMENT("CURRENT_LIABILITIES",1)

 File   Edit   Formula   Format   Data   Options   Macro   Window

| C12 | =Macro24!Current_Ratio(C9,C10) |

Macro24

	A
9	Current_Ratio
10	=ARGUMENT("CURRENT_ASSETS",1)
11	=ARGUMENT("CURRENT_LIABILITIES",1)
12	=CURRENT_ASSETS/CURRENT_LIABILITIES
13	=RETURN(A12)
14	
15	
16	

Ratio_Calc

	A	B	C	D	E	F
8						
9	CURRENT ASSETS		$800,000			
10	CURRENT LIABILITIES		$550,000			
11						
12	CURRENT RATIO		1.455			
13						

Fig. 3.15. The Current_Ratio macro (top) and its result in a worksheet (bottom).

Next, you enter the following formula into A12:

=CURRENT_ASSETS/CURRENT_LIABILITIES

To return the result of the calculation, type the following statement into A13:

=RETURN(A12)

Again, name the macro by using Define Name from the Formula menu. In addition to showing the completed macro, figure 3.15 shows a calculated current ratio of 1.455.

Depreciation Macros

Depreciation calculations are necessary for estimating expenses and calculating taxes due. You can use a number of methods for calculating depreciation of your assets. These methods include straight line, double declining balance, sum of the years' digits, and ACRS (accelerated depreciation). All these methods are simply formulas, which you can incorporate into the function macros you create. Then, when you are ready to calculate depreciation, you just include in your worksheet the function macro keyword and its arguments.

The following macros are presented in this section:

- A double-declining-balance macro

- A sum-of-the-years'-digits macro

- An ACRS macro

A Double-Declining-Balance Macro

For the first depreciation calculation, you can create a useful function macro that uses the double-declining-balance method. With this macro, you can determine depreciation expense for any year within the useful life of an asset. You can use the basic worksheet model to test this depreciation macro.

To create the macro, begin with a new macro sheet on the screen. Type into A1 the label *Dbl_Decline*, which you will use for the macro name (see fig. 3.16).

The next step is to set up the arguments required. The first argument is LIFE, for the useful life of the asset. Enter into A2 the following statement:

=ARGUMENT("LIFE",1)

The second argument, YEAR, represents the current year of the asset's life. To define this argument, type into A3 this statement:

=ARGUMENT("YEAR",1)

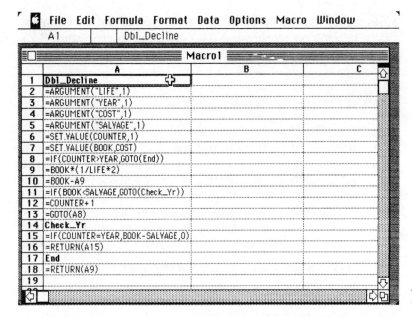

File Edit Formula Format Data Options Macro Window

A1 | Dbl_Decline

	A	B	C
	Macro1		
1	Dbl_Decline		
2	=ARGUMENT("LIFE",1)		
3	=ARGUMENT("YEAR",1)		
4	=ARGUMENT("COST",1)		
5	=ARGUMENT("SALVAGE",1)		
6	=SET.VALUE(COUNTER,1)		
7	=SET.VALUE(BOOK,COST)		
8	=IF(COUNTER>YEAR,GOTO(End))		
9	=BOOK*(1/LIFE*2)		
10	=BOOK-A9		
11	=IF(BOOK<SALVAGE,GOTO(Check_Yr))		
12	=COUNTER+1		
13	=GOTO(A8)		
14	Check_Yr		
15	=IF(COUNTER=YEAR,BOOK-SALVAGE,0)		
16	=RETURN(A15)		
17	End		
18	=RETURN(A9)		
19			

Fig. 3.16. The Dbl_Decline macro.

You enter into A4 the next argument, COST, for the original cost of the asset:

=ARGUMENT("COST",1)

The final argument is SALVAGE, for the salvage value of the asset. Define this argument by typing into A5 the following statement:

=ARGUMENT("SALVAGE",1)

Note that all four arguments are numeric arguments, as indicated by a *type* of 1.

Because depreciation under the double-declining-balance method is always calculated on the book value of an asset (that is, its cost less accumulated depreciation), you must set up a loop in order to obtain the depreciation for the year you want. In setting up this loop, you need to initialize some values before moving into the loop's instructions.

You use the SET.VALUE function to establish the beginning variable values, but first you need to assign variable names to some macro cells. This step is necessary because the SET.VALUE function must have a cell in which to store the values. You use Define Name and assign the name *BOOK* to cell A10 and *COUNTER* to A12.

After naming the macro cells, enter into A6 the first initialization statement as

=SET.VALUE(COUNTER,1)

This statement initializes a loop counter to 1.

The next step is to set at cost the book value of the asset. To do this, you type into A7 the following statement:

=SET.VALUE(BOOK,COST)

You are now ready to establish the beginning of the loop. Type into A8 the following statement:

=IF(COUNTER>YEAR,GOTO(End))

This instruction checks the counter against the year for which you want to calculate depreciation expense. If COUNTER is greater than YEAR, the macro branches to End (which you will establish later as the end of the macro). If COUNTER is not greater than YEAR, control passes to the instruction that follows in A9. There, the depreciation expense for the first year will be calculated by multiplying the BOOK value by the fraction 1 over the life of the asset times 2. You supply this formula in A9 as

=BOOK*(1/LIFE*2)

The next step is to provide in A10 a formula to calculate a new BOOK value. Enter the formula as

=BOOK-A9

This formula subtracts the depreciation just calculated from the BOOK value. Your next concern is whether BOOK value has been reduced to less than the SALVAGE value. This check can be accomplished with the IF function. Type into A11 the following statement:

=IF(BOOK<SALVAGE,GOTO(Check_Yr))

If BOOK is less than SALVAGE, the macro alters the execution flow and checks the year for which you are trying to determine depreciation expense.

For now, assume that the BOOK value is not less than the SALVAGE value. Control moves to the next macro instruction, which increments the loop counter by 1. You provide this instruction in A12 by typing

=COUNTER+1

You use A13 as a means of branching to the top of the loop. To provide this branch, enter the following statement into this cell:

=GOTO(A8)

Here you specify A8 because that is the location of the IF statement that begins the loop.

Next, you enter *Check_Yr* into cell A14. The macro branches to this line only when the condition in A11 is met (that is, when the BOOK value is less than the SALVAGE value).

Now you must determine whether COUNTER has reached the year for which you want the depreciation expense. If COUNTER is equal to YEAR, you want the depreciation expense to be equal to the BOOK value less the SALVAGE value. If COUNTER has not yet reached YEAR, the depreciation expense will be zero. In other words, if BOOK value equals SALVAGE value for the year for which you are calculating depreciation, then BOOK value is equal to zero. To provide these calculations in the macro, enter into A15 the following formula:

=IF(COUNTER=YEAR,BOOK-SALVAGE,0)

Your next step is to return the value in A15 to the worksheet cell containing the Dbl_Decline function. Type the following statement into A16:

=RETURN(A15)

This statement ends this path of the macro. But you must still account for those cases in which BOOK is not less than SALVAGE, yet the condition test on COUNTER has been met. For these instances, you will need another section of code. Recall that in cell A8, at the top of your loop, you set up a branch to GOTO End if COUNTER became greater than YEAR. Now type the label *End* into A17.

Finally, the RETURN function in A18 will return the value in A9, which is the latest depreciation calculation. To return that value to the worksheet cell, you enter into A18 the following statement:

=RETURN(A9)

Before testing this macro, you must name it. Using Formula Define Name, assign the name Dbl_Decline.

You now are ready to test the depreciation macro. All you do is supply the LIFE, YEAR, COST, and SALVAGE values. Bring up a new worksheet on your screen by using the File New command, or use the Window menu to access an existing worksheet. Type *10* into B3, *2* into C3, and *10000* into D3. Next, move to cell F3 and either type the reference to the macro sheet and function name or use the Paste Function command from the Formula menu. Between the parentheses, you will include references to B3, C3, D3, and E3. Format the cells in columns D through F as dollars, using the Format Number command. You should get a result of $1,600.00, as shown in cell F3 of figure 3.17. This figure shows similar calculations for other depreciation expenses as well.

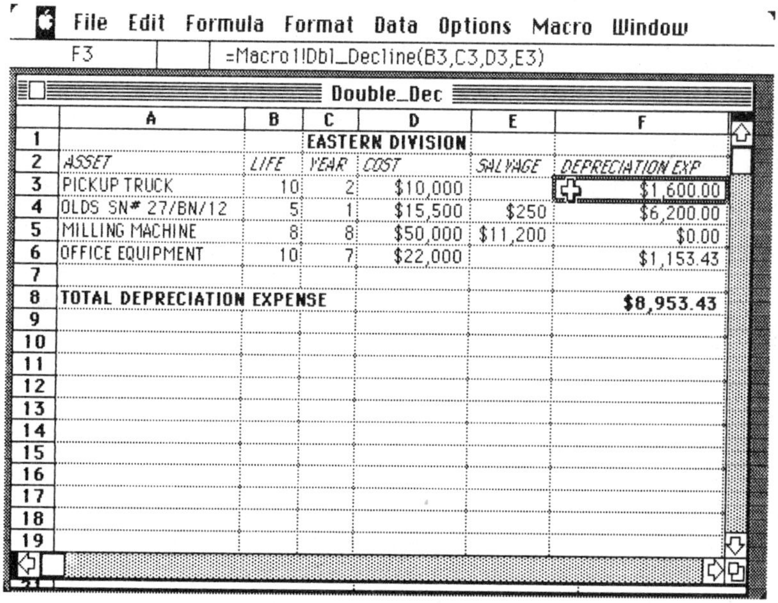

Fig. 3.17. Depreciation expense calculated with the Dbl_Decline macro.

| File | Edit | Formula | Format | Data | Options | Macro | Window |

| F3 | | =Macro1!Dbl_Decline(B3,C3,D3,E3) |

Double_Dec

	A	B	C	D	E	F
1				EASTERN DIVISION		
2	*ASSET*	*LIFE*	*YEAR*	*COST*	*SALVAGE*	*DEPRECIATION EXP*
3	PICKUP TRUCK	10	2	$10,000		$1,600.00
4	OLDS SN# 27/BN/12	5	1	$15,500	$250	$6,200.00
5	MILLING MACHINE	8	8	$50,000	$11,200	$0.00
6	OFFICE EQUIPMENT	10	7	$22,000		$1,153.43
7						
8	TOTAL DEPRECIATION EXPENSE					$8,953.43
9						
10						
11						
12						
13						
14						
15						
16						
17						
18						
19						

A Sum-of-the-Years'-Digits Macro

With the next macro, Sum_Yr, you can look at the result of using another depreciation method. Although this method involves only one formula, that formula is very complicated. You will be glad to have the macro do the work for you.

To create this function macro, first you type the label *Sum_Yr* into A1 of a new macro sheet, and then you provide the arguments (see fig. 3.18). For the sum-of-the-years'-digits method, you need the same variables you used for the double-declining-balance macro. You therefore can include the same ARGUMENT statements. Enter the following statements into A2 through A5, respectively:

=ARGUMENT("LIFE",1)

=ARGUMENT("YEAR",1)

=ARGUMENT("COST",1)

=ARGUMENT("SALVAGE",1)

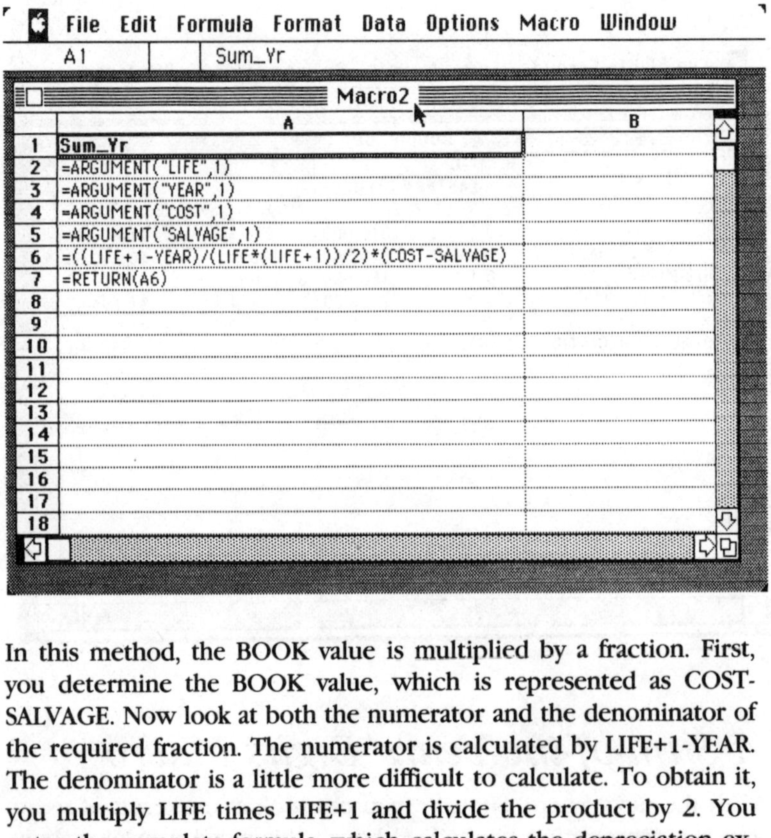

Fig. 3.18. The Sum_Yr macro.

In this method, the BOOK value is multiplied by a fraction. First, you determine the BOOK value, which is represented as COST-SALVAGE. Now look at both the numerator and the denominator of the required fraction. The numerator is calculated by LIFE+1-YEAR. The denominator is a little more difficult to calculate. To obtain it, you multiply LIFE times LIFE+1 and divide the product by 2. You enter the complete formula, which calculates the depreciation expense, into A6:

=((LIFE+1-YEAR)/(LIFE*(LIFE+1))/2)*(COST-SALVAGE)

A RETURN statement in cell A7 will return the calculated result to the worksheet cell containing the Sum_Yr function. Type into A7 the following statement:

=RETURN(A6)

The completed macro appears in figure 3.18, and its use is shown in figure 3.19. You will notice a substantial difference in the depreciation expense under the two methods.

| File | Edit | Formula | Format | Data | Options | Macro | Window |

| F3 | | =Macro2!Sum_Yr(B3,C3,D3,E3) |

Sum_Yr

	A	B	C	D	E	F
1				EASTERN DIVISION		
2	ASSET	LIFE	YEAR	COST	SALVAGE	DEPRECIATION EXP
3	PICKUP TRUCK	10	2	$10,000		$409.09
4	OLDS SN# 27/BN/12	5	1	$15,500	$250	$1,270.83
5	MILLING MACHINE	3	3	$50,000	$11,200	$1,616.67
6	OFFICE EQUIPMENT	10	7	$22,000		$400.00
7						
8	TOTAL DEPRECIATION EXPENSE					$3,696.59
9						
10						
11						
12						
13						
14						
15						
16						
17						
18						
19						

Fig. 3.19. Depreciation expense calculated with the Sum_Yr macro.

An ACRS Macro

The macro for determining accelerated depreciation uses a lookup table to find the appropriate percentage for the computation. Although you could store the lookup table on the worksheet and access the table with the LOOKUP function, using a function macro provides an advantage. You can maintain on a macro sheet one lookup table, which can be accessed by all applications. This means that the auditing, accounting, finance, and treasury departments all can access the macro. In this way, the same macro can be used to assess internal performance or potential investment. Therefore, you can build a macro that calculates accurately, and you can be confident that the depreciation calculations will be consistent throughout the business operation.

Begin by entering into A1 the label *ACRS*, which you will use as the macro name (see fig. 3.20). The three arguments required for this macro are similar to those for the previous two macros: LIFE, YEAR, and COST. Enter these ARGUMENT statements into A2 through A4, respectively:

    =ARGUMENT("LIFE",1)

    =ARGUMENT("YEAR",1)

    =ARGUMENT("COST",1)

```
  File  Edit  Formula  Format  Data  Options  Macro  Window

     A1                ACRS

                          Macro3
              A                    B        C    D    E    F
 1  ACRS                                        ACRS TABLE
 2  =ARGUMENT("LIFE",1)                    3    5    10   15
 3  =ARGUMENT("YEAR",1)                  0.25 0.15 0.08 0.05
 4  =ARGUMENT("COST",1)                  0.38 0.22 0.14 0.1
 5  =HLOOKUP(LIFE,C2:F17,YEAR+1)         0.37 0.21 0.12 0.09
 6  =COST*A5                                  0.21 0.1  0.08
 7  =RETURN(A6)                               0.21 0.1  0.07
 8                                                  0.1  0.07
 9                                                  0.09 0.06
10                                                  0.09 0.06
11                                                  0.09 0.06
12                                                  0.09 0.06
13                                                       0.06
14                                                       0.06
15                                                       0.06
16                                                       0.06
17                                                       0.06
18
19
```

Fig. 3.20. The ACRS macro.

Next, provide a formula in A5 for calculating the correct depreciation percent. Enter the formula as

    =HLOOKUP(LIFE,C2:F17,YEAR+1)

In this HLOOKUP statement, the first argument, LIFE, is the value to be looked up in the table. The second argument is the location of the table, which you later will store in C2 through F17. The last argument is the row number in the table. If the YEAR number is 1, you will want to read row 2 of the table; therefore, you add 1 to the YEAR to obtain the correct row number.

The formula in A6 calculates the depreciation expense. Enter the formula as

    =COST*A5

This formula multiplies the cost of the asset by the depreciation percentage from the table. This percentage is stored in A5.

The final result is returned by the following statement, which you enter into A7:

=RETURN(A6)

The ACRS macro and its associated table appear in figure 3.20. The use of the ACRS macro is shown in figure 3.21.

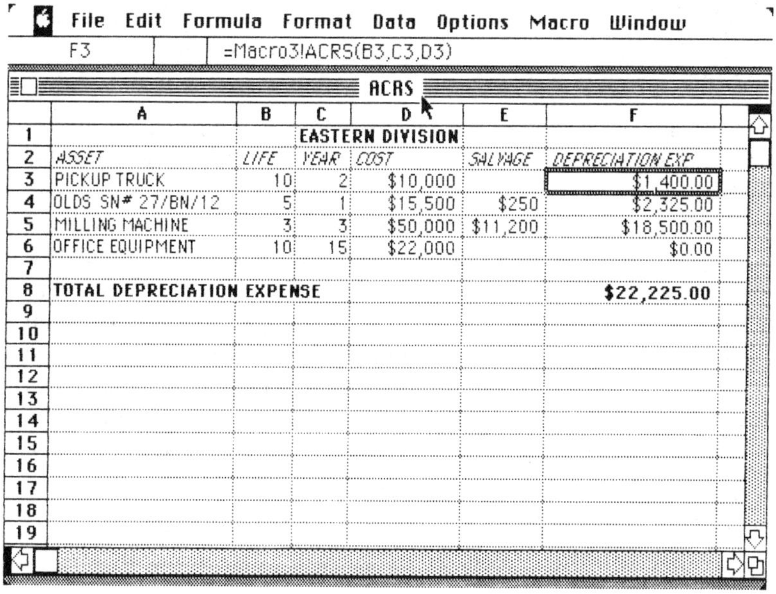

	A	B	C	D	E	F
				EASTERN DIVISION		
2	*ASSET*	*LIFE*	*YEAR*	*COST*	*SALVAGE*	*DEPRECIATION EXP*
3	PICKUP TRUCK	10	2	$10,000		$1,400.00
4	OLDS SN# 27/BN/12	5	1	$15,500	$250	$2,325.00
5	MILLING MACHINE	3	3	$50,000	$11,200	$18,500.00
6	OFFICE EQUIPMENT	10	15	$22,000		$0.00
7						
8	TOTAL DEPRECIATION EXPENSE					$22,225.00

F3   =Macro3!ACRS(B3,C3,D3)

Fig. 3.21. Depreciation expense calculated with the ACRS macro.

Permutation and Probability Macros

Every day, you make intuitive judgments about the likelihood of certain events occurring or the number of possibilities. These intuitive decisions can be formalized with mathematical techniques that provide a quantitative answer to the problem being considered. Two of these techniques are permutation calculations and combination (probability) calculations.

The following macros are presented in this section:

- A permutation macro

- A combination macro

A Permutation Macro

Permutation calculations provide the number of possible combinations of a set of objects. If you have three letters—such as x, y, and z—how many possible letter combinations are there? There are six possible combinations:

```
x y z    z x y
y z x    z y x
y x z    x z y
```

The permutation of x objects is x factorial (commonly written as x!) or x times x-1, x times x-2, and so on, until the last factor is 1. With this logic, 3! is 3*2*1, or 6.

A function macro that calculates permutations can provide useful information to business people who must make decisions daily. For instance, a permutation macro can aid a marketing representative who is trying to decide how to display the company's 5 new products at a trade show. In considering all possible layouts, the representative can use the macro to determine quickly that 5! is 120. The representative also can stipulate that the locations of products 1 and 3 be at the front of the display booth and leave variable the location of the other products. Using the macro, the representative again can determine quickly that 3! is 6 and that only 6 possible display combinations must be evaluated. As you can see, permutation calculations can be performed on all objects in a group or on a subset only.

To create the permutation macro, you need to begin with a new macro sheet on the screen. Enter the label *Permutation* into A1 (see fig. 3.22).

Next, you need an ARGUMENT statement for the number. To define this argument, enter the following statement into A2:

    =ARGUMENT("NUMBER",1)

A loop is necessary for performing the required multiplication calculations. You can establish a counter to store the factorial result. Enter into A3 the following statement:

    =SET.NAME("COUNTER",NUMBER)

The initial value of the counter will be the factorial number you will need.

Next, type into A4 the label *Loop*. Then enter into A5 an IF statement, which will check whether NUMBER has been decremented to 1. If

```
 ┌ ᴄ  File  Edit  Formula  Format  Data  Options  Macro  Window          ┐
 │    A1              │          =Macro1!Permutation(6)                    │
```

	A	B
	Macro1	
1	Permutation	
2	=ARGUMENT("NUMBER",1)	
3	=SET.NAME("COUNTER",NUMBER)	
4	Loop	
5	=IF(NUMBER=1,GOTO(Return))	
6	=SET.NAME("NUMBER",NUMBER-1)	
7	=SET.NAME("COUNTER",COUNTER*NUMBER)	
8	=GOTO(Loop)	
9	Return	
10	=COUNTER	
11	=RETURN(A10)	
12		
13		
14		
15		
16		
17		
18		
19		
20		

Worksheet10

	A	B
1	720	
2		
3		
4		

Fig. 3.22. A macro that calculates the permutations for any number of objects and the macro's result.

NUMBER is 1, the macro will branch to the RETURN function so that the current value of COUNTER can be returned. To provide these calculations in the macro, enter the following statement into A5:

    =IF(NUMBER=1,GOTO(Return))

If NUMBER is not 1, you will need to decrement it by 1. You accomplish this by using the SET.NAME function in A6:

    =SET.NAME("NUMBER",NUMBER-1)

Now continue with the multiplication required for the factorial calculation. Enter the following statement into A7:

    =SET.NAME("COUNTER",COUNTER*NUMBER)

This instruction multiplies the current value of COUNTER by NUMBER. Cell A8 will contain the branch to the top of the loop. Enter into that cell the statement

    =GOTO(Loop)

The macro will end with a Return section. Type the label *Return* into A9. Set A10 equal to the value of COUNTER by entering the following statement into that cell:

    =COUNTER

Use A11 for the RETURN function. Type the following statement into that cell:

   =RETURN(A10)

Now use Formula Define Name to define the names *Permutation, Loop,* and *Return.* Permutation, which is the macro name, is the only name for which you will need to click Function.

To test the macro, move to the worksheet environment. Enter into a worksheet cell a reference to the Permutation macro and also provide an argument. Figure 3.22 shows the completed macro and a worksheet cell containing =Macro1!Permutation(6). This macro calculates the number of possible permutations of 6 objects. The result, in cell A1 of the worksheet, is 720.

You can create a variation of this permutation macro. This second macro examines a certain number of objects at one time and looks at the number of possibilities for this subset. Two arguments are required for the modified macro: NUMBER, for the number of objects; and AT_ONCE, for the number of objects taken at one time. The formula, which calculates the permutations of x objects taken y at a time, is the following:

   $x!/(x-y)!$

If you use a new macro sheet, assign the same name, Permutation, to this second macro (see fig. 3.23). If you use the macro sheet that contains the first permutation macro, then use a different macro name here. Enter both arguments, NUMBER and AT_ONCE, into A2 and A3, respectively:

   =ARGUMENT("NUMBER",1)

   =ARGUMENT("AT_ONCE",1)

Next, you must initialize COUNTER to the value of NUMBER. Do this by typing the following statement into A4:

   =SET.NAME("COUNTER",NUMBER)

Now you need a number that corresponds to the number of objects minus the number taken at one time. This number corresponds to x-y in the first permutation macro. You can have the result stored in SAVE_NO by typing the following statement into A5:

   =SET.NAME("SAVE_NO",NUMBER-AT_ONCE)

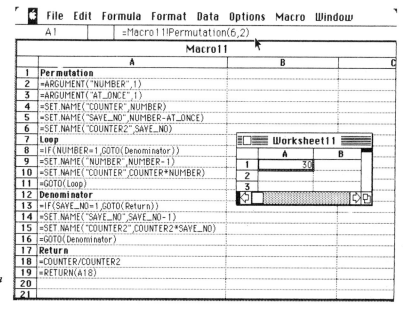

File Edit Formula Format Data Options Macro Window

A1 = =Macro11!Permutation(6,2)

Macro11

	A	B	C
1	Permutation		
2	=ARGUMENT("NUMBER",1)		
3	=ARGUMENT("AT_ONCE",1)		
4	=SET.NAME("COUNTER",NUMBER)		
5	=SET.NAME("SAVE_NO",NUMBER-AT_ONCE)		
6	=SET.NAME("COUNTER2",SAVE_NO)		
7	Loop		
8	=IF(NUMBER=1,GOTO(Denominator))		
9	=SET.NAME("NUMBER",NUMBER-1)		
10	=SET.NAME("COUNTER",COUNTER*NUMBER)		
11	=GOTO(Loop)		
12	Denominator		
13	=IF(SAVE_NO=1,GOTO(Return))		
14	=SET.NAME("SAVE_NO",SAVE_NO-1)		
15	=SET.NAME("COUNTER2",COUNTER2*SAVE_NO)		
16	=GOTO(Denominator)		
17	Return		
18	=COUNTER/COUNTER2		
19	=RETURN(A18)		
20			
21			

Worksheet11

	A	B
1	30	
2		
3		

Fig. 3.23. A macro that calculates permutations of a specified number of objects taken a specified number at a time and the macro's result.

You also need a counter to store the second factorial result. Enter into A6 the statement

=SET.NAME("COUNTER2",SAVE_NO)

This statement makes the initial value of COUNTER equal to NUMBER minus AT_ONCE.

Now type the label *Loop* into A7, which begins the loop that will calculate the numerator of the fraction. Cell A8 checks whether NUMBER has been decremented to 1 yet. Once NUMBER is decremented, you will want to calculate the denominator. Enter the following statement into A8:

=IF(NUMBER=1,GOTO(Denominator))

NUMBER is decremented with the following statement, which you type into A9:

=SET.NAME("NUMBER",NUMBER-1)

You use the SET.NAME function to perform the factorial calculation. Enter the following statement into A10:

=SET.NAME("COUNTER",COUNTER*NUMBER)

A11 will contain a branch to the beginning of the loop. Type into that cell the statement

=GOTO(Loop)

When the factorial for NUMBER finally is obtained, the macro will branch to Denominator in A12. You enter the label *Denominator* into that cell.

In this loop, you will be working with the factorial for SAVE_NO. Cell A13 checks whether SAVE_NO is 1. If SAVE_NO is 1, your work is finished, and you will move to the Return section of the macro. You type the following statement into A13:

=IF(SAVE_NO=1,GOTO(Return))

SAVE_NO will be decremented with the following statement, which you enter into A14:

=SET.NAME("SAVE_NO",SAVE_NO-1)

The factorial counter is incremented with the following statement in A15:

=SET.NAME("COUNTER2",COUNTER2*SAVE_NO)

In this section of the macro, the last instruction, which you enter into A16, is

=GOTO(Denominator)

Here the macro branches to the top of the Denominator loop. Once this branch is taken, both the numerator and the denominator will be calculated.

You label the last section of the macro by typing *Return* into A17. Then you enter into A18 this formula:

=COUNTER/COUNTER2

A RETURN function will return the result of this formula. Enter into A19 the following statement:

=RETURN(A18)

Use Formula Name Define to define the names Permutation, Loop, Denominator, and Return. Figure 3.23 contains the completed macro and a sample worksheet showing the result of the macro, which calculates the number of permutations of 6 items taken 2 at a time. The formula was entered as

=Macro11!Permutation(6,2)

A result of 30 appears in A1 of the worksheet.

A Combination Macro

The combination calculation is similar to the permutation calculation. With a combination, however, you are looking at the number of combinations of a subset of all the objects. In other words, with the three-letter group of x, y, and z, you can determine how many unique two-letter combinations can be formed. You are not concerned with the arrangement of the letters, as you were with the permutation calculation. The combinations for x, y, and z, taken two at a time, are x y, x z, and y z.

The formula for determining combinations of x objects taken y at a time is

$x!/(y!*(x-y)!)$

You can use this combination formula in probability calculations, such as determining the likelihood that an event will occur.

Suppose, for example, that you work with a quiz show host, and you want to know how likely it is that a contestant will win two of the three big prizes after passing the qualifying rounds. The winner of the day's show gets to draw two prize cards from a fish bowl. What is the probability that the contestant will pick cards for two of the big prizes?

In the combination calculation, the probability is equal to the number of ways to pick 2 big prizes divided by the number of ways to pick any 2 prizes. If there are 12 cards from which the contestant can select, the probability can be represented in combination notation as

$_3C_2/_{12}C_2$

If you use the combination formula, the result is 3/66, or 1/22. Therefore, a little more than 4 percent is the likelihood that the contestant will choose cards for 2 of the big prizes.

You can create a combination macro that will calculate the number of combinations of objects taken only some at a time. The formula you use is

$$x!/(y!*(x-y)!)$$

In this formula, x is the total number of items, and y is the subset selected at one time. Notice that this equation contains a third factorial calculation. You therefore must set up a third loop in your macro. You also will need additional variables to store the factorial calculation and to control the loop.

To create the macro, move to a new macro sheet and enter the label *Combine* into A1 (see fig. 3.24). You use the same two arguments you used for the previous macro: NUMBER and AT_ONCE. Enter the following ARGUMENT statements into A2 and A3:

=ARGUMENT("NUMBER",1)

=ARGUMENT("AT_ONCE",1)

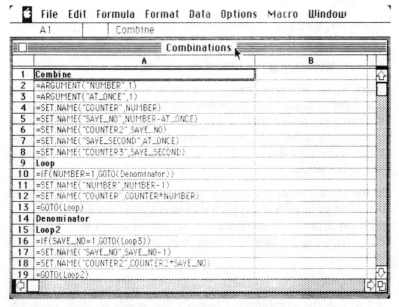

Fig. 3.24. The first section of the Combine macro.

Your next step is to initialize the variables. You begin as you did in the last macro, but you also must handle the third factorial. To initialize COUNTER, you enter the following statement into A4:

=SET.NAME("COUNTER",NUMBER)

To initialize SAVE_NO, you enter into A5 this statement:

=SET.NAME("SAVE_NO",NUMBER-AT_ONCE)

Next, you initialize COUNTER2 to have the same value as SAVE_NO (A6). A new variable, SAVE_SECOND, is introduced to control the new loop. You initialize this variable in A7 with the statement

=SET.NAME("SAVE_SECOND",AT_ONCE)

Finally, you initialize the factorial counter, COUNTER3, by entering the following statement into A8:

=SET.NAME("COUNTER3",SAVE_SECOND)

The first loop, which establishes the numerator, is identical to the calculation that performed the same function in the preceding macro. Type the label *Loop* into A9. You also must provide a check to see whether NUMBER has been decremented to 1 yet. Enter the following statement into A10:

=IF(NUMBER=1,GOTO(Denominator))

You can decrement NUMBER with the following statement, which you enter into A11:

=SET.NAME("NUMBER",NUMBER-1)

The next macro instruction, in A12, increases the factorial counter. Type the following statement into that cell:

=SET.NAME("COUNTER",COUNTER*NUMBER)

Now you are ready to branch to the beginning of the loop with the statement in A13:

=GOTO(Loop)

The next section of the macro will calculate the denominator of the formula. This calculation is handled in two loops because two different factorials are required. Type the label *Denominator* into A14, and the label *Loop2* into A15. Although you could use just one label, two are included in this example; notice that using more than one level of labels in a macro can make the organization clearer. The first statement checks whether the factorial for the denominator needs to be calculated (that is, whether the number is 1, because 1! is 1). If the factorial does not need to be calculated, you will be able to branch to the final loop. Type into A16 the first instruction for Loop2 as

=IF(SAVE_NO=1,GOTO(Loop3))

Next, the loop counter will be decremented, and the factorial calculation will be augmented. For these macro instructions, you enter the following statements into A17 and A18, respectively:

=SET.NAME("SAVE_NO",SAVE_NO-1)

=SET.NAME("COUNTER2",COUNTER2*SAVE_NO)

Then you place into A19 the branch statement

=GOTO(Loop2)

Now you are ready to type into A20 the label *Loop3*, for the loop for the last factorial calculation (see fig. 3.25). Cell A21 is used to check whether the last factorial calculation has been completed. Enter into that cell the following statement:

=IF(SAVE_SECOND=1,GOTO(Return))

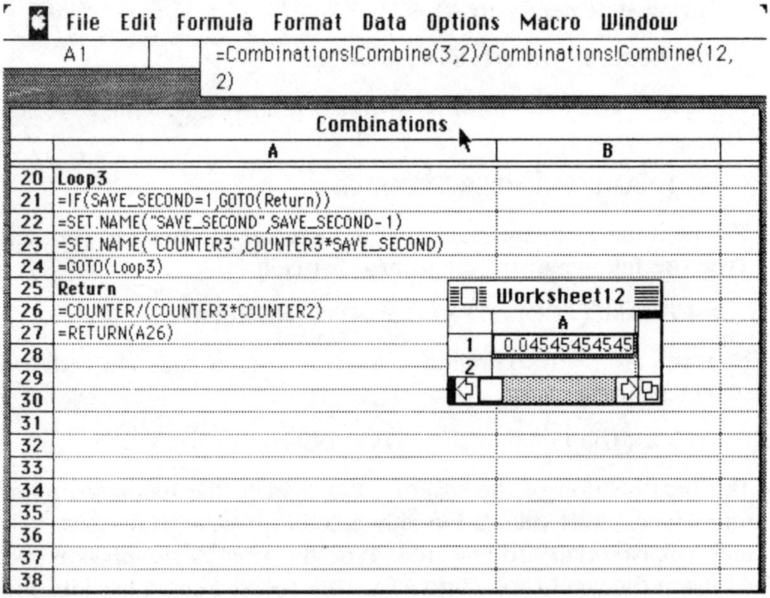

Fig. 3.25. The last section of the Combine macro and the macro's result.

Because SAVE_SECOND is your counter for this third factorial loop, SAVE_SECOND is decremented for each pass through the program. Cell A22 will contain the instruction that decrements this counter in each pass through the loop. Enter into A22 the following statement:

=SET.NAME("SAVE_SECOND",SAVE_SECOND-1)

The third factorial counter is incremented with the following statement, which you enter into A23:

=SET.NAME("COUNTER3",COUNTER3*SAVE_SECOND)

And the last loop instruction takes you to the top of the loop. For this instruction, enter the following statement into A24:

=GOTO(Loop3)

When Loop3 is finally completed, SAVE_SECOND will be equal to 1, and you can move to the Return section, where the final result is calculated. Type the label *Return* into A25. The combination formula uses the three factorials just calculated. You enter into A26 the formula

=COUNTER/(COUNTER3*COUNTER2)

This formula is the same factorial expression that was mentioned in the combination overview that preceded these calculations (the factorial expression described in the second paragraph at the beginning of the section).

Cell A27 will return the result of the formula to the worksheet. Enter into that cell the statement

=RETURN(A26)

Cell A1 of Worksheet12 contains the probability calculation—that is, the likelihood of one contestant winning more than one large prize (see fig. 3.25).

Customized Function Macros

One of the advantages of Excel's function macro capability is that you easily can customize function macros for highly specialized calculations. Once you learn how to apply the macro concepts presented in this chapter, you can design useful, timesaving function macros that perform specific calculations whenever necessary. In this section are the following customized macros:

- A shipping cost macro
- A macro that calculates square footage
- A macro that calculates capacity
- A macro that calculates purchase costs

- A macro that calculates sales commission

- A macro that calculates surface area

- A macro that calculates benefits

As you examine these macros, watch for ways to alter them for use in your own applications. For instance, the square footage macro for determining material costs could be adapted for determining building rents computed by square footage. And the macro for calculating purchase costs could be used for computing project or construction costs. You even could design a similar macro to compute closing costs for a real estate customer if you wanted to make the necessary modifications.

The sample macros in the following sections represent just a few of the many custom functions you can add to Excel's own set of functions.

A Shipping Cost Macro

A shipping cost macro is useful for a company that ships materials from different warehouses. Shipping costs can vary depending on the location of the warehouse. This function macro provides an easy-to-modify method for looking up shipping costs for various orders. This macro should be helpful to catalog houses, customers researching shipping alternatives, common carriers, and any others who must factor transportation costs into their decisions. And the table can be expanded easily to handle additional weight classes or shipping alternatives.

In this example, goods can be shipped from three warehouses. The costs for shipping from these warehouses are stored on a unit basis, but several additional factors must be considered in determining the shipping costs. A minimum shipping charge of $2.00 and a handling charge of $0.75 are added to all orders. The maximum shipping and handling costs on any order are $50.00. Although you could compute these "exceptions" (varying factors) on the worksheet, using a function macro is preferable because you easily can modify the shipping charges if postal rates increase. In addition, all sales organizations within the company can access the one rate schedule stored as part of a macro.

Creating the Shipping Cost Macro

To create the shipping cost macro, you first need a macro sheet on the screen. You can use File New Macro Sheet to create a new sheet, or you can use an existing one and place the macro in a blank area of the sheet. Before entering the macro itself, you should enter the table of shipping rates the macro will access. First, move your cursor to cell B2 and enter *1* through *8* into B2:B9, *10* into B10, *12* into B11, and *15* into B12 (see fig. 3.26). These numbers represent the shipping weight breaks for the different per-pound rates contained in the table. Next, move to C1, the column for the rates for warehouse 1. Enter *1* into C1 and then *1.65, 1.6, 1.55, 1.25, 1.25, 1.25, 1, 1, 0.95, 0.9,* and *0.8* into C2:C12. Warehouse 2 has rates of $0.85 per pound regardless of the weight class; therefore, enter *2* into D1 and *0.85* into D2:D12. For warehouse 3, enter *3* into E1 and *1.1, 1, 0.85, 0.8, 0.8, 0.75, 0.75, 0.7, 0.6, 0.6,* and *0.6* into E2:E12.

| ⬢ | File | Edit | Formula | Format | Data | Options | Macro | Window |

| D3 | | =Shipping!Shipping(B3,C3) |

Shipping

	A	B	C	D	E	F
			1	2	3	
1	Shipping_Macro					
2	=ARGUMENT("LBS",1)	1	1.65	0.85	1.1	
3	=ARGUMENT("WAREHSE",1)	2	1.6	0.85	1	
4	=VLOOKUP(LBS,B2:E12,WAREHSE+1)	3	1.55	0.85	0.85	
5	=(A4*LBS)+0.75	4	1.25	0.85	0.8	
6	=IF(A5<2,2,A5)	5	1.25	0.85	0.8	
7	=IF(A6>50,50,A6)	6	1.25	0.85	0.75	
8	=RETURN(A7)	7	1	0.85	0.75	
9		8	1	0.85	0.7	
10		10	0.95	0.85	0.6	
11		12	0.9	0.85	0.6	
12		15	0.8	0.85	0.6	

Invoice

	A	B	C	D	E	F
1	INVOICE	POUNDS	WAREHOUSE	SHIPPING COSTS		
2						
3	23-4567	10	3	$6.75		
4	32-4568	4	1	$5.75		
5	44-9991	1	2	$2.00		

Fig. 3.26. The shipping cost macro and its result in a worksheet.

After completing the table, you begin entering the macro instructions. First, enter into cell A1 the label *Shipping_Macro,* which you will use as the macro name. This function macro has two arguments: LBS, for the pounds shipped; and WAREHSE, for the type of warehouse from which they are shipped. Now enter the first ARGUMENT statement into A2:

   =ARGUMENT("LBS",1)

LBS is a numeric argument. Next, enter the second argument into A3:

   =ARGUMENT("WAREHSE",1)

WAREHSE determines whether the shipping rates for warehouse 1, 2, or 3 will be used.

Now you are ready to enter the calculations. Enter into cell A4 the following:

   =VLOOKUP(LBS,B2:B12,WAREHSE+1)

Here, you are using one of Excel's built-in functions. The VLOOKUP function will look up the number of pounds in B2:B12 and return the matching value with an offset of WAREHSE+1. In other words, if WAREHSE is 3, the value from the fourth column of the table will be returned.

The next step is to multiply the number of pounds by the per-pound shipping cost listed in the table. You also will want to add the $0.75 handling charge. Type the following statement into A5:

   =(A4*LBS)+0.75

You have two checks yet to perform. You must ensure that the shipping charge is at least equal to the $2.00 minimum but does not exceed the $50.00 maximum. Use the built-in IF function to handle both these checks. First, enter into A6 the statement

   =IF(A5<2,2,A5)

This statement checks the current value of cell A5. If the value is less than 2, 2 is stored in A6. If the value is not less than 2, the current value of cell A5 is stored in A6. Second, type into A7 the statement

   =IF(A6>50,50,A6)

This statement checks the value just placed in A6. If the value is greater than 50, 50 is stored in A7. If the value is not greater than 50, the current value of A6 is stored in A7.

Your last macro instruction will contain a RETURN function, which returns the value in A7. Enter the following into A8:

   =RETURN(A7)

The final step is to name the macro. First, move to cell A1 and click the mouse button to activate the cell. Then select Define Name from the Formula menu, click Function, and click OK.

Using the Shipping Cost Macro

To try the macro, you must move to a worksheet. Enter *10* into B3 and *3* into C3. Copy the shipping cost macro into D3 by using the Paste Function command from the Formula menu. In this example, both the macro sheet and the macro are named Shipping. Your macro sheet may have a different name, such as Macro2. If you have already saved the macro sheet, its name will depend on the name you used when you saved the sheet. If you have not yet saved the sheet, its name is determined by how many new macro sheets you have requested during the current session with Excel; each new sheet is assigned the next sequential number.

Your arguments for the shipping cost macro will be B3 and C3. You can type these cell references and separate them with commas, or you can point to the references and just type the commas.

The use of the macro is shown in the lower part of figure 3.26. This example is "spruced up" a bit with additional invoice numbers and headings, but the result shown in D3 (the $6.75 minimum charge) is what you should see when you run the macro using the data supplied. Here the result appears in currency format. For this format, you need to use the Number command from the Format menu.

Modifying the Shipping Cost Macro

You can modify the shipping cost macro to handle calculations when a variety of items are being shipped. You can have multiple weights as arguments to a macro that would add the weights. You can design the macro to allow for preferential rates for certain customer classifications or to provide free shipping for new customers. To make these changes, you would need a new argument for the customer, and IF statements to determine whether or not to calculate shipping. Whatever your needs, after you define them, you can alter the macro so that it can fulfill the demands of each shipment.

A Macro That Calculates Square Footage

Square footage calculations are necessary for estimating the amount of material needed to cover a floor, compare the floor space of two houses, or build a product. You can record the calculations in a function macro and then use it whenever you need to make such calculations. The function macro described in this section calculates square footage by multiplying length by either height or width, depending on whether you are measuring floors or walls.

Square footage calculations are required for many commercial applications. Carpet, tile, and paneling installers need to know the square footage to be covered with the product and its adhesive before they can determine what to charge for the job. Although these calculations are simple, this function macro enables you also to determine the cost for multiple installations of the same size.

Suppose that you work for High-Rise Construction, a company that builds multiple-unit dwellings. You need to calculate the square footage of multiple units in order to determine material costs. To make this calculation, you can include in the macro an option for looking at the square footage of multiple units. If you use an extra argument that specifies the number of rooms with particular dimensions, you will be able to calculate the square footage of one room or many rooms of the same size. Because of the varying requirements of High-Rise Construction, your macro should be able to calculate square feet or square yards. Square footage is needed for determining ceramic tile costs, but square yardage is needed for carpeting costs.

Creating the Square Footage Macro

Create this function macro on a new macro sheet. Type the macro name *Sqft* into A1 (see fig. 3.27).

This macro requires four arguments, one for each of the four potential variables: length, width, number of rooms, and an indicator for measuring square yards or square feet.

In this example, the name of the first argument is LEN. To provide the argument name and to specify that only numeric data is acceptable, enter the following statement into A2:

```
=ARGUMENT("LEN",1)
```

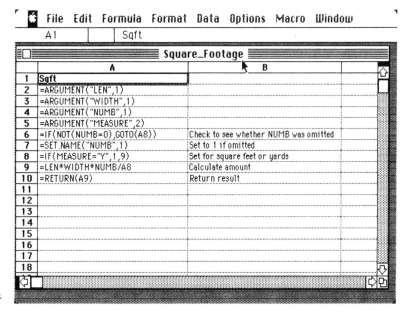

File Edit Formula Format Data Options Macro Window

| A1 | | Sqft |

Square_Footage

	A	B	
1	**Sqft**		
2	=ARGUMENT("LEN",1)		
3	=ARGUMENT("WIDTH",1)		
4	=ARGUMENT("NUMB",1)		
5	=ARGUMENT("MEASURE",2)		
6	=IF(NOT(NUMB=0),GOTO(A8))	Check to see whether NUMB was omitted	
7	=SET.NAME("NUMB",1)	Set to 1 if omitted	
8	=IF(MEASURE="Y",1,9)	Set for square feet or yards	
9	=LEN*WIDTH*NUMB/A8	Calculate amount	
10	=RETURN(A9)	Return result	
11			
12			
13			
14			
15			
16			
17			
18			

Fig. 3.27. A macro that calculates square footage.

Now you provide the remaining three ARGUMENT statements. Add an ARGUMENT statement for width, specifying WIDTH as the name of the second argument, and 1 for a numeric value. Place this second argument into cell A3:

=ARGUMENT("WIDTH",1)

To create an ARGUMENT statement for the number of rooms, again indicating a numeric value, enter into A4 the statement

=ARGUMENT("NUMB",1)

Then type the last argument statement into A5:

=ARGUMENT("MEASURE",2)

This statement indicates that an argument can be provided for a unit of measure and that the argument's *type* will be text.

If you do not supply an argument when you use a function macro, Excel substitutes the error value #N/A for a missing text argument and zero for a missing numeric argument. If you want to have arguments as optional entries, you must assign a default value to be used if the user of your macro omits an argument. In the Sqft macro, for example, you may want LEN and WIDTH to be supplied each time but NUMB and MEASURE to be optional entries. To avoid having a value of zero jeopardize the correct result, you may want to provide default values for these arguments if a user does not enter them. You can provide default values in two ways: by checking for the value zero or by checking for a particular entry for an argument. Both methods are used in building this macro.

The first method is used for NUMB, the argument for the number of rooms. You enter into A6 the statement

    =IF(NOT(NUMB=0),GOTO(A8))

In the IF portion of the statement, Excel checks the condition NOT(NUMB=0). If the condition is true, the program takes the TRUE condition branch (GOTO A8) of the macro. If the condition is false, because a FALSE condition is not specified, the statement in the next macro cell, A7, is executed.

The macro branches to A8 if an entry was supplied for NUMB. You can use A7 to set the default value because the only condition under which you move to A7 is that no entry was supplied for NUMB. To establish a default value of 1 for NUMB, use the SET.NAME function in cell A7 by typing

    =SET.NAME("NUMB",1)

The second method for establishing a default value is useful when you are checking for a particular entry for an argument. You check for the acceptable value and establish a result based on that value. If any other value exists, it will be converted back to a default setting. And if the argument was not supplied, the default value will be substituted. This method is used for the argument named MEASURE. A value of Y indicates that the calculation should return square yards. If no value is provided, the calculation will return square feet. Because one square yard contains nine square feet, the adjustment is easy to make.

You enter into A8 the following statement:

    =IF(MEASURE="Y",1,9)

This formula will cause A8 to assume the value of 9 if MEASURE is equal to Y, but the value of 1 if MEASURE has not been provided or is any other text character.

You enter into A9 the following formula, which calculates the result returned:

    =LEN*WIDTH*NUMB/A8

This formula calculates the total square feet by multiplying length times width times the number of rooms. The product is divided by the value in A8. If A8 is 1, the result is provided in square feet. If A8 is 9, the result is provided in square yards.

The last macro statement is in cell A10. The RETURN function will return the value in cell A9 to the location of the function macro in your worksheet. You enter the following statement into A10:

=RETURN(A9)

Notice that this macro contains comments, or annotation, for some of the macro lines. These comments are placed in column B (B6 through B10 of this example). You should use comments with all your macros. Comments are not used for all the macros in this book because the screen is not wide enough to show both the macro instructions and a written description.

To name the macro, use Formula Define Name. First, make A1 the active cell and click the mouse button. Then select the Define Name command from the Formula menu. When the dialog box appears, click Function and then click OK. Your new macro is now ready for action.

Using the Square Footage Macro

Figure 3.28 shows construction costs for the Diamond Tower construction project of the High-Rise company. Cell G5 contains information for performing similar calculations for all the rooms in this high-rise apartment complex. All the carpet estimates require using Y for MEASURE so that the results will be in square yards. Because ceramic tile requirements are measured in square feet, Y for MEASURE does not appear in the formulas in G14 and G15.

To try the macro, move to a blank worksheet window by selecting Window and choosing a worksheet name. If you don't have a blank worksheet open at this time, select File New Worksheet. In the sample worksheet, enter *14* for room length into cell C5, and *16* for room width into D5. Then enter *500* for the number of rooms into E5. Next, enter *$6.50* as the cost per square yard into F5. Last, enter into G5 the reference to the function macro:

=Square_Footage!Sqft(C5,D5,E5,"Y")

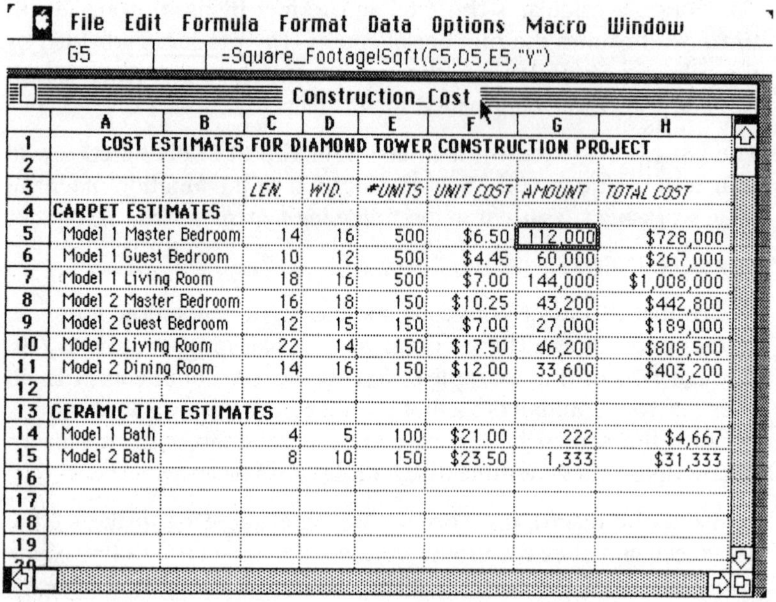

	A	B	C	D	E	F	G	H
1	COST ESTIMATES FOR DIAMOND TOWER CONSTRUCTION PROJECT							
2								
3			LEN.	WID.	#UNITS	UNIT COST	AMOUNT	TOTAL COST
4	CARPET ESTIMATES							
5	Model 1 Master Bedroom		14	16	500	$6.50	112,000	$728,000
6	Model 1 Guest Bedroom		10	12	500	$4.45	60,000	$267,000
7	Model 1 Living Room		18	16	500	$7.00	144,000	$1,008,000
8	Model 2 Master Bedroom		16	18	150	$10.25	43,200	$442,800
9	Model 2 Guest Bedroom		12	15	150	$7.00	27,000	$189,000
10	Model 2 Living Room		22	14	150	$17.50	46,200	$808,500
11	Model 2 Dining Room		14	16	150	$12.00	33,600	$403,200
12								
13	CERAMIC TILE ESTIMATES							
14	Model 1 Bath		4	5	100	$21.00	222	$4,667
15	Model 2 Bath		8	10	150	$23.50	1,333	$31,333
16								
17								
18								
19								

Fig. 3.28. The square footage macro used in a worksheet.

Typing "Y" as the fourth argument will give the result in square yards. If you don't want square yards, enter any other letter or leave off the last argument. When you compute the formula, the result you should get appears in cell G5 in figure 3.28.

Modifying the Square Footage Macro

The square footage macro can be adapted to determine costs for a variety of materials. These costs can be based, for instance, on the square feet of material needed or the amount of paint used. To alter the macro, you substitute the appropriate formulas for the new calculations. Costs can be determined by multiplying the quantity used by the per-unit cost. You can add an argument for the grade of material to be used. Also, you can add to the macro sheet a lookup table that gives the unit cost to be used for determining material costs.

A Macro That Calculates Capacity

This function macro is useful for calculating the capacity of a variety of containers. Suppose that you work for a candy company that is designing a line of candy-filled Christmas ornaments. Because the

company's main business is candy production, the company has decided to purchase.plastic ornaments and then fill them with candy.
The ornaments will have a spherical shape, but the dimensions have
not yet been determined. This macro would be helpful to the company in its evaluation of a wide range of options.

To create the macro, you first need a new macro sheet on the screen.
Use File New Macro Sheet to bring up the sheet. Enter the macro
name *Capacity_Macro* into A1 (see fig. 3.29). Because you are calculating the capacity of a sphere, you need to indicate only the radius
measurement. Enter the following statement into A2:

=ARGUMENT("RADIUS",1)

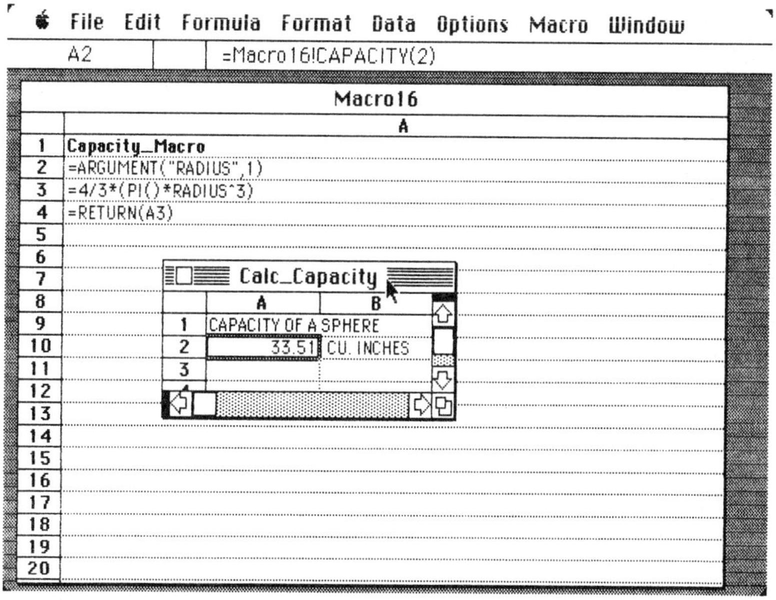

*Fig. 3.29. A macro that
calculates capacity and its result
in a worksheet.*

Now type into A3 the formula for calculating capacity:

=4/3*(PI( )*RADIUS^3)

This calculation is four-thirds times π times the radius cubed. PI( )
is a built-in function representing the value for π.

Finally, enter the following statement into A4:

=RETURN(A3)

To name the macro, use Formula Define Name. Then move to a
worksheet and test the macro. Type *CAPACITY OF A SPHERE* into

A1 and enter into A2 a reference to the new function macro. Type your macro sheet name, an exclamation point, and the function name *Capacity*. Type *2* for RADIUS. Figure 3.29 shows the macro, with the result (33.51 cubic inches) displayed in worksheet cell A2.

A Macro That Calculates Purchase Costs

Now suppose that you work for Kool-Aire, a company that installs air conditioners. The company markets four different models and offers three payment plans as well as an optional two-year maintenance agreement. You can create a macro enabling a salesperson to calculate a monthly payment that reflects the options each customer selects.

This macro has three arguments: (1) MODEL, for the air conditioner model; (2) MAINTENANCE, for the maintenance agreement; and (3) PAYMENT, for the payment plan. The macro will use the air conditioner model to determine the cost of the equipment and the labor hours required for installation. The cost of the optional maintenance agreement will be added if the customer elects to purchase it, and the monthly payment will be calculated on the basis of the payment plan selected.

To create the macro, you first enter the macro name *Cost* into A1 on a new macro sheet (see fig. 3.30). You then enter into A2 the following ARGUMENT statement for MODEL:

    =ARGUMENT("MODEL",1)

To establish a variable for the maintenance agreement, enter the following statement into A3:

    =ARGUMENT("MAINTENANCE",2)

Payment is a number between 1 and 4, indicating which payment plan the customer wants. Enter the following statement into A4:

    =ARGUMENT("PAYMENT",1)

Next, you create the lookup tables for the cost of equipment, labor, and maintenance (see fig. 3.31). Move to C1 on the macro sheet and enter *MODEL #*. Type into C2 through C5 the four model numbers: *1210, 1250, 2110,* and *2150,* respectively. Enter the label *EQUIP.* into D1. Then enter into D2 through D5 the equipment cost

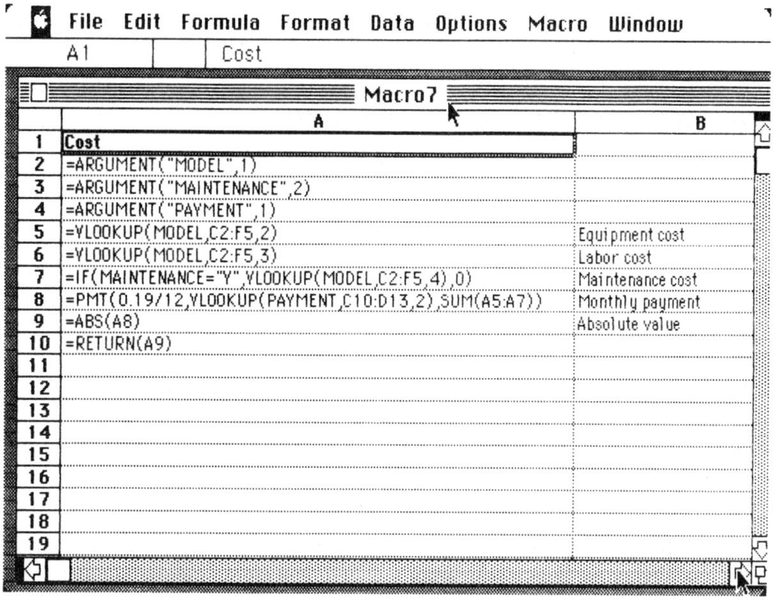

Fig. 3.30. A macro for calculating purchase costs.

for each model: *1200, 1500, 1800,* and 2100. Now provide the labor costs. First, enter into E1 the label *LABOR.* Then type into E2 through E5 the following costs: *150, 180, 210,* and *150.* The last column in the table contains the maintenance costs. Enter *MAINT., 220, 250, 250,* and *250* into F1 through F5.

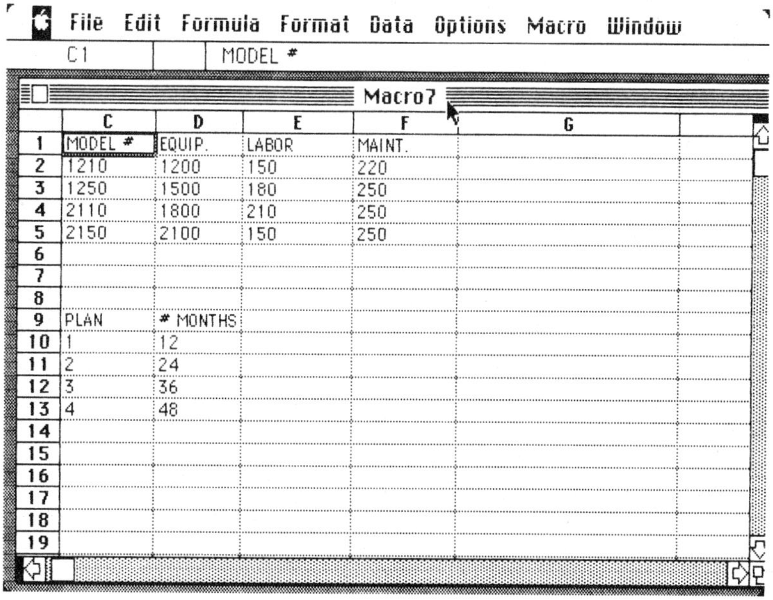

Fig. 3.31. Tables for the purchase cost macro.

You need a second table for the number of payments in each payment plan. Type the following into C9 through C13: *PLAN*, *1*, *2*, *3*, and *4*. For the next column (D9 through D13), enter the number of months: *# MONTHS*, *12*, *24*, *36*, and *48*.

After completing the lookup tables, you are ready to enter the remaining macro instructions (see fig. 3.30). Type into A5 the following statement, which determines the equipment cost for the model selected:

    =VLOOKUP(MODEL,C2:F5,2)

The next instruction will determine the labor costs for the model selected. Again, you use the VLOOKUP function. Enter into A6 this statement:

    =VLOOKUP(MODEL,C2:F5,3)

Like equipment and labor costs, maintenance costs also are determined with a VLOOKUP function, but maintenance costs are optional. You use the logical IF function along with VLOOKUP in order to determine the appropriate charge for a maintenance contract. Enter the following formula into A7:

    =IF(MAINTENANCE="Y",VLOOKUP(MODEL,C2:F5,4),0)

This statement instructs Excel to check the variable MAINTENANCE. If it contains Y, the VLOOKUP function will find the maintenance charge for the model purchased. If MAINTENANCE does not contain Y, the customer elected not to purchase the maintenance agreement, and the maintenance cost will be zero.

Excel's PMT function calculates the monthly payment, using the arguments specified. Type the following statement into A8:

    =PMT(0.19/
    12,VLOOKUP(PAYMENT,C10:D13,2),SUM(A5:A7))

Examine carefully each part of this formula because it contains arguments within arguments. PAYMENT is an argument of VLOOKUP, which is an argument of PMT. The first argument required by PMT is the interest rate. It must be expressed in the same terms as for the number of periods. Because the number of periods is expressed in months, the interest rate also is expressed in months by dividing the annual interest rate of 19 percent by 12:

    =PMT(0.19/12,

The second argument for the PMT function is the number of periods. You use another VLOOKUP function to determine the number of periods for the plan specified:

VLOOKUP(PAYMENT,C10:D13,2)

Here, Excel is instructed to look in the second table to find the number of months.

The third argument for the PMT function is the amount to finance. This amount is the sum of the equipment, labor, and maintenance costs for the project. You calculate the sum with the statement

SUM(A5:A7)

Because payments made are negative numbers and payments received are positive numbers, the sum needs to be converted to a positive number in order to be aesthetically appealing. To convert the sum, you use the ABS function in A9:

=ABS(A8)

Cell A10 will contain the RETURN function. Enter the statement as

=RETURN(A9)

Finally, you name the macro by moving to A1 and selecting Formula Define Name. The example macro was saved on a macro sheet named Macro7.

Test the purchase cost macro by moving to a new worksheet file and entering a model number. Enter *1210* into D6, specifying the model; *"Y"* into D7, indicating the purchase of the maintenance agreement; and *3* into D8, specifying plan 3. Next, move your cursor to D11 and type

=Macro7!Cost(D6,D7,D8)

Note that your macro sheet may be named Macrosheet8, Macro9, or Mac345. Be sure to use the correct macro sheet name in front of the macro name, Cost.

Figure 3.32 presents the information supplied, with a few additional labels. The grid lines and row and column headings were removed from the display with the Display command from the Options menu.

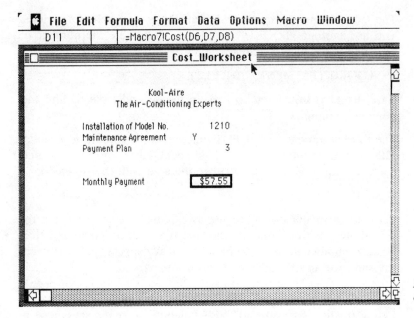

 File Edit Formula Format Data Options Macro Window

| D11 | =Macro7!Cost(D6,D7,D8) |

Cost_Worksheet

Kool-Aire
The Air-Conditioning Experts

Installation of Model No.   1210
Maintenance Agreement   Y
Payment Plan   3

Monthly Payment $57.55

Fig. 3.32. Kool-Aire's customer cost projection.

A Macro That Calculates Sales Commissions

High Roller Company pays sales personnel commissions based on a sliding scale. Sales up to $5,000 earn commissions of 10 percent. Sales between $5,000 and $10,000 earn commissions of 12 percent. All sales of more than $10,000 earn commissions of 15 percent. Suppose that you are an employee whose job is to calculate total commissions for each period. The payout to sales personnel is determined by the company's profile of cash versus charge sales and by the expected payment time for charge sales. Of the total commissions earned, 70 percent is paid in the current month, 20 percent in the month following, and 10 percent in the second month after the sale. You can develop a macro that will calculate the payment results for you. The results are returned in an array of three values.

To create the macro, you first enter the label *Commission* into A1 of a new macro sheet (see fig. 3.33). Because the results will be returned in an array, you then enter the following statement into A2:

=RESULT(64)

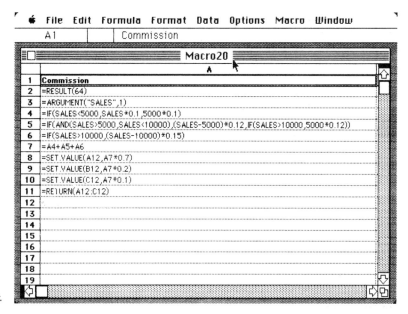

File Edit Formula Format Data Options Macro Window

| A1 | | Commission |

Macro20

	A
1	**Commission**
2	=RESULT(64)
3	=ARGUMENT("SALES",1)
4	=IF(SALES<5000,SALES*0.1,5000*0.1)
5	=IF(AND(SALES>5000,SALES<10000),(SALES-5000)*0.12,IF(SALES>10000,5000*0.12))
6	=IF(SALES>10000,(SALES-10000)*0.15)
7	=A4+A5+A6
8	=SET.VALUE(A12,A7*0.7)
9	=SET.VALUE(B12,A7*0.2)
10	=SET.VALUE(C12,A7*0.1)
11	=RETURN(A12:C12)
12	
13	
14	
15	
16	
17	
18	
19	

Fig. 3.33. A macro that calculates sales commissions.

The only argument is SALES, for the monthly sales total. Enter the following statement into A3:

=ARGUMENT("SALES",1)

You use IF functions to calculate the commission for each of the three established categories. The first IF function calculates commissions for SALES<5000. If sales are less than $5,000, a 10 percent commission will be paid. If sales are greater than $5,000 but less than $10,000, a 10 percent commission will be paid on the first $5,000. To include the first IF function in the macro, type the following statement into A4:

=IF(SALES<5000,SALES*0.1,5000*0.1)

The next calculation is for sales between $5,000 and $10,000. The second IF statement, which you enter into A5, begins with an AND function:

=IF(AND(SALES>5000,SALES<10000),(SALES-5000)
*0.12,IF(SALES>10000,5000*0.12))

If the compound condition is true (that is, if sales are greater than $5,000 but less than $10,000), a 12 percent commission will be paid on the amount above $5,000. That amount is arrived at simply by subtracting $5,000 from SALES. Remember that a 10 percent commission on the first $5,000 of sales is ensured by the preceding statement in A4. If, however, the compound condition is false, then sales were less than $5,000, and no commissions will be paid at the 12 percent rate. However, if sales are greater than $10,000, a 12 percent commission will be paid on the first $5,000.

The last IF function checks whether sales exceeded $10,000. If sales are greater than $10,000, a 15 percent commission will be paid on any sales exceeding $10,000. For this calculation, you enter this statement into A6:

=IF(SALES>10000,(SALES-10000)*0.15)

The following formula, which you enter into A7, adds all three commission calculations:

=A4+A5+A6

Next, you use Excel's SET.VALUE function to calculate the array values to be returned. In this calculation, the total commissions in A7 are multiplied in turn by the three commission distribution percentages. Enter the following statement into A8:

=SET.VALUE(A12,A7*0.7)

Seventy percent of the commissions (the amount to be paid currently) will be stored in A12.

Now enter the following statement into A9 for the commission amount to be paid the next month:

=SET.VALUE(B12,A7*0.2)

The third SET.VALUE function, which you enter into A10, calculates the commissions in the second month after the sales:

=SET.VALUE(C12,A7*0.1)

A RETURN function will return the three array values. For this calculation, enter the following statement into A11:

=RETURN(A12:C12)

Finally, you name the macro by selecting Define Name from the Formula menu.

To use the macro, move to a new worksheet. Enter *JEFF SMITH* into A3 and *20000* into B3. Use Format Number to format B3:E11 as currency, with zero decimal places. Next, select cells C3:E3 and enter the macro formula by holding down the Command key while you finalize the entry by pressing the Return key or clicking the dialog box. Figure 3.34 shows Jeff Smith's commission for the current month. You also will notice that headings and additional calculations have been added to the display.

```
 ⌐  ⬥  File  Edit  Formula  Format  Data  Options  Macro  Window        ⌐
        C3                 {=Macro20!Commission(B3)}
```

	A	B	C	D	E
1			COMMISSION	COMMISSION	COMMISSION
2	EMPLOYEE	SALES	CURRENT MO.	NEXT MO.	2ND MONTH
3	JEFF SMITH	$20,000	$1,820	$520	$260
4	CAROL WOODS	$35,000	$3,395	$970	$485
5	JOHN GOVER	$29,000	$2,765	$790	$395
6	JOE BLOUGH	$65,000	$6,545	$1,870	$935
7	MARILYN JONES	$15,000	$1,295	$370	$185
8	ALICE WALKER	$19,500	$1,768	$505	$253
9	NANCY STETLER	$84,000	$8,540	$2,440	$1,220
10	PAUL HOMER	$26,500	$2,503	$715	$358
11	EILEEN BLUM	$45,000	$4,445	$1,270	$635
12					
13					
14					
15					
16					
17					
18					
19					

Fig. 3.34. Commissions calculated with the Commission macro.

A Macro That Calculates Surface Area

Surface area calculations are useful for a number of tasks. Such calculations are necessary, for instance, if you need to determine the amount of steel sheeting required for construction or if you are going to paint, plate, or laminate objects.

In this section are three macros for calculating surface areas. The first macro calculates a cylinder's surface area, the second macro determines the surface area of a sphere, and the third macro calculates the surface area of a right circular cone (a cone that can contain a right triangle). The formulas you use for these macros are the following:

Cylinder	$(2\pi\text{Radius}*\text{Height})+(2\pi\text{Radius}^2)$
Sphere	$4\pi\text{Radius}^2$
Cone	$(\pi\text{Radius}*\text{Side})+(\pi\text{Radius}^2)$

You begin the first macro in A1, where you enter the label *Cylinder_Area* (see fig. 3.35). Arguments for RADIUS and HEIGHT are required. You type these ARGUMENT statements into A2 and A3:

=ARGUMENT("RADIUS",1)

=ARGUMENT("HEIGHT",1)

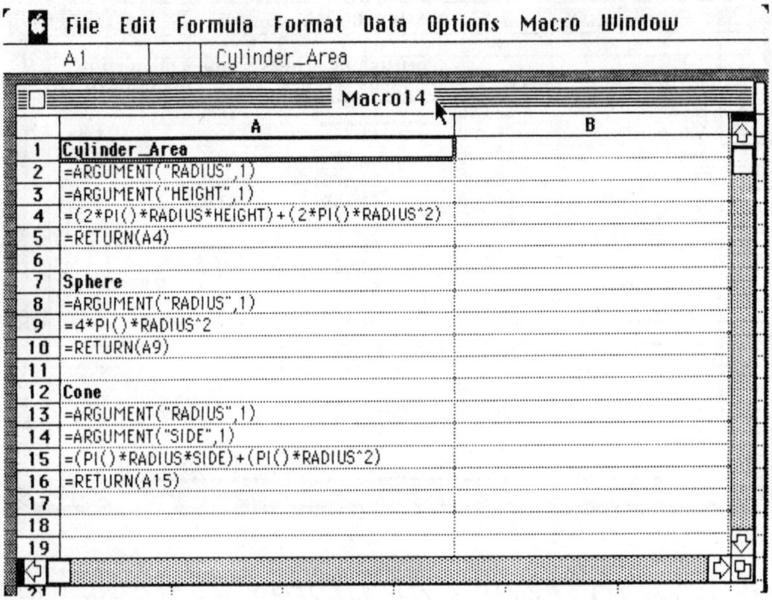

```
 File  Edit  Formula  Format  Data  Options  Macro  Window

    A1              Cylinder_Area

                            Macro14
                    A                              B
 1  Cylinder_Area
 2  =ARGUMENT("RADIUS",1)
 3  =ARGUMENT("HEIGHT",1)
 4  =(2*PI()*RADIUS*HEIGHT)+(2*PI()*RADIUS^2)
 5  =RETURN(A4)
 6
 7  Sphere
 8  =ARGUMENT("RADIUS",1)
 9  =4*PI()*RADIUS^2
10  =RETURN(A9)
11
12  Cone
13  =ARGUMENT("RADIUS",1)
14  =ARGUMENT("SIDE",1)
15  =(PI()*RADIUS*SIDE)+(PI()*RADIUS^2)
16  =RETURN(A15)
17
18
19
```

Fig. 3.35. Surface area macros.

Next, enter the formula for the surface area calculations into A4:

=(2*PI( )*RADIUS*HEIGHT)+(2*PI( )*RADIUS^2)

Notice the use of parentheses to ensure that operations are given the correct priorities. Notice also the use of the built-in function PI( ), which returns an approximation of the constant π.

Finally, provide a RETURN function by typing the following statement into A5:

=RETURN(A4)

Now you name the macro, using Formula Define Name. Try running this first macro, using a radius of 3 and a height of 5. Figure 3.36 shows the calculated result in cell A2.

The second macro, which calculates the surface area of a sphere, requires only one argument: RADIUS. To create the macro, you first

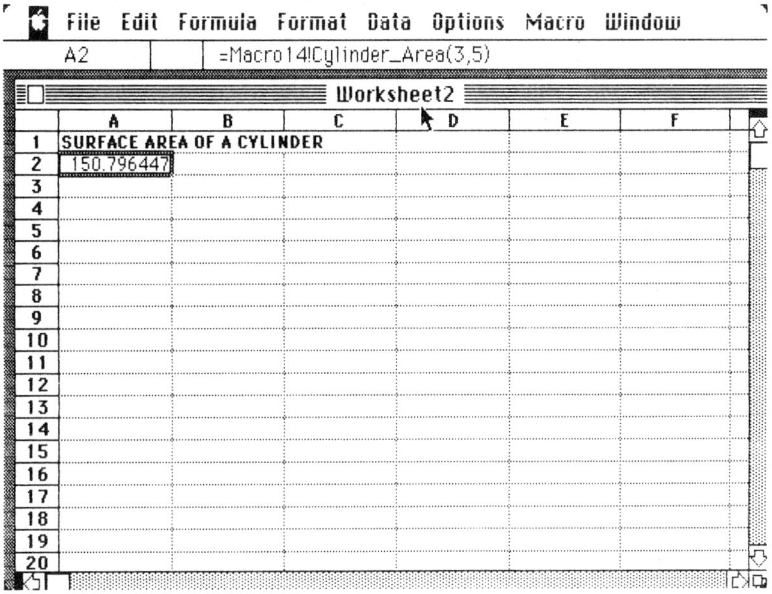

Fig. 3.36. The surface area of a cylinder calculated.

enter the label *Sphere* into A7 of the macro sheet (fig. 3.35) and then type the following ARGUMENT statement into A8:

=ARGUMENT("RADIUS",1)

Next, enter this formula into A9:

=4*PI( )*RADIUS^2

A RETURN function will return the value in A9. Type the following into A10:

=RETURN(A9)

Now name the macro, using Formula Define Name. A sample execution of the macro is shown in figure 3.37. The radius is 5.

The third macro calculates the surface area of a cone. Two arguments, RADIUS and SIDE, are required. To create the macro, you first enter the label *Cone* into A12 (see fig. 3.35). Next, you enter the following ARGUMENT statements into A13 and A14:

=ARGUMENT("RADIUS",1)

=ARGUMENT("SIDE",1)

File   Edit   Formula   Format   Data   Options   Macro   Window

A2	=Macro14!Sphere(5)

≣ Worksheet2 ≣

	A	B	C	D	E	F
1	SURFACE AREA OF A SPHERE					
2	314.159265					
3						
4						
5						
6						
7						
8						
9						
10						
11						
12						
13						
14						
15						
16						
17						
18						
19						
20						

Fig. 3.37. The surface area of a sphere calculated.

Now type the following formula into A15 and then provide a RE-TURN function in A16:

=(PI( )*RADIUS*SIDE)+(PI( )*RADIUS^2)

=RETURN(A15)

Again, you use Formula Define Name to name the macro. Figure 3.38 shows the calculation for a cone with a radius of 2 and a side of 5. The function macro name and its sheet name were placed in A2, and the macro returned a result of 43.9822972 for the surface area of the cone.

A Macro That Calculates Benefits

Suppose that you work for a company named Friendly Employer and your job is to determine basic benefits for the employees. The comprehensiveness of an employee's benefit package depends on the individual's location code and level within the company. For example, only level 3 employees, who are senior managers, are eligible for profit sharing. Yet all employees qualify for pension plans, except level 1 employees, who are part time.

File Edit Formula Format Data Options Macro Window

A2 =Macro14!Cone(2,5)

Worksheet2

	A	B	C	D	E	F
1	SURFACE AREA OF A CONE					
2	43.9822972					
3						
4						
5						
6						
7						
8						
9						
10						
11						
12						
13						
14						
15						
16						
17						
18						
19						
20						

Fig. 3.38. The surface area of a cone calculated.

You can create a macro that will save you time by calculating the various benefits for you. The results will be returned as an array of three values: a value for basic benefits, a value for profit sharing, and a value for the pension plan.

Begin this macro in a new macro sheet. Type into A1 the label *Benefits*, which you will use as the macro name (see fig. 3.39). Enter the following RESULT function, specifying an array, into A2:

    =RESULT(64)

Next, you define the arguments for SALARY and JOBCODE. Enter into A3 and A4 the following ARGUMENT statements:

    =ARGUMENT("SALARY",1)

    =ARGUMENT("JOBCODE",1)

Now you are ready to create the table of job codes with associated levels and locations. Use cells C1:E11 for the table entries. Enter the following job codes into column C: *CDE, 13, 24, 43, 54, 55, 113, 121, 134, 144,* and *167*. Notice that the job codes are entered in ascending sequence. Next, type the following levels into column D: *LVL, 1, 1, 1, 2, 3, 1, 1, 1, 2,* and *3*. Finally, enter the location data into column E: *LOC, 1, 1, 1, 1, 1, 2, 2, 2, 2,* and *2*.

   File   Edit   Formula   Format   Data   Options   Macro   Window

	A	B	C	D	E
	Benefits		CDE	LYL	LOC
1	Benefits		CDE	LYL	LOC
2	=RESULT(64)		13	1	1
3	=ARGUMENT("SALARY",1)		24	1	1
4	=ARGUMENT("JOBCODE",1)		43	1	1
5	=VLOOKUP(JOBCODE,C2:E11,2)		54	2	1
6	=VLOOKUP(JOBCODE,C2:E11,3)		55	3	1
7	=INDEX({0.15,0.16,0.18;0.17,0.18,0.21},A6,A5)		113	1	2
8	=SALARY*A7		121	1	2
9	=IF(A5=3,SALARY*0.1,0)		134	1	2
10	=IF(A5=1,0,SALARY*0.075)		144	2	2
11	=SET.VALUE(A16,A8)		167	3	2
12	=SET.VALUE(B16,A9)				
13	=SET.VALUE(C16,A10)				
14	=RETURN(A16:C16)				
15					
16					
17					
18					
19					

Fig. 3.39. A macro that calculates benefits.

The job code classification can determine both the level and location of a position. Excel's VLOOKUP function finds the level of a position, using the values in the second column of the job code table. To provide this calculation, you enter the following statement into A5:

    =VLOOKUP(JOBCODE,C2:E11,2)

VLOOKUP also finds the location of a position, using the values in the third column of the table. You enter this second VLOOKUP statement into A6 as

    =VLOOKUP(JOBCODE,C2:E11,3)

The two values determined in A5 and A6 will be used to index a list of percentages for estimating benefits. To provide this calculation, you use Excel's INDEX function. The statement in A7 contains a reference to two rows and three columns of information. You enter the statement into that cell by typing

    =INDEX({0.15,0.16,0.18;0.17,0.18,0.21},A6,A5)

This statement will return the correct percent to A7, where the INDEX function is stored.

The salary field is then multiplied by the percent just determined. For example, if A5 contains a value of 3, which indicates a job code for executive management, then profit sharing is calculated at 10 percent of sales. To provide this calculation, you enter the following statement into A9:

=IF(A5=3,SALARY*0.1,0)

The pension plan is for all employees except level 1 employees, who are part time. Enter into A10 the following statement:

=IF(A5=1,0,SALARY*0.075)

With this statement in the macro, no pension fund expenditures will be made for level 1 employees, but any other level will have a pension payment of 7 1/2 percent of salary.

Excel's SET.VALUE function is used to place the values just calculated into an array. The statements you enter into A11, A12, and A13, respectively, are the following:

=SET.VALUE(A16,A8)

=SET.VALUE(B16,A9)

=SET.VALUE(C16,A10)

These three statements place the values from A8 through A10 into A16 through C16. The values then will be in horizontal array format.

Finally, you provide a RETURN function by typing this statement into A14:

=RETURN(A16:C16)

Now you are ready to name the macro, using Formula Define Name.

To test the macro, move to a worksheet window and enter a job code of 55 into B3 and a salary of *56000* into C3 (see fig. 3.40). Select cells D3:F3 and enter a reference to the benefits macro. In this example, the macro was saved on a macro sheet named Macro5, and the reference was entered as Macro5!Benefits(C3,B3).

Because the macro is an array macro, remember to hold down the Command key while you press the Return key or click the dialog box to finalize this entry.

As shown in figure 3.40, basic benefits are calculated at $10,080, profit sharing at $5,600, and pension plan contributions at $4,200. Headings, formatting, and additional examples have been added to the display.

File Edit Formula Format Data Options Macro Window

D3   {=Macro5!Benefits(C3,B3)}

Benefit_Wrksht

	A	B	C	D	E	F
1	EMPLOYEE NAME	JOB_CODE	SALARY	BASIC	PROFIT	PENSION
2				BENEFITS	SHARING	PLAN
3	JOHN SMITH	55	$56,000	$10,080	$5,600	$4,200
4	MARY JONES	13	$25,000	$3,750	$0	$0
5	HARRY PAULSON	43	$32,000	$4,800	$0	$0
6	BOB MATTESON	144	$41,000	$7,380	$0	$3,075
7	JERRY BROWN	167	$75,000	$15,750	$7,500	$5,625
8						
9						
10						
11						
12						
13						
14						
15						
16						
17						
18						
19						

Fig. 3.40. Employee benefits calculated.

Conclusion

In this chapter, you have examined many types of function macros. You can put some of them to use right away by building a macro library that suits your own application needs. You probably can use the macros that determine dates or financial ratios immediately. Macros like those that calculate sales commission and benefit calculations, however, will almost certainly need to be changed to conform with policies in your company. You will be able to use the function macros in this chapter as patterns for macros containing calculations that will work in your company.

As you read about command macros in the next several chapters, you may find ways to incorporate some of the function macros into the command macros. You can accomplish this task easily by using the Paste Function command to copy the function name, just as you would for any other Excel built-in function.

4

Creating Macros for the Worksheet Environment

Worksheet macros serve two primary purposes. First, macros save time in the performance of repetitive tasks. Second, worksheet macros automate tasks so that even a novice can achieve successful results with a complex model.

In Chapter 3, you learned about function macros that handle calculations. Those function macros are one type of macro you can use in the worksheet environment. In this chapter, you will learn to create another type of macro for the worksheet: command macros. Those presented in this chapter can handle such tasks as cursor movement and cell selection, data entry and formatting, worksheet printing and storage, and window creation and manipulation.

Command macros vary in sophistication. For example, you can create a simple one- or two-line macro to make a menu selection. Or you can create a complex command macro that interprets a menu selection, retrieves and creates files, and prints a final report. Naturally, the second type requires many lines of instructions to complete all the tasks specified.

The macros in this chapter are designed to be used as stand-alone tools to assist you with your worksheet tasks. You can group several macros together in order to perform a multipurpose task. Grouping is a useful technique because it allows you to test each unit of the macro before you integrate the units into a macro that is too long for efficient testing.

This chapter discusses the following types of macros:

- Macros for cell selection and cursor movement
- Macros for entering, checking, and changing functions and data
- A macro to process menu selections
- Macros that change the worksheet format
- A macro to name individual cells in a column
- A macro that combines command and function macros
- Macros to save and retrieve files
- Macros to print worksheet data
- A macro to enter formulas
- A macro that manipulates windows
- A macro to protect your worksheet data

Macros for Cell Selection and Cursor Movement

When you are not executing a macro, you select a cell by moving the mouse and clicking it. You can select more than one cell by pressing the mouse button while you are dragging the mouse. Once you have selected a range of cells, you may want to change the active cells in the range so that you can make entries or alterations. Normally, you change the active cells by moving the cursor up or down the first column of the range with the Return key and Shift-Return sequence. After you have traveled down the first column, you move to the next column.

In macro mode, this progression is not automatic. You must take charge of changing the active cell. Leaving macro mode to do this is time-consuming. This approach also opens the way for operator errors while the application is not under macro control. In the following section, you will learn how you can allow the operator to move the cursor within a macro, but restrict the operator's other activities.

This section presents several macros that put the operator in charge of cursor movement and cell selection while the program remains in macro mode. The macros include the following:

- Macros for selection of cells by the operator

- Macros that control cursor movement

The first two macros provide a means of selecting cells from within a macro. The sample macros change the width of the columns in the range of cells the operator selects. The next macros control cursor movement in the worksheet. The last macro, which has two versions, lets you navigate from within a selected range in order to enter a list of account names.

Macros for Selection of Cells by the Operator

If the operator selects cells before the macro is executed, all that the macro has to do is complete the desired task for the selected cells. When you design an automated application, however, you usually do not want the operator to leave the controlled environment of the macro in order to select cells. For one reason, the operator accidentally may make other changes before resuming the desired task. Another problem with leaving macro mode is that the operator may misinterpret the reason for the cell selection; outside the macro environment, you cannot display a prompt that gives the operator instructions. To prevent these problems, you can require that the operator select the cells from within the macro.

The example macro, Select_Width, uses the SELECT function to change the column width for the specified cells. The macro is simple to create. You need to enter only two INPUT statements and the command for changing the column width (see fig. 4.1). You enter these instructions in the same way that you enter function macros (see Chapter 3).

After you have entered all the macro statements, assign a name to these cells by using the Define Name command. Naming a command macro is not like the procedure you used in Chapter 3 to name function macros. Instead, you click the command macro indicator in the dialog box. If you want to, you also may assign a letter code to provide quick execution of the macro.

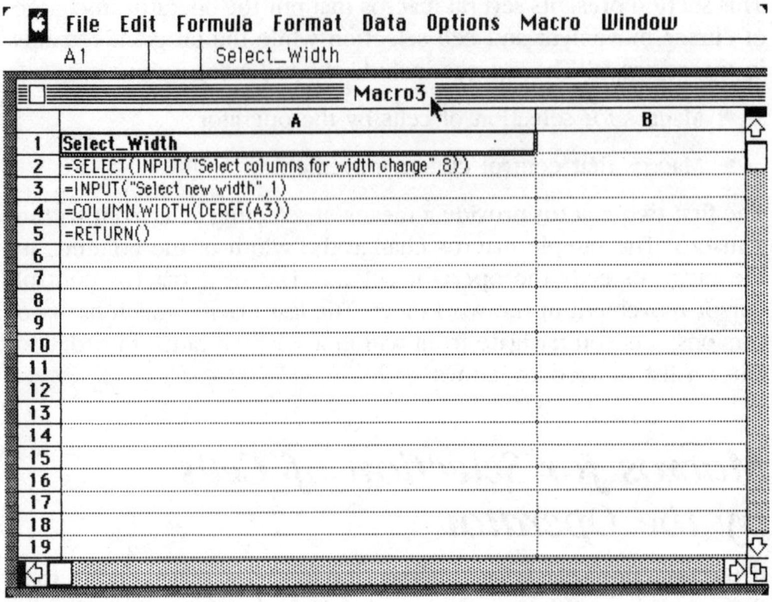

Fig. 4.1. A macro for the selection of cells.

Examine the individual statements in the example more closely before you try to duplicate the macro. The first statement (in A2) contains an INPUT function nested in the SELECT function; this statement establishes the selected cells. Because this statement does not code specific cell selection in the macro, it has flexibility. This INPUT function allows the operator to select a new area each time the macro is executed. In cell A3, another INPUT statement prompts the operator for the width of the columns.

After the operator specifies the cells and column width, the COLUMN.WIDTH statement alters the width of the cells selected. The macro uses the value stored by the INPUT statement in A3 to determine this width. The value is accessed by the DEREF function, which makes available the value rather than the cell address.

When you test this macro, you will find that it functions regardless of the width specified or the number of columns selected. Used within a larger macro, this macro frees the operator from having to remember that cells must be selected before the Column Width command can be executed. The operator does not even need to know that the Column Width command is on the Format menu.

The advantage of obtaining a column width by using an INPUT statement is that it gives the operator clear directions for the entry needed. This method, however, does not draw on the Column Width command's capability to capture this information. To use the COLUMN.WIDTH function's facility for data entry, replace the entries in A3 and A4 with a single statement: COLUMN.WIDTH?( ). The revised macro is illustrated in figure 4.2. When these macro instructions are executed, the normal dialog box for Column Width will appear on the screen. With this approach, you also know the current column width, at least for the column that contains the active cell.

	File Edit Formula Format Data Options Macro Window	
A1	Select_Width	

	Macro4	
	A	B
1	Select_Width	
2	=SELECT(INPUT("Select columns for width change",8))	
3	=COLUMN.WIDTH?()	
4	=RETURN()	
5		
6		
7		
8		
9		
10		
11		
12		
13		
14		
15		
16		
17		
18		
19		

Fig. 4.2. A more flexible selection macro.

Macros That Control Cursor Movement

The active cell in a selected range normally is controlled by the Tab and Return keys in combination with the Shift key. Within a macro, however, these keys have no representations. You can use the SELECT function to simulate the pressing of these keys. The SELECT function has two arguments: a reference to a range of cells you want selected and a reference to a cell you want to designate as the active cell within the range. To create a macro that moves the cursor within a selected range, you need only the second argument.

❖ File Edit Formula Format Data Options Macro Window

| A1 | | Right |

Direction

	A	B	C
1	Right	Up	
2	=SELECT("RC[1]")	=SELECT("R[-1]C")	
3	=RETURN()	=RETURN()	
4			
5	Left	Down	
6	=SELECT("RC[-1]")	=SELECT("R[1]C")	
7	=RETURN()	=RETURN()	
8			
9			
10			
11			
12			
13			
14			
15			
16			
17			
18			
19			

Fig. 4.3. Four macros that control cursor movement.

The four simple macros shown in figure 4.3 move the cursor right, left, up, or down. You can combine these macros with other macro statements in order to create headings, to insert frequently used text, or to supply standard labels for all your worksheets.

For example, you can create a macro that places your standard set of account names in a column of the spreadsheet. Before executing this macro, you select the cells where the account names should be placed.

The easiest way to create this macro is to use the Recorder. As you enter the account names in a column of worksheet cells, you can have the macro capture these keystrokes. A sample macro created in this fashion is shown in figure 4.4.

Notice that the Accounts macro uses the FORMULA and SELECT functions repeatedly for each account name. The FORMULA function enters the required text for the account names. After each name is entered in the selected area, the cursor is moved down one cell by the SELECT function.

	A
1	Accounts
2	=SELECT("RC:R[9]C")
3	=COLUMN.WIDTH(18)
4	=FORMULA("SALARY EXPENSE")
5	=SELECT(,"R[1]C")
6	=FORMULA("RENT")
7	=SELECT(,"R[1]C")
8	=FORMULA("UTILITIES")
9	=SELECT(,"R[1]C")
10	=FORMULA("POSTAGE")
11	=SELECT(,"R[1]C")
12	=FORMULA("TEMPORARY PERSONNEL")
13	=SELECT(,"R[1]C")
14	=FORMULA("MAINTENANCE")
15	=SELECT(,"R[1]C")
16	=FORMULA("LANDSCAPING SERVICE")
17	=SELECT(,"R[1]C")
18	=FORMULA("VEHICLE LEASING")
19	=SELECT(,"R[1]C")
20	=FORMULA("VEHICLE MAINTENANCE")
21	=SELECT(,"R[1]C")
22	=FORMULA("ENTERTAINMENT")
23	=SELECT("R[-9]C[1]:RC[1]")
24	=RETURN()

Fig. 4.4. A macro to enter account titles.

Macros for Entering, Checking, and Changing Functions and Data

Whether you are entering data, formulas, or functions, the process of entering information is one of the most time-consuming worksheet activities. In addition, a mistake in this process can be costly in terms of erroneous results and time-consuming corrections.

Macros can take some of the drudgery out of the input process because they can enter repetitive information for you. Macros also can perform inspection and clean-up activities that ensure the data entered by the operator is accurate.

The macros in this section can help you save time and effort when you enter, check, and change functions and data. The following macros are included:

- Macros to input built-in functions

- A macro to handle error checking and alterations

- A macro for rounding

- A macro to change the internal storage accuracy

- A string manipulation macro

Macros To Input Built-In Functions

Although built-in functions are a powerful feature of the Excel package, they can be time-consuming to enter, because they require many accurately placed parentheses and commas. If you need to enter a column of built-in function data and if the functions are not similar enough to use the Copy command, a macro can be a real time-saver.

This section presents two examples of function entry through a macro. The first macro, a date stamp, can be used any place you want to include the current date on your spreadsheet. Aside from providing the date, which is always updated, the macro records constant times, for example, the times of truck deliveries. This macro fits nicely in any automated application where a time stamp is needed.

You will want to use the Recorder to create this macro. Any time that you create a macro that includes a number of macro commands that have menu selection equivalents, the Recorder is your best choice for timesavings and accuracy.

The first macro enters the date as a formula that is updated each time the worksheet is recalculated (see fig. 4.5). The first entry in this macro is the FORMULA function; this places the label TODAY'S DATE in the active cell. This cell is then formatted with a column width of 14. Next, the macro moves the active cell one cell to the right and enters =NOW( ) as a formula. Notice the required quotation marks around the formula entries. This cell is formatted with one of Excel's established date formats and is set at a column width of 11 in cell E7.

The NOW( ) function is used a second time in E8. This time, the function is entered in a macro cell. The macro then selects the worksheet cell that is one cell to the right of the last entry and places the current value of NOW( ) in that cell. The cell is then formatted as time, providing a time stamp that will not change.

This one macro demonstrates both methods of time-stamping. The date entry is a formula that will be updated every time the sheet is calculated. The time stamp uses the NOW( ) function in a different way and places a permanent time stamp in the cell.

With this last task completed, you can end this macro with RETURN. This useful macro can place a date stamp anywhere you like in the spreadsheet. That date always will be updated to reflect the current date.

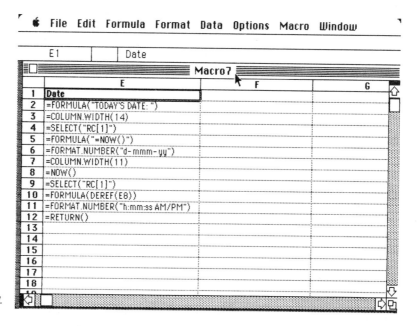

Fig. 4.5. A macro to place the current date in a worksheet cell.

Sometimes you do not want to update the cell. You may want the cell to display the date of the last update or the date of the receipt of an invoice, just like the time stamp in figure 4.5. On these occasions, the macro in figure 4.5 is useless because it does not store the date as a constant.

To store a date as a constant, you have several alternatives. One method is to edit the date formula. While editing the cell, use Calculate Now from the Options menu to freeze the value in the cell. Another method is to copy the macro to itself with Paste Special. However, less complex options are available. You can use Excel's built-in DATE function. This method is best for instances when you know the date that you want to place in the cell. You can code the arguments for *year*, *month*, and *day* in the macro or use INPUT statements to obtain them from the operator.

Another alternative is to incorporate the NOW( ) function in the macro. The result is stored in a macro cell. You use a FORMULA statement that uses the DEREF function to reference the storage cell for NOW to obtain the cell's value. This function places the serial date number in the worksheet cell.

Figure 4.6 provides an example of the last approach. In the worksheet, DATE LAST UPDATED: is the label that precedes the date. This macro updates the date only when the macro is executed.

Therefore, the macro provides an ideal time stamp to indicate budget versions or project plan revisions.

The macro begins in E2 by placing the label, DATE LAST UPDATED:, in the current cell. This cell is widened to allow a full display of the entry. The current date is stored in E4 of the macro. The cell immediately to the right of the cell used for the label is selected in E5. The statement in E6 places in that cell the value in E4, and the value is formatted in E7. Then the macro changes the width so that a proper date display is provided.

| File | Edit | Formula | Format | Data | Options | Macro | Window |

| B1 | | 30051.433634259 | | | |

Macro8

	E	F	G
1	Date		
2	=FORMULA("DATE LAST UPDATED: ")		
3	=COLUMN.WIDTH(18)		
4	=NOW()		
5	=SELECT("RC[1]")		
6	=FORMULA(DEREF(E4))		
7	=FORMAT.NUMBER("d-mmm-yy")		
8	=COLUMN.WIDTH(11)		
9	=RETURN()		
10			
11			
12			
13			
14			

Worksheet6

	A	B	C	D	E	
1	DATE LAST UPDATED:	11-Apr-86				
2						

Fig. 4.6. A macro to place a fixed date in a worksheet cell.

A Macro To Handle Error Checking and Alterations

Now that you have learned how to move the cursor around in the selected area, you may want to check for a specific value or for error values in the selected area so that you can make an alteration. This facility works for changing job codes, part numbers, or warehouse assignments, or for replacing a value like #N/A with a zero.

Assume that you are teaching a graduate class in management. You have assigned a number of tests and projects over the semester and have used an Excel worksheet like the one in figure 4.7 to record the grades from each project. At the beginning of each semester, the worksheet contains #N/A in every grade cell. As projects and tests are completed, the not-available indicators are replaced by the scores. At a glance, you can see which students haven't completed a project, because #N/A stands out more clearly than a zero.

Although you are lenient with makeup exams and late projects because your students travel frequently for work, you still must set a time when the grade for uncompleted work is changed to a zero. The time you have chosen for this change is at the end of the semester when you will be grading the final exams. Because this is a busy time, you want Excel to check the grades and change all the remaining #N/As to zeros. The macro in figure 4.8 handles this task.

The macro has three sections. The first is the initialization section in cells A2 through A8. In A2, the name GRADES is assigned to the current selection. The counter for the Outer_Loop, OUT_LOOP, is assigned a value equal to the number of columns. IN_LOOP is given a value equal to the number of rows. In A7 and A8, counters are established to ensure that all rows and columns are checked. These counters are initialized at 1.

The Outer_Loop starts in A9 and ends in A20. The Inner_Loop starts in A10 and ends in A16. The Outer_Loop changes columns in the inspection process, and the Inner_Loop changes rows.

	A	B	C	D	E
1	STUDENT	EXAM 1	EXAM 2	EXAM 3	FINAL EXAM
2	BROWN, JERRY	#N/A	79	81	91
3	CARLSON, MARY	55	63	71	77
4	DWIGHT, MARK	45	72	78	73
5	EGGERS, PAUL	95	98	99	90
6	FALLON, TIM	88	82	#N/A	86
7	MORRIS, JOHN	67	71	79	75
8	NELSON, TROY	72	81	85	84
9	PETERSON, DEBBIE	99	95	91	93
10	ROGERS, MARY	85	80	88	91
11	STILSON, ROY	#N/A	77	79	78
12	TAYLOR, JANE	91	89	93	91
13	WRIGHT, CAROLE	82	#N/A	88	84
14					
15					
16					
17					
18					
19					

Fig. 4.7. A worksheet for grade entry.

	A
1	Grade_Macro
2	=SET.NAME("GRADES",SELECTION())
3	=ROWS(SELECTION())
4	=COLUMNS(SELECTION())
5	=SET.NAME("OUT_LOOP",A4)
6	=SET.NAME("IN_LOOP",A3)
7	=SET.NAME("COUNT_ROWS",1)
8	=SET.NAME("COUNT_COLUMNS",1)
9	Outer_Loop
10	Inner_Loop
11	=IF(NOT(ISNA(INDEX(GRADES,COUNT_ROWS,COUNT_COLUMNS))),GOTO(A14))
12	=SELECT(INDEX(GRADES,COUNT_ROWS,COUNT_COLUMNS))
13	=FORMULA(0)
14	=IF(COUNT_ROWS=A3,GOTO(A17))
15	=SET.NAME("COUNT_ROWS",COUNT_ROWS+1)
16	=GOTO(A10)
17	=IF(COUNT_COLUMNS=A4,GOTO(A21))
18	=SET.NAME("COUNT_COLUMNS",COUNT_COLUMNS+1)
19	=SET.NAME("COUNT_ROWS",1)
20	=GOTO(A9)
21	=RETURN()

Fig. 4.8. A macro to replace #N/A with zero.

In the Inner_Loop, each entry is checked for a value of #N/A. When #N/A is found, the statements in A12 and A13 select that cell and change the value to zero. If #N/A is not found, a check is made for more rows in the column to be examined. If more rows remain, the row count is incremented in A15. If not, the column count is checked and incremented if appropriate (A18). When the column count is incremented, the row count is set at 1.

The only limitation of this macro is that you must use #N/A for missing grades at the time you record the grades. The macro will not change a blank cell to zero.

Parts of the macro, such as the SET.NAME statements, could be handled with the Recorder; but other instructions, such as the IF statements, must be entered from the keyboard. The easier method is to enter the entire macro from the keyboard.

A Macro for Rounding

Excel provides an option that lets you change to the same precision all your numeric results that appear on the display. This option is Precision As Displayed from the Options menu. Because this is an all-or-nothing approach, it may not always meet your needs. Sometimes you may want to round the figures that appear in one column of cells but leave the others untouched. You can change selected figures by incorporating the ROUND function in the appropriate formulas.

If you enter the ROUND function when you create your formulas, you do not need to use a macro. However, you can use a macro to add the ROUND function to a formula you already have entered. To edit your formula in this way, you can move the cursor to the cell that needs the ROUND function and execute the macro in figure 4.9.

	B	C
	Macro5	
26	Try	
27	=SET.NAME("ACTIVE",SELECTION())	
28	=GET.FORMULA(ACTIVE)	
29	=FORMULA("=ROUND("&MID(B28,2,LEN(B28)-1)&",2)")	
30	=RETURN()	
31		
32		
33		
34		
35		
36		
37		
38		
39		
40		
41		
42		
43		
44		

Fig. 4.9. A macro to round formula results.

You can create this macro and execute it whenever you need to round a formula entry. When you create the macro, keep two points in mind. First, this is a command macro for which the Recorder feature will not help. Because the required actions are not part of the menu structure, you must enter the commands. Second, in constructing this macro, you should not use absolute cell references. They would limit the usefulness of the macro to certain cells.

Examine the functions required to build this macro. The first macro function, SET.NAME (in cell B27), attaches the name ACTIVE to the selected cells.

This macro is designed to edit only the first cell in the selection but easily can be changed to edit all the cells in the selection. You use the same editing techniques explained earlier in this chapter. These editing features allow you to change the contents of cells by adding or subtracting characters in the entry. This technique is used frequently with the ROUND function or one of the text functions.

After the active cell has been assigned a name, the GET.FORMULA function (B28) obtains the formula stored in the cell. This command gets the entire formula including the equal sign.

Next, you build the replacement formula for the active cell. Remember that the formula stored in B28 has an equal sign, which must be removed rather than embedded in the new formula. The argument for the FORMULA function in B29 is a string formula. The first part of this string formula is "=ROUND(". This part provides the fixed components at the beginning of the formula. The next component is the existing formula minus the equal sign at the beginning. The MID function, by beginning in the second position of the entry, strips off the equal sign. The number of characters used is the length of the formula minus one. The last part of the new formula is ",2)". This last component ends the function and specifies that two decimal places of accuracy are desired.

You can enhance this FORMULA function by adding an INPUT statement that requests the level of rounding desired. The rounding level then can be supplied as a variable. This variation expands the usefulness of the macro.

You can apply the concept used in the ROUND function to the DOLLAR function, which has a parallel construction. In addition to rounding figures, the DOLLAR function formats the results as currency and stores them as text.

A Macro To Change the Internal Storage Accuracy

One way that you can change the internal storage accuracy is from within the Options menu structure. If you are designing applications for others, however, you may want to steer away from using this menu. When you use the Options menu, you have no warning before Excel permanently alters your data to the display precision. Inadvertently choosing this option can cause permanent loss of the extra decimal accuracy.

One means of preventing this problem is to establish a macro for handling precision accuracy (see fig. 4.10.) Operators can be instructed to make changes in precision through the macro only. You can write the macro so that it displays a warning message and prompts the operator to enter a confirmation code.

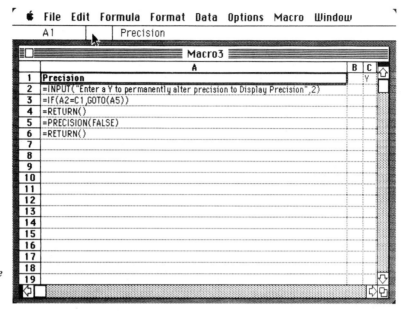

Fig. 4.10. A macro to change the precision accuracy of stored values.

The first step in the creation of the macro is to enter an INPUT function that provides a prompt for the change in the storage accuracy. The operator can choose to proceed by entering Y. Any other entry is disregarded and does not affect the accuracy of the stored data. The entry made by the operator in response to the Input prompt is stored in cell A2.

To see this macro in action, create a worksheet with the entries 3.3, 3.3, and 3.3 in cells A1 through A3. Next, enter a formula in A4 to sum the three values. Select all four cells and format them as whole numbers (select 0). Because of the internal precision, 3, 3, and 3 will add up to 10. Now try using the macro to correct this problem. All three occurrences of 3.3 will be changed internally to 3 to match the display precision.

The next macro statement compares the value stored in A2 with the value stored in C1. If the values are equal, control branches to A5, which contains the PRECISION function with a logical value of FALSE. A logical value of FALSE changes Full Precision to Precision As Displayed. If the values compared in A3 are not equal, control passes to the instruction in A4. Because A4 contains a RETURN function, the macro ends without changing the internal accuracy of the active worksheet.

You can apply the concepts presented in this macro to many applications. Any time that you want to be cautious with the use of a command, this method is valuable. It provides an opportunity for the operator to verify that the command should be enacted. This method is useful when you are archiving historic data, deleting large sections of a worksheet, or rolling history off a sheet in order to make room for data for the new year. The key element in this approach is the INPUT statement; this statement provides confirmation for the requested action.

A String Manipulation Macro

All text data, which is considered to be string data, can be manipulated by string functions such as MID and LEN. Manipulating text is especially useful for restructuring data transferred to Excel from other programs. The string functions allow you to restructure data that otherwise would prove unsuitable. For example, suppose that you have part numbers that are too long to be used in the format you desire. These part numbers, however, can be identified by the first six characters plus the last digit. You can use a macro to manipulate the strings in order to obtain the characters you need. You then can overlay the old column of data with the new part numbers.

Your first step is to have the operator select the part numbers for conversion. The macro for this selection, shown in figure 4.11, first determines the size of the selection. Then the existing part numbers are manipulated by the macro's string functions to create the new list of part numbers shown in figure 4.12.

The macro has two sections (see fig. 4.11). You probably will want to enter this macro from the keyboard rather than use the Recorder. The first section, Fix_Partnumbers, initializes variables and performs housekeeping tasks so that the macro will operate in an organized fashion. The second part, Top_Loop, contains instructions for looping through the selected cells and changing each part number.

Because ORIG_DATA refers to the entire selection, the macro uses COUNT to change one entry at a time. Notice that the text formula in A9 uses COUNT to access just one entry. Until all the part numbers are changed, the macro stores the revised numbers in an area called ALTERED. Then ALTERED is cut and pasted over the original data.

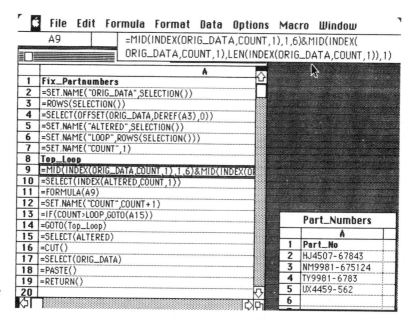

Fig. 4.11. A macro to manipulate string data.

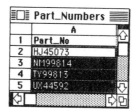

Fig. 4.12. Converted part numbers.

A Macro To Process Menu Selections

Although Excel's menus are easy to use, the options focus on spreadsheet capabilities rather than on business functions. To automate business functions, you need a menu that includes options like Update Accounts Receivable or Print Payroll Report rather than the spreadsheet commands.

Excel does not have a menu command specifically for creating a menu. However, through the available commands, Excel provides two methods for creating custom menus. One approach provides a dialog box for the operator's entry, and the other allows free-form screen design and entry.

With the dialog box, you start with a blank screen and design a menu. To make your menu display more attractive, you probably will want to remove the grid lines. You use an INPUT statement in your macro to accept the operator's menu choice. You can have the operator type the correct letter or use the mouse to select the cell containing the desired option. A disadvantage of this approach is that the dialog box for input takes up space on the screen.

The free-form screen design, which does not use a dialog box for input, provides more aesthetic screen design for menu options (see fig. 4.13). The menu is completely free form and can be designed to suit your needs. Because menus are created on regular work-sheets, you can arrange your menu selections any way you like. You can make two columns of selections or place everything in one column. If you are going to have the operator select an option number from the menu, you may want to have the option numbers in one column and the selections they represent in the second column. To complete the design, you can remove the grid lines with the Display command from the Options menu. This method creates a professional-looking menu screen.

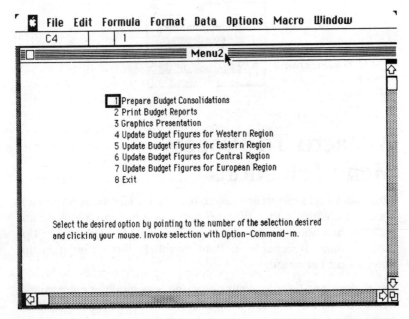

Fig. 4.13. A menu screen.

In the sample menu, created with the free-form screen design, the operator selects a menu option number. After the selection is made, the operator has to execute a macro that will process the response. The letter *m* has been assigned to the macro that processes the menu selection. Therefore, the operator invokes the processing macro by pressing the Option-Command-m key sequence.

Study the inner workings of the Excel macro, Process_Selection (see fig. 4.14). The purpose of this macro is to process the option selected from the menu. The macro in the figure shows only the code for the selection of each menu option. The subroutine code that processes each of the menu selections is not shown here.

The instruction in A7 of the macro returns the value of the selected cell (1, 2, 3, and so on) and serves as the basis of all further activity in the macro. DEREF is used to obtain the value of the selected cell rather than its address. If the selection is a valid menu item, the macro directs control to the set of instructions that provide the required capability. The IF statements in A8 through A15 perform checks for valid menu responses and cause the macro to take the branch to the location containing the special processing. To use this macro, you would have to create a separate macro for each branch. The value of the selected cell determines which macro is executed. For example, when A7 equals 1, the branch to the Consol macro is taken.

If the program does not find a valid menu selection to process, control passes to A16. The ALERT function in A16 causes the program to pause and display an Alert message for the operator. Cell A16 contains a level 1 Alert that informs the operator that the menu selection is invalid. You can have the program examine the menu choice further by adding extra instructions before the ALERT statement. You also can provide a more descriptive error message concerning the selection. The macro instruction following the ALERT statement (A17) branches to the Budget_Menu macro in A1 through A3. This macro displays the menu and starts the entire process again.

When you are creating the processing for each menu option, you can apply the shell programming concepts discussed in Chapter 2. Notice that the options in the processing routines shown in figure 4.15 are not coded. Instead of coding, you can use the MESSAGE function to indicate that you have reached the specified routine. The first argument in each MESSAGE statement must be a logical value with TRUE indicating that the message in the statement should be displayed. This approach gives you an opportunity to test the menu logic before you write the instructions for each menu selection.

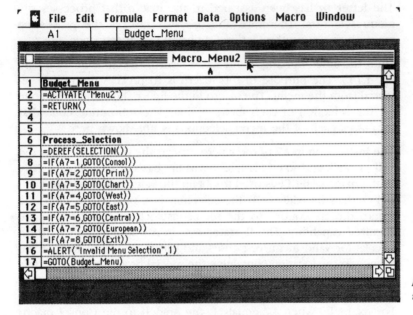

```
 File  Edit  Formula  Format  Data  Options  Macro  Window
         A1                    Budget_Menu

════════════════════════ Macro_Menu2 ════════════════════════
                                A
 1  Budget_Menu
 2  =ACTIVATE("Menu2")
 3  =RETURN()
 4
 5
 6  Process_Selection
 7  =DEREF(SELECTION())
 8  =IF(A7=1,GOTO(Consol))
 9  =IF(A7=2,GOTO(Print))
10  =IF(A7=3,GOTO(Chart))
11  =IF(A7=4,GOTO(West))
12  =IF(A7=5,GOTO(East))
13  =IF(A7=6,GOTO(Central))
14  =IF(A7=7,GOTO(European))
15  =IF(A7=8,GOTO(Exit))
16  =ALERT("Invalid Menu Selection",1)
17  =GOTO(Budget_Menu)
```

Fig. 4.14. A macro to process menu selections.

```
 File  Edit  Formula  Format  Data  Options  Macro  Window
         A1                    Budget_Menu

════════════════════════ Macro_Menu2 ════════════════════════
                                A
18  Consol
19  =MESSAGE(TRUE,"Consolidations")
20  =RETURN()
21  Exit
22  =MESSAGE(TRUE,"Exit")
23  =RETURN()
24
25
26
27
28
29
30
31
32
33
34
```

Fig. 4.15. A shell structure for the menu options.

Applications for menu processing abound. Rather than have the operator remember the sequence of commands for different tasks, you can create a menu choice for each task. The processing steps for each task can be coded and then processed when that option is selected from the menu. You can handle file reads and saves, window processing, budget consolidations, and any other application that requires more than one choice. This approach improves accuracy and saves time. It is especially useful for less experienced users, but even the experienced user will appreciate the timesavings.

Macros That Change the Worksheet Display

Although the Excel package offers many options for the display of your worksheet, you normally work with only a few. Because most of your applications have certain similarities, you probably use the same display options repeatedly. The instructions for these display options can be recorded in a macro you invoke whenever you need to change the worksheet display.

Macros for some of the frequently used display options are explained in this section. The macros include

- A macro for displaying formulas

- A macro to freeze formula values

- Macros to change the numeric format

- A macro to provide alignment options

- A macro to change the column width

- A macro for transposing column and row data

A Macro for Displaying Formulas

Sometimes, you will want to display formulas instead of the results of calculations. To examine a single formula, you make the cell that contains the formula the active cell and study the formula in the formula bar. If you want to examine a number of formulas, you select Display from the Options menu and then select Formulas to display the entire worksheet as formulas. Because this command is not used frequently, you may forget that it is available.

The macro to display formulas is simple and can save you time. You probably will want to create the macro with the Recorder to ensure that you code the arguments of the DISPLAY function correctly. The arguments correspond to the options in the Display dialog box. These options are Formulas, Gridlines, and Row & Column Headings. Each argument can have a value of TRUE, equivalent to checking the option it represents, or FALSE, representing unchecked. The completed macro, named Formulas, is shown in figure 4.16.

You can assign a letter name to the macro so that you can execute it with the Option-Command-key sequence. Remember that unlike some other packages, Excel differentiates between upper- and lowercase letters.

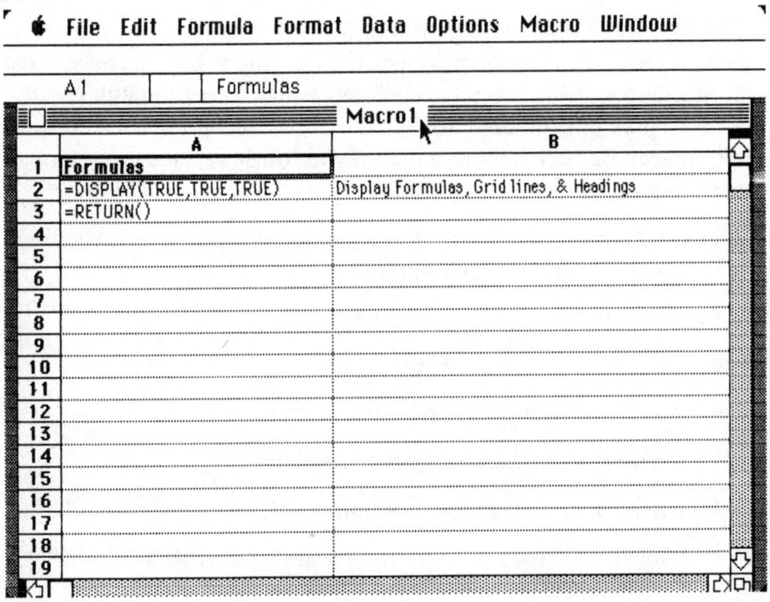

Fig. 4.16. A macro to display worksheet formulas.

You can enhance this macro so that it expands the column width. You can use a fixed width-expansion beyond the 15-character width the package allows for formulas. Or you can use the INPUT function and allow the user to specify the width. Each enhancement requires new macro statements. To change the column width, for example, you incorporate the COLUMN.WIDTH function.

A Macro To Freeze Formula Values

A formula result changes when any variable in the formula changes. Most of the time, the new result is just what you want. In certain situations, however, you want to retain the current value of a formula and then only make changes to the variables. For instance, you may want to place a fixed date or time stamp on a menu. Or, you may want to change budget projections to constants after the current year's figures have been determined. Whenever you have decided on an optimal value for a formula, you can "freeze" the results of your calculations.

One way to freeze formula values is shown in the macro in figure 4.17. This macro copies cells to themselves by using the Paste Special command with the Values option. This process has the effect of freezing the formulas to their current values.

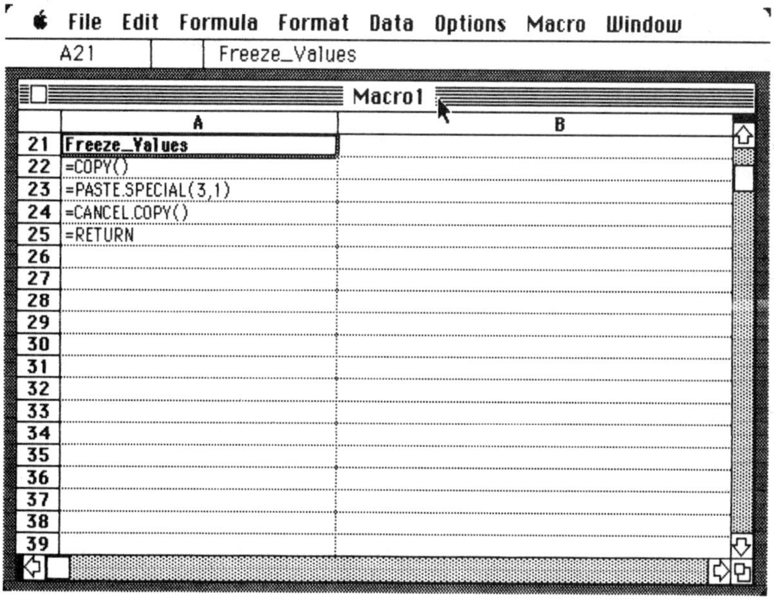

Fig. 4.17. A macro to freeze formula values.

Before invoking the macro, the user must select the cells to be altered by the macro. The first function in the macro is COPY( ). Because you don't want to copy to a different range of cells, a second selection is not required. The only other statement required to freeze the values is PASTE.SPECIAL. The first argument, 3, specifies values. The second argument, 1, means that no mathematical operation (addition, subtraction, multiplication, or division) is being performed during the Paste operation.

Although the macro could end after this statement, the selected cells still would have a highlighted border around them; this is because the Copy To and From ranges are the same. This situation is remedied by adding the CANCEL.COPY( ) statement.

Macros To Update the Worksheet Format

The worksheet Format menu provides a variety of options, including different formats for displaying cell values. These options range from Currency and Percentage formats to Date and Time display options. Worksheet formats also control the alignment of data in cells and the style and size of type used for worksheet entries. You can use macros to handle any of these tasks. However, you will want to automate only the format tasks you perform frequently because the time required to create seldom used macros could offset any potential time savings. Some useful formatting macros are macros to change the numeric format and a macro to provide alignment options.

Macros To Change the Numeric Format

The first examples in this section are macros that change the format of numeric cell entries. You should study these macros and then create your own variations to meet your particular needs.

The simplest type of formatting macro executes the Format Number command for the cells selected. The macro is straightforward and contains only a macro name, one macro function, and the RETURN statement. For example, the macro shown in figure 4.18 formats cells as percentages. The correct cells must be selected before the macro is executed.

You can create a macro just like this for each format you use frequently. Using macros saves considerable time, because you do not have to select the menu option and search the list of dialog box options for the format you want.

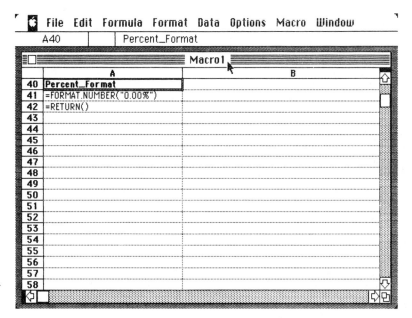

Fig. 4.18. A macro to format cells as percentages.

A different approach to numeric formatting would be to create a menu of the formats you use frequently. In the next example, a macro displays a list of five menu options, and the operator selects the option desired. The macro uses the INPUT statement to obtain the operator's choice from the menu.

The macro shown in figure 4.19 does not generate the menu. You create the menu on a worksheet for permanent storage before you enter the macro instructions. (This macro could be modified easily by using the approach given earlier in this chapter's section "A Macro To Process Menu Selections.")

The macro is named Format and has been assigned the letter *f* for quick execution. This macro first activates the window that contains the menu screen. The INPUT statement (A3), executed next, causes a dialog box to appear on the screen with the menu (see fig. 4.20). The dialog box expects the letter of the desired format as input. This input is examined to determine the type of formatting requested. Notice that one of the menu options is *No Change*. You may elect not to alter the format after you issue the macro command.

If you don't enter an acceptable option, an Alert error message is displayed, and you are requested to reenter your choice. Until a value is entered, the macro loops between displaying the menu and check-

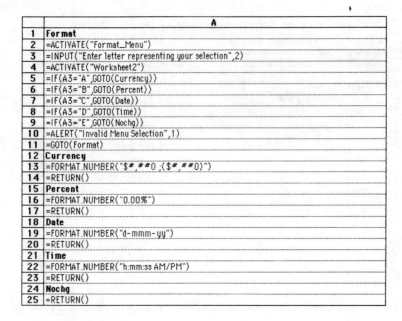

	A
1	**Format**
2	=ACTIVATE("Format_Menu")
3	=INPUT("Enter letter representing your selection",2)
4	=ACTIVATE("Worksheet2")
5	=IF(A3="A",GOTO(Currency))
6	=IF(A3="B",GOTO(Percent))
7	=IF(A3="C",GOTO(Date))
8	=IF(A3="D",GOTO(Time))
9	=IF(A3="E",GOTO(Nochg))
10	=ALERT("Invalid Menu Selection",1)
11	=GOTO(Format)
12	**Currency**
13	=FORMAT.NUMBER("$#,##0_);($#,##0)")
14	=RETURN()
15	**Percent**
16	=FORMAT.NUMBER("0.00%")
17	=RETURN()
18	**Date**
19	=FORMAT.NUMBER("d-mmm-yy")
20	=RETURN()
21	**Time**
22	=FORMAT.NUMBER("h:mm:ss AM/PM")
23	=RETURN()
24	**Nochg**
25	=RETURN()

Fig. 4.19. A macro to provide several formatting options.

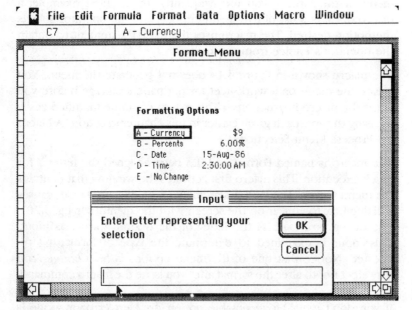

Fig. 4.20. The menu presented by the Format macro.

ing the response. When a valid entry is processed, the worksheet window remains active, and the macro performs the formatting requested.

A macro that provides menu-driven formatting options is suitable when you want to limit the alternatives presented to the operators. Because Excel has many formatting options, limiting the operators' options can reduce the inconsistencies in formatted reports.

A Macro To Provide Alignment Options

The macro in figure 4.21 illustrates the use of the question mark (?), which is available with many macro functions. Commands like Alignment, Calculation, Column Width, and Format Number produce dialog boxes when selected from the menu. To build flexibility into your macros, you can use these menu commands along with a question mark as macro functions: ALIGNMENT?( ), CALCULATION?( ), COLUMN.WIDTH?( ), and FORMAT.NUMBER?( ). When these macro functions are executed, their dialog boxes appear on the screen. Because the operator makes selections from within the macro, you can limit the selections offered.

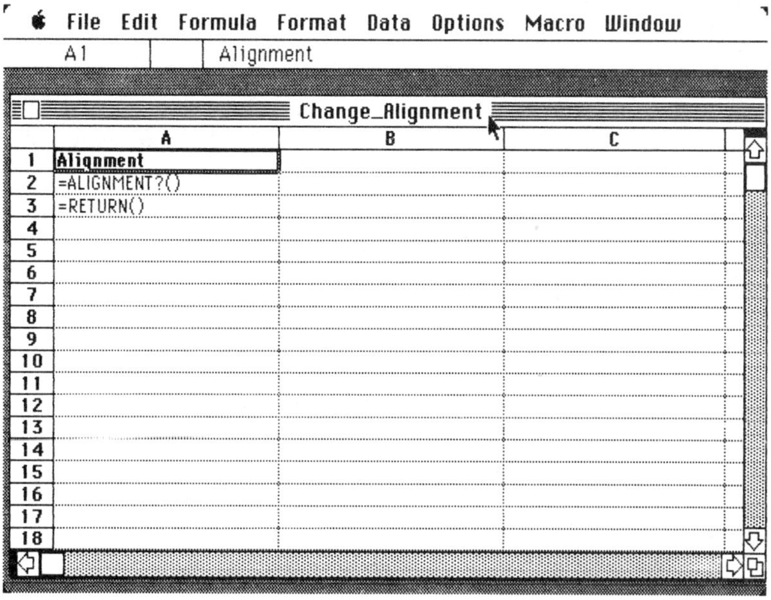

Fig. 4.21. A macro to handle alignment.

When the Alignment macro in figure 4.21 is executed, a dialog box is displayed (see fig. 4.22). The operator can select General, Left, Center, Right, or Fill. All the choices are identical to those under the Alignment option of the Format menu. Of the five options, three—Left, Center, and Right—do what the names imply. General aligns text to the left and numbers to the right and centers error values and logicals. Fill repeats the cell value until the cell is filled.

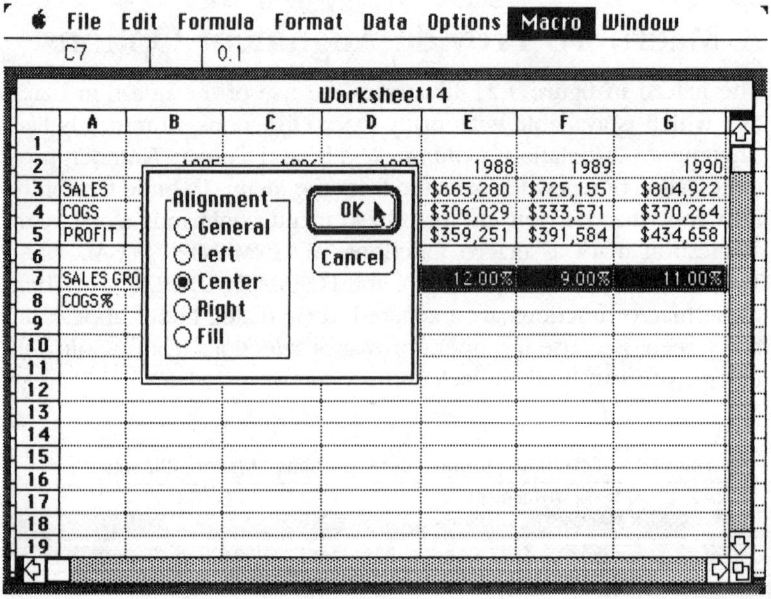

Fig. 4.22. The dialog box generated by the Alignment macro.

A Macro To Change the Column Widths

You can use a number of methods to build a macro that alters column widths. You can use the question mark (?) option (introduced in the preceding section). The advantage of this method is that it lets you control selections within the macro, but at the same time allows the operator flexibility. For frequently used column widths, you may want to set up a macro for each width. If you need to build many models having the same basic format, you can create a single macro to establish the varying widths required for each worksheet.

Suppose, for example, that you must build 10 models, each listing account names and certain other information. All the models require that the first column have a width of 20; the second, 3; the third, 5; and the fourth, 11; the width of the fifth column varies. By altering the column widths with a macro, you do not have to remember the appropriate widths from sheet to sheet. All you need to do is execute the macro.

Before you execute the macro (shown in fig. 4.23), you must position the cursor in the first column of your worksheet. The first COLUMN.WIDTH function pertains to the column containing the active cell. In the example, a value of 20 is given as the width of the first column. The macro then moves the cursor one column to the right before the second COLUMN.WIDTH statement is executed. The other functions operate in the same manner until processing reaches the last COLUMN.WIDTH function. This function uses the question mark option to allow the operator to specify through a dialog box the width for that column.

File Edit Formula Format Data Options Macro Window

A21		Width	

	Macro25	
	A	B
21	Width	
22	=COLUMN.WIDTH(20)	
23	=SELECT("RC[1]")	
24	=COLUMN.WIDTH(3)	
25	=SELECT("RC[1]")	
26	=COLUMN.WIDTH(5)	
27	=SELECT("RC[1]")	
28	=COLUMN.WIDTH(11)	
29	=SELECT("RC[1]")	
30	=COLUMN.WIDTH?()	
31	=RETURN()	
32		
33		
34		
35		
36		
37		
38		
39		

Fig. 4.23. A macro to handle a variety of column widths.

Unlike the column width macros shown in figures 4.1 and 4.2, this macro establishes predetermined widths in order to customize the columns in a range of a worksheet. For example, one column in your worksheet may contain a part number; another, a quantity; and a third, a price. You can specify in the macro specific widths for each of these columns.

A Macro for Transposing Column and Row Data

The Cut and Paste commands are useful when you want to copy data from one row to another or from one column to another. You cannot, however, use the Cut and Paste commands to copy values in a column to cells in a row, or data from a row to a column.

Being able to copy between columns and rows can save time. Perhaps the months of the year are listed across a row on your worksheet, and you want to list them down a column. The division names for your company may be listed down column 2, and you want them across row 100 as labels for a few summary statistics. Although you cannot perform this copy operation with menu selections, you can create a macro that handles the task.

The macro for transposing data between rows and columns is shown in figure 4.24. Examine the functions used in the macro. The first statement, which combines the SELECT and INPUT functions, lets the operator select a contiguous group of cells in either a row or a column. Next, the DEFINE.NAME function is used to assign a name to these cells so that the operator can select that range to be transposed. Unless you assign a name to these original cells, the selection will be lost when the second group of cells is selected. You use the range name to reaccess the original cells.

The second group of cells is selected with the nested macro functions in A4. If the original group of cells was stored as a column, this selection must be a row. Likewise, if the original group of cells was a row, this group must be a column. If the orientation of the two selections is not different, Excel cannot transpose the values.

The FORMULA.ARRAY function is used to put an array formula in the second group of cells. This statement produces the same effect as pressing the Option key when a formula is entered from the keyboard. Because the cells in the second range must store the results of this array formula, the area selected must be the right size. If the original values are stored as a column of eight values, eight cells in one row are required to hold the results of the TRANSPOSE function, which changes the orientation.

The transposed cells rely on the original cells for their values. If you delete the original cells at this point, the second group of cells cannot contain their transposed values. To make the transposed cells no longer dependent on the original values, you must change the

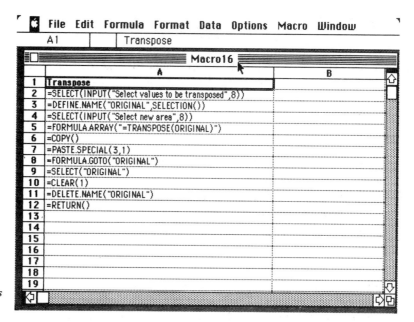

File Edit Formula Format Data Options Macro Window

| A1 | | Transpose |

Macro16

	A	B
1	**Transpose**	
2	=SELECT(INPUT("Select values to be transposed",8))	
3	=DEFINE.NAME("ORIGINAL",SELECTION())	
4	=SELECT(INPUT("Select new area",8))	
5	=FORMULA.ARRAY("=TRANSPOSE(ORIGINAL)")	
6	=COPY()	
7	=PASTE.SPECIAL(3,1)	
8	=FORMULA.GOTO("ORIGINAL")	
9	=SELECT("ORIGINAL")	
10	=CLEAR(1)	
11	=DELETE.NAME("ORIGINAL")	
12	=RETURN()	
13		
14		
15		
16		
17		
18		
19		

Fig. 4.24. A macro for transposing data between rows and columns.

array formula to a set of constant values. This is accomplished with the COPY and PASTE.SPECIAL functions. COPY accesses the cells currently selected, and the PASTE.SPECIAL(3,1) statement copies only the values. Because the range selected was not changed, the cells are copied to themselves. After the PASTE.SPECIAL statement is executed, the cells no longer contain references to the original array. This means that the original array can be deleted.

The macro moves the cursor to the original cells in order to provide visual verification of their deletion. The statement =SELECT("ORIGINAL") is what actually alters the cells selected. The CLEAR function is used with an argument of 1, indicating that everything should be cleared from the selected cells. The name ORIGINAL is deleted with DELETE.NAME because you do not need to retain names assigned to handle the temporary needs of a macro.

If you had chosen to end the macro after the PASTE.SPECIAL operation, a highlighted border would have appeared around the transposed cells after they had been converted to values. The macro eliminates the border by including an instruction to format the columns or to select new cells, as is done in cell A9. Another way to eliminate this highlighting is to include a CANCEL.COPY statement.

If you choose, you can enhance this macro by making it copy from one document to another. To add this next level of sophistication, you must be sure that the other file is open and use the ACTIVATE function to access the window that contains the information you need. You would insert the ACTIVATE statement immediately after the COPY statement. You then would proceed to select cells in the new worksheet before pasting data in them.

A Macro To Name
Individual Cells in a Column

Excel's Define Name command is efficient for assigning names to a cell or group of cells. In fact, you don't even have to type the names; Excel uses the information in an adjacent cell to name a value. Suppose, however, that you have a column of account names, and you want to assign those names to the account balances stored in the cells immediately to the right of each name. Even though you don't have to type each name, you do have to select each cell and issue the Define Name command for each—a time-consuming process without macro support.

You can create a macro like the one shown in figure 4.25 to assign range names. This macro works regardless of the length of the columns of names and data or where the names begin. The macro is based on the assumption that you will select two adjacent columns. The column to the left will contain the names, and the column to the right will contain the values.

As a first step, the macro uses SET.NAME to initialize the looping COUNTER to a value of 1. You then must determine the number of rows in the selection because this number is the limiting factor for the looping process. The statement in A3 handles this process. The IF statement in A4 monitors the number of iterations and branches to the RETURN statement when COUNTER exceeds the number of rows in the selection.

The INDEX function (A5) plays a major role in this macro. INDEX, one of Excel's built-in functions, is very versatile and operates on a range of cells. The INDEX function refers to a single cell within the range. The cell is specified by the *row* and *column* that follow the function name.

INDEX is used once to obtain the name to be assigned to a cell and again to specify the cell address. In cell A5, INDEX is telling Excel

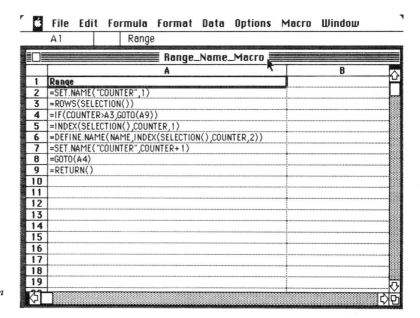

 File Edit Formula Format Data Options Macro Window

A1 | Range

	Range_Name_Macro	
	A	**B**
1	**Range**	
2	=SET.NAME("COUNTER",1)	
3	=ROWS(SELECTION())	
4	=IF(COUNTER>A3,GOTO(A9))	
5	=INDEX(SELECTION(),COUNTER,1)	
6	=DEFINE.NAME(NAME,INDEX(SELECTION(),COUNTER,2))	
7	=SET.NAME("COUNTER",COUNTER+1)	
8	=GOTO(A4)	
9	=RETURN()	
10		
11		
12		
13		
14		
15		
16		
17		
18		
19		

Fig. 4.25. A macro to assign range names.

to look at the selected cells for the required cell range. INDEX uses COUNTER to access the row in this range and specifies column 1 because the name from the left column is the data being accessed.

Cell A5 in the macro is assigned the name NAME with Formula Define Name, just as you name any other macro cell. Each range name used in the DEFINE.NAME function will be stored in A5. The function in A6 actually assigns NAME to each cell one at a time for each iteration of the loop. NAME contains the text in the left column to be used for the cell name; the cell that the name is assigned to, in the right column, is indicated by the statement INDEX(SELECTION( ),COUNTER,2). Therefore, the first INDEX statement references cells in column 1, and the second INDEX statement references cells in column 2. Execution of the statement in A6 assigns the name from the cell in the left column to the adjacent cell to the right.

To repeat this process for the cells in the next row of the selected cells, the SET.NAME statement in A7 increments COUNTER by 1. Cell A8 branches back to the top of the loop. After all rows of the selected cells have been processed, RETURN ends the macro.

You can create this macro quickly. However, you should not use the Recorder because it will record in the macro the specific labels from your examples. You want a macro that works in all situations, not one that assigns a specific set of names to cell values.

To try this macro, create a new worksheet file and enter the following labels in A1 through A3, respectively: SALES, COGS, and PROFIT. Enter values of 1,000,000, 550,000, and 450,000 in B1 through B3, respectively. Select cells A1 through B3 and run the macro. Cell B1 will be assigned the range name SALES; cell B2, the name COGS; and cell B3, the name PROFIT. To see these new range names, select Formula Define Name.

A Macro That Combines Command and Function Macros

In the last chapter, you learned how to use function macros to tailor calculations to your exact needs. The primary purpose of function macros is to streamline calculations that must be performed repeatedly. Function macros provide custom built-in functions to meet your needs exactly. Because these special macros normally are used as formulas in the worksheet setting, you may not think of using them in a command macro; but using a function you have built in a command macro can be very effective at times.

You saw some examples of built-in functions used in command macros earlier in this chapter. As you used built-in functions like IF and MID in your command macros, the arguments were supplied as constants or as references to cells in the macro. Using function macros in a command macro is exactly the same as using a built-in function. You follow the same rules. The function macros are entered as formulas in the command macro. The arguments are supplied as constants or references to cells in the macro or active worksheet.

Here is an example of how function macros are used in a command macro. Assume that you want to design a spherical container that has a volume greater than 25 cubic inches and the smallest possible radius. You also want measurements of the radius to be in even 10ths of an inch. You already have a function macro to calculate volume when you supply a radius: the Capacity macro you created in Chapter 3. To obtain the desired radius, you could use a trial-and-error approach, but the Capacity macro can provide a better method.

You can check the radius length by combining the features of the function macro with a command macro structure as shown in figure 4.26. The first statement in the command macro establishes a minimum radius size of 1 with the SET.VALUE function. The next statement contains a reference to the function macro, Capacity. The argument for the Capacity macro is B5, the cell in which you are storing the current value of the radius. When cell B3 is evaluated, the instructions in the Capacity macro are executed. The function macro calculates the capacity of a sphere with the current radius size. This result is stored in cell B3, the cell containing the reference to the function macro.

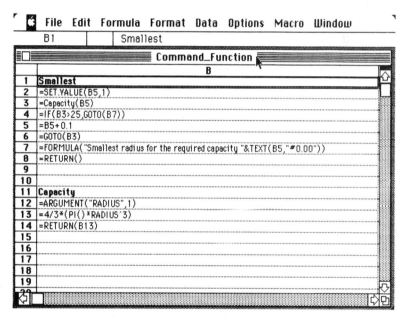

Fig. 4.26. A command macro
that uses a function macro.

The IF function (B4) checks the computed result stored in B3. If the required capacity was not achieved, the radius must be increased. The instruction in B5 increases the radius by an increment of 0.1. Control then branches to B3 to recalculate the capacity with the new radius.

When the check in B4 shows that the result in B3 is greater than 25, the condition specified has been met and the required radius size can be returned to the active worksheet. The GOTO function in B4 sends processing to B7, where the return of the required information is handled. The FORMULA function in B7 is executed only after the required capacity has been achieved. This instruction displays a message giving the radius size. Because text and values cannot be combined, the radius value must be converted to a text value with the TEXT function. The result of this macro is shown in figure 4.27.

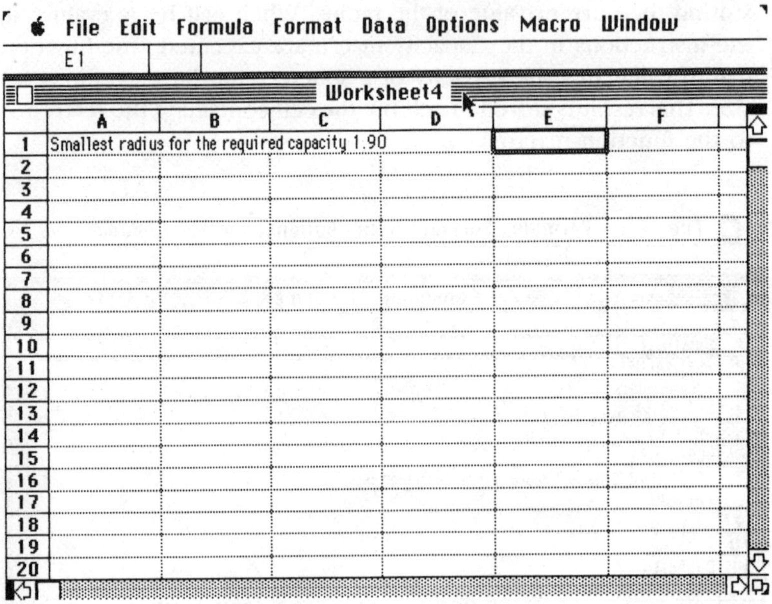

Fig. 4.27. *The result of the combined command and function macros.*

If you must perform this calculation for a variety of container sizes, you may want to modify the macro. You can add an INPUT statement before B3 so that the operator can enter the desired volume. You can modify the IF statement in B4 so that it refers to the value entered by the operator.

Because Excel has such an extensive list of built-in functions, you may not have frequent opportunities to use function macros in your command macros. Just remember that the capability exists and can be used with the same ease as using a built-in function.

Macros To Save and Retrieve Files

You should save files regularly to minimize the risk of losing data. In addition to the original copy of your file, which you will want to keep updated, backup copies on a separate disk are a good precaution for important data. A macro can handle file saves and create backup copies of your file.

Another file task that a macro can handle nicely is producing a list of files on a disk. Using macros for file operations also can help you establish standards for file names. This practice eliminates the risk of an operator's using a nonstandard file name.

The Save macro given in figure 4.28 saves a copy of the original file (cell A2) and gives you an opportunity to create a backup file and save it (cell A3). The macro uses two SAVE.AS functions with the question mark option. Using SAVE.AS?( ) provides the opportunity to eject the original disk and insert a backup copy before the SAVE.AS?( ) statement is executed.

File Edit Formula Format Data Options Macro Window

	A	B	C
	A1		Save
	Macro19		
1	Save		
2	=SAVE.AS?("Budgets",1)		
3	=SAVE.AS?("Bkup_Budget",1)		
4	=RETURN()		
5			
6			
7			
8			
9			
10			
11			
12			
13			
14			
15			
16			
17			
18			
19			
20			

Fig. 4.28. A macro that makes a backup copy.

Retrieving a whole list of files is easy with a macro. You can open the files once with the Recorder turned on, and your macro will be available every time you need to access those files. The sample macro shown in figure 4.29 retrieves three files. This sample macro was created with the Recorder.

 File Edit Formula Format Data Options Macro Window

| D3 | | Open_All |

	D	E	F
3	Open_All		
4	=OPEN("Budgets")		
5	=OPEN("Employee")		
6	=OPEN("Growth")		
7	=RETURN()		
8			
9			
10			
11			
12			
13			
14			
15			
16			
17			
18			
19			
20			
21			
22			

Fig. 4.29. A macro to open a list of files.

Macros To Print Worksheet Data

You may want to print a report from the information contained in
a number of document files or you may want to print several copies
of the same report. Manually specifying print requirements can be
a time-consuming task. A print macro can make printing an updated
copy of a report a simple process that requires just a keystroke combination. Examples of print macros, which are presented in the next
section, are

- A macro to print several copies of a document

- A macro to print data from different documents

A Macro To Print Several Copies of a Document

The macro in figure 4.30 prints an entire worksheet according to
the settings established when you create the macro. This means that
you don't have to be concerned with how the settings were left the
last time you printed this worksheet. Running this macro establishes
the correct settings. You should use the Recorder to capture the

keystrokes in this type of macro because of the many parameters of the PRINT functions.

The first macro function is PAGE.SETUP. Notice the string of arguments following the function name. The first argument is the *header*. This is set at the standard setting of *&F*, which prints the document name in the header. As a variation, you can add the date or time by including the remaining symbols before the comma. For example, to print the time on the left, the document name in the center in bold, and the date on the right, you enter *&L&T&C&B&F&R&D* as the first argument for the function. The second function argument is the *footer*. *Page &P* prints at the bottom of each page the constant *Page* and the correct page number. Any option of the Page Setup command from the File menu is a valid entry in the macro.

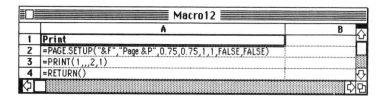

Fig. 4.30. A macro to print several copies of a document.

The four numbers that follow *header*—0.75, 0.75, 1, and 1—are the settings for the left, right, top, and bottom margins, respectively. You can modify these settings easily by changing the function's arguments. If you want one setting to vary, you can build the function with a reference to a variable; you can use an INPUT statement to capture the required argument before executing the command.

The last two arguments contain logical values. The first indicates whether you want the row and column headings printed. FALSE indicates that headings will not be printed, and TRUE specifies that you want them printed. The option to have grid lines printed is represented by the last argument. FALSE means that grid lines will not be printed.

The next function in the sample macro is the PRINT function. This command has five arguments. The first argument is the *range*. The 1 indicates that the entire document will be printed. A 2 would indicate that only a section of the document would be printed. That section is specified by the *from* and *to* arguments that follow. The *from* and *to* arguments are needed only if the range setting is a 2, which prints part of the report. If the *range* is set as 1, commas replace these two arguments, as in the example. The number of *copies* you want printed is the next argument. In the example, this number is 2, so the macro will print two copies of the report. The last argument, *feed*, indicates the type of paper you want to use. A 1 in this position specifies continuous-feed paper, and a 2 indicates cut sheets. The example specifies continuous paper.

The PRINT function starts the printing process. If you are printing a long report, now is the perfect time to fill your coffee cup. When you return, both copies of your report will be ready. Just be sure to turn on your printer before you initiate the macro.

A Macro To Print Data from Different Documents

Updating a budget, financial projection, or cyclical accounting report may entail the printing of a number of reports. You can design a macro to print the entire package of reports. This means that once the update is completed, your work is finished. The macro shown in figure 4.31 has been set up to print reports from three document files. You are not limited to this number; follow the pattern established to add more reports to the macro.

	A	B
	Macro13	
6	**Prt_Budget**	
7	=OPEN("Expenses")	
8	=OPEN("Employee")	
9	=OPEN("Total_Company",TRUE)	
10	=SELECT("RC:R[16]C[5]")	
11	=SET.PRINT.AREA()	
12	=PRINT(1,,,1,1)	
13	=ACTIVATE("Employee")	
14	=PRINT(1,,,1,1)	
15	=ACTIVATE("Expenses")	
16	=SELECT("R[9]C:R[20]C[3]")	
17	=PRINT(1,,,1,1)	
18	=SET.PRINT.AREA()	
19	=RETURN()	
20		

Fig. 4.31. A macro to print data from several documents.

You have some options for constructing this macro. You can place all the OPEN statements at the beginning of the macro (as in the example). This approach has an advantage if different disks are required to load the files. The operator can do all the disk swapping at the beginning of the macro's execution. Once the files all have been opened, the operator can attend to other tasks while the reports are being printed. You should use this approach if you have sufficient room in memory for all your files. If you have too many files to fit in memory at once, you can group the OPEN statements in two sections of the macro so that the operator will not have to interrupt other tasks in order to load one file at a time.

Notice that the third OPEN function contains an argument in addition to the file name. This argument is used only for files with external references. The logical value is TRUE if you want the references updated and FALSE if you don't want them updated. Omitting this argument has the same result as entering TRUE.

Because Total_Company is the last document opened, it becomes the active file. The cells selected in A10 are the range of cells to be printed from Total_Company. After the cells are selected, the function in A11, SET.PRINT.AREA, uses the selected cells for the print area. A PRINT function similar to the one in the preceding macro is used. Note that 1 specifies one copy of the report. Also notice that the PAGE.SETUP function does not appear. This causes the existing settings to be used. You may want to add the PAGE.SETUP function to this macro if you are concerned about setting changes between print requests.

After printing the Total_Company summary, the macro prints the entire Employee sheet. This is executed with the ACTI-VATE("Employee") statement. Because the document already is open, you need to activate only the window that contains the document. Note that you must enclose the document name in quotation marks in order for this command to function correctly. Because the macro lacks a SET.PRINT.AREA statement for area selection, the entire report will be printed.

The last report to be printed is taken from the Expenses document. This time, the entire report is not needed, and an area is selected with the SELECT statement in A16 before printing is requested.

Print macros like the two preceding ones can be created quickly. Everything can be handled with the Recorder. You can use these macros as part of a larger application or just to save you some time in printing your reports.

A Macro To Enter Formulas

Entering long formulas can be a tedious process. Fortunately, most formulas can be entered once and copied to a number of other locations, thereby reducing the number of formulas that must be entered from the keyboard.

Formulas that contain built-in functions, however, require special handling. First of all, the arguments specified for a built-in function allow you to tailor each calculation to your specific needs. Although this provides an advantage in terms of flexibility, it frequently precludes copying these functions to other locations. In the new locations, you will want new argument values. In addition, entering the functions each time predisposes the data-entry process to error. With a number of arguments, each of which is position dependent, the operator easily can make a mistake and enter the values in an incorrect sequence.

Macros can solve the problems of entering formulas. Two macro functions facilitate the entry of a formula into the active cell: FORMULA and FORMULA.ARRAY. You can enter a simple formula or value with these, or you can construct elaborate formulas that require the TEXT functions for completion. Using INPUT statements from within a macro can eliminate the problem of errors and ease the entry of these functions. This method also allows you to edit each value to ensure that it meets the criteria established for that particular argument. Whenever repetitive processing is required, macros are a viable option.

Suppose that you have to record transactions and to time-stamp grain deliveries throughout the day. You plan to use the TIME function to record this information. Although you can enter the TIME function to record the time of each delivery from the delivery receipt, this method is unnecessarily time-consuming. A better approach is to create a macro that can be executed with a macro letter code (see fig. 4.32).

For this type of macro, the Recorder will not be of benefit. You have to enter the macro instructions from the keyboard.

The macro creates an entry containing the built-in TIME function and prompts the operator for the values for the three variables. First, the hour, minute, and second are captured in three separate INPUT statements. This method offers the advantage of allowing you to display a prompt to the operator as each component of the time is requested.

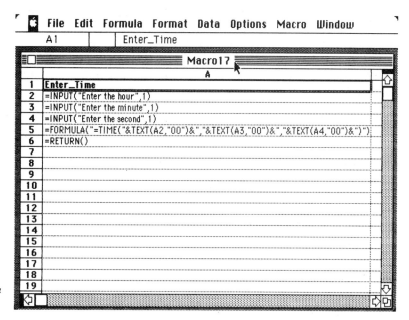

File Edit Formula Format Data Options Macro Window

A1 | Enter_Time

Macro17

	A
1	Enter_Time
2	=INPUT("Enter the hour",1)
3	=INPUT("Enter the minute",1)
4	=INPUT("Enter the second",1)
5	=FORMULA("=TIME("&TEXT(A2,"00")&","&TEXT(A3,"00")&","&TEXT(A4,"00")&")")
6	=RETURN()
7	
8	
9	
10	
11	
12	
13	
14	
15	
16	
17	
18	
19	

Fig. 4.32. A macro to enter a built-in function for time.

The heart of this macro is the FORMULA function. It is especially lengthy because the input values are numbers, and each must be converted into text. The first component of the FORMULA statement is "=TIME(". This is a constant that is used regardless of the values entered. This constant is joined to the next component with the ampersand (&) used for constructing text formulas.

The three components for the variable values are similar to each other. Each uses the TEXT function. This function gives the cell reference for the value to be converted to text and the format to be used in the conversion. Notice that the format is enclosed in quotation marks. Because the TIME function always separates its three arguments with commas, quotation marks must be added to the formula. The commas are enclosed in quotation marks and flanked with ampersands.

To modify the macro, you can add a last step that formats as a valid time the active cell where this entry was made. You can make this modification with the FORMAT.NUMBER function.

You also can enhance this macro by adding logical tests to check whether valid data is entered. For example, you can check the number of minutes stored in A3 to ensure that the number is greater than zero and less than 60. To add these checks to this macro, the best approach is to put an IF statement after each INPUT statement. You can have processing branch back up one instruction and reexecute the INPUT statement when an invalid number is entered. A more sophisticated approach is to build a section of error-processing code for mistakes in any of the three entries. Each routine would have its own appropriate error message.

If you need to enter a whole column of time values, this macro can be modified to include a loop. Cells can be selected within the macro or before its execution. Once the cells are selected, the number of rows can be used as the iteration count. After all values are entered, the last step can do the formatting.

A Macro That Manipulates Windows

With the window features of Excel, you can make maximum use of the limited size of your monitor screen. You can create a number of windows in order to look at different parts of the same document, or you can display at the same time information from different documents. Macro functions allow you to build all these features into your macros.

One use of the windowing functions in the macro environment is to provide help windows for the users of your application. You have two methods for providing this information. You can use a separate area of the active worksheet or use another file to hold the help information.

If you choose to store help information in another area of the active worksheet, your task is to change the area of the screen displayed. A number of macro functions affect cursor movement in the active window: HLINE and VLINE, HPAGE and VPAGE, and HSCROLL and VSCROLL. HLINE and VLINE scroll the screen a line or column at a time. HPAGE and VPAGE are a little faster and scroll a page at a time. HSCROLL and VSCROLL are probably the most practical for accessing information stored in a separate location because these functions scroll to the row or column specified.

Another approach is to store your help information in a separate file. This method offers the advantage of allowing you to use different options, such as type styles, to differentiate your help information from the active worksheet data. You can design your macro to use window functions that will size and move the worksheet so that both help and worksheet information can appear on the screen at the same time.

The sample macro shown in figure 4.33 allows you to request help information stored in another file. The Help window is designed and saved before you create the macro. You must decide whether this Help document will be open at all times or whether the macro that requests help must open the file. In the example shown, the file is assumed to be open.

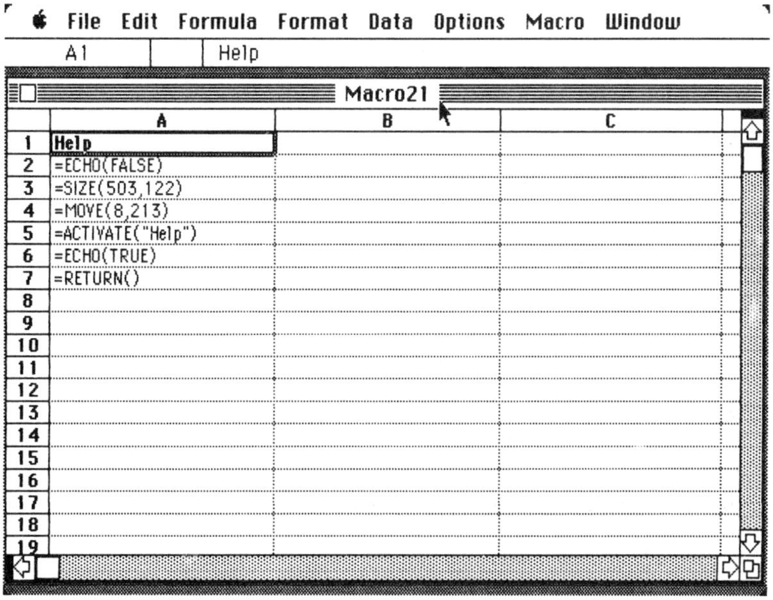

Fig. 4.33. A macro to display a Help window.

The first function in this macro, ECHO, controls screen updating while a macro is being calculated. Using FALSE for the argument eliminates updating and reduces the flicker effect during macro execution. Next, the active window is reduced by the SIZE function. The first argument provides a window width of 503 (512 is the maximum). The second argument controls the height. The example calls for a height of 122 (342 is the maximum).

Next, the reduced active window is moved to the bottom of the screen by the MOVE statement. The first argument specifies the window's distance from the left edge of the screen. The second argument is the distance from the top of the screen.

The Help window is activated next. This window must be designed to fit in the open space on the screen. Likewise, the size of the Help window determines how you must change the size of the active window to allow both windows to appear on the screen at once.

The last instruction, ECHO, turns the updating of the screen back on. ECHO with a TRUE argument is all that is required. At the completion of the macro, the screen appears as shown in figure 4.34.

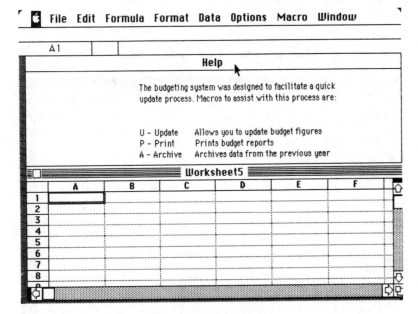

Fig. 4.34. The result of the Help macro.

Using this approach, you need another macro to reactivate the worksheet window and restore its original size. This second macro would follow the same pattern as the macro in figure 4.33.

Consider providing help windows for your automated applications. Whether you elect to store this information on the active worksheet or in another file, a help window can save a new user of your application considerable time. A help window also can save you many hours because you will not have to answer the same questions repeatedly.

A Macro To Protect
Your Worksheet Data

With Excel, you can protect your worksheet data in either of two ways: You can lock all the worksheet cells, or you can lock just the cells that contain critical formulas. The default setting locks all cells. Therefore, if you want to allow data entry in certain cells even when the worksheet has been protected, you need to unlock those cells. Usually, you unlock cells with the Format Cell Protection option, and you make changes manually. After the changes are made, you need to protect the document again because some cells now are unprotected.

You can create a macro to unlock or lock cells, but first you need to understand the locking process. In the normal course of events, you probably will enact protection from the menu when you first complete testing for a new model. Subsequent changes may be made from within a macro.

Once the decision is made to lock or unlock cells, you must decide whether to hide formulas from display in the formula bar. This also is accomplished with the Cell Protection command. At this point, you choose Protect Document from the Options menu. Again protection can be enacted from the menu or with a macro.

To observe the protection features in action, suppose that you have an application where you store three months of summary statistics for the executive management of your company. Each month, as new data becomes available, a month of history is rolled off the storage area in the model and new data is added. To ensure that the historical data is not disturbed by individuals updating other portions of the model, you decide to lock those cells and use a macro for rolling off the data and updating the storage area.

A macro that can handle this task is shown in figure 4.35. The first statement in this macro is the PROTECT.DOCUMENT function with the question mark option. This is the only form of PROTECT.DOCUMENT that works for macros that have a password assigned with protection. When this command is executed, the operator must supply the password for the document, or protection is not disabled.

Assuming correct entry of the password, A3 is executed next. This command selects the two most recent months of data. These are cut from the worksheet with the next command. Then the command

	File	Edit	Formula	Format	Data	Options	Macro	Window

A1		Protect

Macro18

	A	B
1	Protect	
2	=PROTECT.DOCUMENT?()	
3	=SELECT("R2C2:R4C3")	
4	=CUT()	
5	=SELECT("R2C3")	
6	=PASTE()	
7	=SELECT("R2C2")	
8	=FORMULA(INPUT("Enter sales",1))	
9	=SELECT("R3C2")	
10	=FORMULA(INPUT("Enter inventory",1))	
11	=SELECT("R4C2")	
12	=FORMULA(INPUT("Enter salaries",1))	
13	=SELECT("R2C2:R4C2")	
14	=FORMAT.NUMBER("$#,##0_;($#,##0)")	
15	=PROTECT.DOCUMENT?()	
16	=RETURN()	
17		
18		
19		

Fig. 4.35. A macro to handle protection features.

in A5 selects the cell at the top of the second month's history and the cut cells are pasted in place. This cut-and-paste process rolls the history data off the storage area in the model to make room for the latest month. The Absolute Record option was selected when this macro was recorded to ensure that the macro is not dependent on cursor location at the outset of the process.

The next macro function (A7) selects the first input cell. The content of this cell is established with the nested macro functions, FORMULA and INPUT, in A8. This means that the value returned from INPUT is used as a formula in the active cell. This process continues for the remaining two cells in the example. In an application, these instructions are likely to be contained in a loop, and looping would continue to satisfy the required number of entries. When all the entries have been made, the new data is formatted to match the data for the other months.

As a last step, protection is enabled (A15) by using the same command used to disable protection in A2. Because the protection feature is still desired, the question mark option must again be used. The second occurrence of this statement in the macro acts as a toggle switch to enable again the protection capabilities for the worksheet.

Conclusion

You will want to add many of the macros in this section to your macro library. You can put a number of them to use right way to handle tasks such as date-stamping worksheets, formatting cells, and controlling windows. You may want to combine macros to create a macro that handles several functions together. You might create a menu macro that will read and write your files. You can use the code for the menu macro in this chapter and then use the code from other macros to provide the code for each selection. Regardless of the approach you choose, you now should have a basic understanding of how macros can improve your productivity in the worksheet environment.

In the next chapter, you will learn how macros can help when you are working with data management tasks. You need to remember the lessons of this chapter because you can modify many of these examples for use in the database environment.

5

Creating Macros for the Data Management Environment

In addition to worksheet features, Excel has data management capabilities. Whereas the emphasis in the worksheet environment is on calculations, the emphasis in data management is on data storage. With Excel, you can perform the fundamental data management activities. You can create a database of customers, vendors, or employees and search for records in that database. You also can sort a database into different sequences for different reporting needs.

Although the data management capabilities of Excel are adequate for many data management applications, the features are not as automatic or sophisticated as those of specialized database packages. This fact makes the data management macros you add to your macro library especially valuable. These macros simplify the use of data management commands and extend the capabilities of the program to produce some of the same results as dedicated database packages. For example, from database records, you can have formatted screens for data entry, for error checking procedures, and for creating mailing labels.

This chapter presents the following macros:

- Macros for creating prompts and data entry screens

- Macros for sorting data

- Macros for finding information in a database

- Error-processing macros

- Macros for word-processing tasks

- A macro to create a report from two files

As you study the macros covered in this chapter, you will find familiar macro constructs such as looping and setting counters. These are used in the same manner as in worksheet applications except that the statements in the loop perform data management tasks. You also will learn new techniques that are especially useful in the database environment. These include the use of functions such as OFFSET, which selects another reference of the same size as the current selection. Another technique is using an INPUT statement from within a SELECT statement to allow a new selection with each execution of the macro. These functions can be used in other environments, but are particularly useful when you are working with database records. Finally, you will find specialized data management functions. These functions correspond to selections from the Data menu, such as Data Find, Data Extract, and Data Sort.

You also will see the STEP function at the beginning of several macros. This function causes the macro to execute one step at a time. Because the data management macros can be a little more difficult to follow than worksheet macros, you should include the STEP function where it is shown. STEP, which is a good debugging tool, executes the macro slowly so that you can see exactly what is happening. After the first run of the macro, you can delete this function and run the macro at normal speed.

Macros for Creating Prompts and Data Entry Screens

Data entry is an ongoing process whether you are working in the worksheet, where figures must be updated each month, or in the database, where records must be added regularly. This section introduces ways to speed and improve accuracy in data entry in the database environment.

Excel uses a spreadsheet approach to database management. The columns are used as fields, and the rows are the records. Information is entered as entries in cells in the database, just as in a spreadsheet.

The cell-oriented approach to data entry in a database causes some difficulty because in a database you do not enter a string of like numbers; you enter combinations of numbers and text. One result of this difference is a greater possibility for errors during data entry. The formatted entry screens of dedicated database software products avoid many errors because of the instructions displayed to the user. Cell entries, however, don't provide much guidance to the operator. Data management macros eliminate this problem and add other desirable features to the data entry process.

In this section, you will learn two approaches for handling data entry. One uses INPUT statement prompts to guide the operator's actions. The other uses a formatted screen for the entry of individual database records. The macros in this section are

- A macro to create INPUT statement prompts for data entry

- A macro to create a formatted data entry screen

A Macro To Create INPUT Statement Prompts for Data Entry

Using INPUT statement prompts for data entry provides a separate Input box for each field in the record you are entering. The advantage of this method is the display of a descriptive prompt as each item of data is entered. These instructions provide a focus for each entry and thereby considerably lower the error rate.

A macro that creates prompts is shown in figure 5.1. The macro is based on the premise that the worksheet containing the database is active. The database range on this worksheet also is assumed to have been assigned the range name *DATA*. A portion of the database is shown in figure 5.2.

As you work with a database, you want to add new records to the end of the database. Records added at the end of a range are not included in that range, however, unless you rename the range each time. A better method is to stretch the range to make room for a new record. By inserting a record immediately before the last record in a range, you can expand that range without having to redefine it. Then the last record can be copied up to the new location and the new record added over the last record.

	A
1	Input_Prompts
2	=SELECT(INDEX(IDATA,ROWS(IDATA),0))
3	=INSERT(2)
4	=SELECT(OFFSET(SELECTION(),1,0))
5	=COPY()
6	=SELECT(OFFSET(SELECTION(),-1,0))
7	=PASTE()
8	=SELECT(OFFSET(SELECTION(),1,0))
9	=SET.NAME("CURRENT",SELECTION())
10	=SELECT(INDEX(CURRENT,1,1))
11	=FORMULA(INPUT("Enter branch number",1))
12	=SELECT(INDEX(CURRENT,1,2))
13	=FORMULA(INPUT("Enter region number",1))
14	=SELECT(INDEX(CURRENT,1,3))
15	=FORMULA(INPUT("Enter state code for location",2))
16	=SELECT(INDEX(CURRENT,1,4))
17	=FORMULA(INPUT("Enter receivables in whole dollars",1))
18	=SELECT(INDEX(CURRENT,1,5))
19	=FORMULA(INPUT("Enter branch manager's last name",2))
20	=SELECT(INDEX(CURRENT,1,6))
21	=FORMULA(INPUT("Enter number of employees",1))
22	=SELECT(CURRENT)
23	=INPUT("Do you wish to enter additional records - Y or N?",2)
24	=IF(A23="Y",GOTO(A3))
25	=RETURN()

Fig. 5.1. A macro to create prompts.

File   Edit   Formula   Format   Data   Options   Macro   Window

A20   9988

Branch_Data

	A	B	C	D	E	F	G
1	BRANCH	REGION	LOCATION	RECEIVABLES	MANAGER	NO_EMP	
2	8712	6	GA	$985,632	Tower	9	
3	6731	4	IL	$1,290,000	Clark	18	
4	5612	3	LA	$1,209,875	Brown	12	
5	9430	2	LA	$999,812	Jacobs	14	
6	2214	6	LA	$1,200,975	Black	10	
7	2459	3	LA	$1,178,900	Douglas	12	
8	6652	7	MD	$13,456,332	Yancy	15	
9	3312	4	MD	$980,765	Harris	15	
10	2345	1	MD	$78,999	Myer	15	
11	1235	3	MD	$67,890	Jackson	14	
12	5691	4	MD	$56,900	York	8	
13	3349	8	MI	$865,490	Rogers	7	
14	5609	2	OR	$10,223,469	Stark	20	
15	4435	5	SC	$1,100,673	Jasper	10	
16	5619	6	TX	$1,200,897	Smythe	13	
17	9200	3	TX	$75,908	Ford	11	
18	9311	1	YA	$1,118,500	Woods	15	
19	4328	5	WA	$95,700	Hanson	11	
20	9988	1	MD	$76,000	Bauch	9	

Fig. 5.2. Database records entered with the macro.

Copying may seem like a strange choice because the last record is duplicated until the new record is copied into the last line. Because the CUT function will cause the range for DATA to shrink back to its original size, you have to stay with COPY. The instructions to INSERT and COPY and then PASTE are located in cells A3 through A7 of the macro. Notice the use of the OFFSET function to select records above and below the selected record.

After the PASTE operation is completed, the record below the copied record is selected. This record is named CURRENT because it represents the record currently being entered (A9). Separate fields in the row labeled CURRENT are accessed for the entry of each field.

As might be expected, column 1 of CURRENT is selected first (cell A10). In cell A11, an INPUT function is placed in a FORMULA statement in order to enter the value from the INPUT function in the selected cell. The Input box that is generated displays the message *Enter branch number* (see fig. 5.3). Excel expects a branch number because the entry is restricted to numeric data by the *type* code of 1. Note, however, that this macro contains no check for valid numeric values.

	⚫ File Edit Formula Format Data Options Macro Window						
A23		3334					
			Branch_Data				
	A	**B**	**C**	**D**	**E**	**F**	**G**
12	5691		4 MD	$56,900	York	8	
13	3349		8 MI	$865,490	Rogers	7	
14	5609		2 OR	$10,223,469	Stark	20	
15	4435		5 SC	$1,100,673	Jasper	10	
16	5619		6 TX	$1,200,897	Smythe	13	
17	9200		3 TX	$75,908	Ford	11	
18	9311		1 VA	$1,118,500	Woods	15	
19	4328			**Input**			
20	9988						
21	5511		**Enter branch number**		**OK**		
22	3334						
23	3334				**Cancel**		
24							
25							
26			5685				
27							
28							
29							
30							
31							

Fig. 5.3. First Input box generated by the macro.

The cell immediately to the right is selected (A12), and an INPUT statement is used to place a formula in this cell (A13). The instructions to the operator request a region number. Because the *type* code is 1, this entry too must be numeric.

A state code with a *type* of 2 for text is next (A15). At the Input box, the user must enter a letter code rather than a numeric one.

The last three fields for which INPUT statements display prompts are RECEIVABLES; MANAGER, for the branch manager's last name; and NO_ EMP, for the number of employees. These entries continue across the current row. The Input box for RECEIVABLES is shown in figure 5.4.

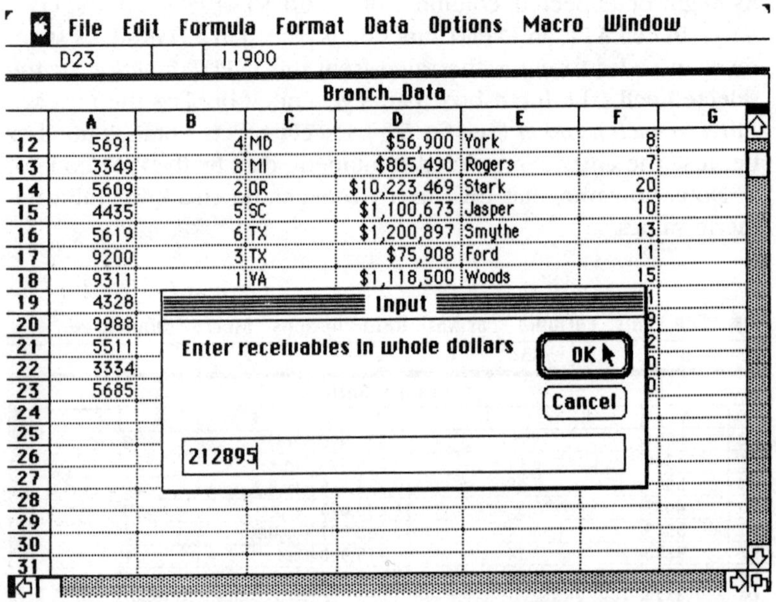

Fig. 5.4. The Input box for receivables.

After all the fields have been entered, the entire record named CURRENT is selected (A22). This step sets up the macro for adding another record.

The last INPUT statement displays a question concerning the addition of more records. If the operator chooses N, not to add more records, the macro ends. On the other hand, if the response is Y, the macro branches to A3, adds another blank record, and repeats the entire process.

A Macro To Create a Formatted Data Entry Screen

This macro requires you to design a screen layout suitable for data entry before you begin. You should place this formatted screen on the worksheet where the data management information will be stored. Next, you establish the database fields across a row of this worksheet and select the field names and any existing records. The example presented here uses only the first two fields in a database, but you easily can extend the macro to work with a full database by adding more fields and duplicating the processing code in the macro. Figure 5.5 shows the two data records already entered and an input area in another window on the same sheet. Figure 5.6 shows the entry of data on the form.

With these preliminary steps accomplished, your next step is to create the macro. Actually, two macros are required. The first macro, Display, presents the initial display of the formatted screen for data entry (see fig. 5.7). The purpose of this macro is to activate the window containing the formatted screen. The operator can read the instructions stating that each field should be entered. After the data is entered, the operator can read the next instruction: invoke the macro in order to add the data to the database.

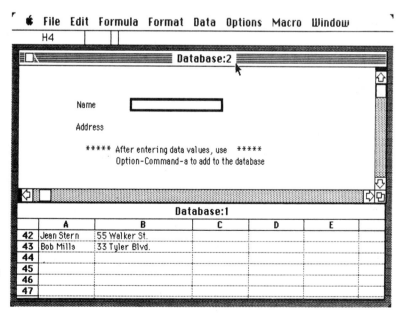

Fig. 5.5. Database records in one window and input area in another window.

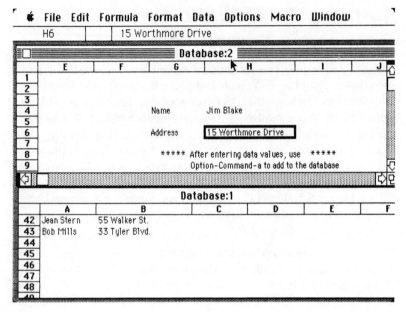

Fig. 5.6. Data entered in the input screen.

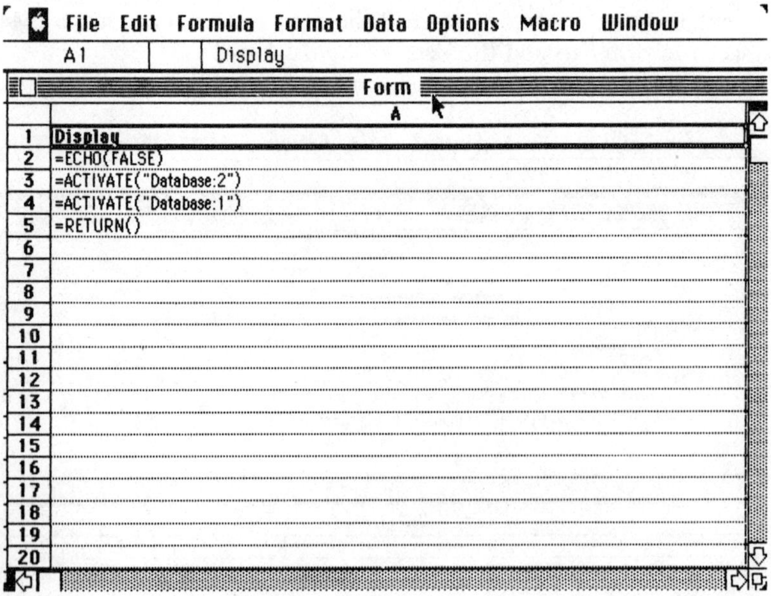

Fig. 5.7. The Display macro.

The Display macro has only four statements. The first statement (in A2) eliminates screen flickering. Because the macro requires more

than one change to the screen, the better procedure is to turn updating off and wait for the automatic screen update that occurs at
the end of each macro.

The ACTIVATE statements bring windows 1 and 2 from the Database
document to the screen. The document must be open before the
macro is invoked. As an enhancement, you may prefer to add an
OPEN statement. The RETURN statement in A5 ends the macro.

Pressing Option-Command-a invokes the Update macro shown in
figure 5.8. This macro activates the record storage area of the database after disabling the screen updating process with ECHO(FALSE).
Notice that both functions are combined in one cell (A10). The
plus sign (+) joins the two functions. The macro next selects the
last row of the database. This choice is based on the INDEX function
and the number of rows in the selection. All the database columns
are selected because the *column* argument is 0.

	A
9	**Update**
10	=ECHO(FALSE)+ACTIVATE("Database:1")
11	=SELECT(INDEX(!DATA,ROWS(!DATA),0))
12	=INSERT(2)
13	=SELECT(OFFSET(SELECTION(),1,0))
14	=COPY()
15	=SELECT(OFFSET(SELECTION(),-1,0))
16	=PASTE()
17	=SELECT(OFFSET(SELECTION(),1,0))+SET.NAME("PLACE",SELECTION())
18	=SELECT(!H4)
19	=CUT()
20	=SELECT(INDEX(PLACE,1,1))
21	=PASTE()
22	=SELECT(!H6)
23	=CUT()
24	=SELECT(INDEX(PLACE,1,2))
25	=PASTE()
26	=ACTIVATE("Database:2")
27	=SELECT(!H4)
28	=ECHO(TRUE)
29	=RETURN()

Fig. 5.8. The Update macro.

The same insertion process used in the preceding example (fig. 5.1)
is used. The last database row is selected, and the INSERT function
is used to add a blank record. This blank record is placed immediately before the last record in the database. As previously noted,
this insertion may seem strange; but if a blank record is added to
the end, the database range is not extended. Inserting within the
database range, on the other hand, expands the range.

The record at the end of the database now has a blank row above it. This record must be copied up one row and the new record added in the place of the last record. Because the inserted record is now the selected record, you will have to use the OFFSET function (A13) to access the last completed record and copy it up one row. An offset of 1 for *row* and 0 for *column* is used. COPY is invoked next for the new selected record. Now, you must select the blank row above the last record (A15). An offset of -1 for *row* handles this task. That leaves the PASTE function (A16) to complete the process of placing the record in its proper slot.

The last record is again selected with a *row* offset of 1 and assigned the name PLACE (A17). This is another example of joined function entries. In cell A18, the first cell of the entry form is selected as the macro begins to move the data from the entry form to the selected database record. The function in this first cell is CUT (A19). The area where the information is placed is determined by the place in the database for the current record. PLACE is the name used to store the current database record for this information. A row location of 1 and a column location of 1 are specified by the function in A20, and the information is pasted with the instruction in A21.

This process, which entails selection of a data entry form value, the CUT operation, selection of the next database field, and pasting, must be repeated for each field in the database. You must be sure that when each update is completed, the blank form is available for the next entry. You call up the blank form by executing the Display macro.

The entire process will repeat for each record you want to add. For applications that normally need multiple updates, you can set up an automatic loop. You also may want to add other enhancements. You may choose to use a trigger value to stop data entry. As an example, you might use *ZZZ* for the entry when processing is to stop. Another approach is to have each update add a fixed number of records. This is appropriate if your application requires the addition of a record for each branch. With this approach, you can set up a specific iteration count.

Your first feeling about these two macros may be that they slow data entry. In some ways, you are correct; but you may discover time savings that counteract this. Although the actual data entry process may take a few extra seconds, this approach still can save significant time because of fewer errors. Correcting errors can be time-consuming, and you may find that reducing errors more than pays back your time investment in this approach.

Macros for Sorting Data

After you add new records to the end of a database, it is no longer in sequence according to the last sort. If you plan to produce a report from the database, you probably will want to re-sort the data before printing. You can build a macro that automatically sorts the data before printing the report. The macro begins with the statements that place the data in the report sequence you specify. With this approach, you will know that the report will be correct every time because it cannot be printed without the macro's first executing the sorting code.

The macros explained in this section help you sort your database. They include

- A macro for sorting and printing

- A macro to provide flexibility in the sort process

A Macro for Sorting and Printing

The first macro has a predefined report sequence, as is likely to be the case with a sort preceding a report. The database contains information about branches in the company. In the set of data that you will examine are the BRANCH number, the REGION code, the state code (LOCATION), the total RECEIVABLES outstanding, the branch manager's last name (MANAGER), and the number of employees in the branch (NO_EMP). Although the complete database has many more fields, this discussion and examples are confined to these six fields (see fig. 5.9).

The macro that performs the sort is named Sort_by_Branch (see fig. 5.10). The first instruction in this macro (A13) is an INPUT statement, which is added as a precaution to ensure that all the database records have been selected before the execution of the macro. In this example, the operator would select cells A2:F12 before running the macro. If the user forgets to select the database cells, the SORT will not function, and the report will be incorrect. The INPUT statement instructs the operator to enter a Y to proceed or an N to cancel the macro. Actually, as seen in cells A14 and A15, any response other than Y ends the macro's execution. This ap-

🍎 File Edit Formula Format Data Options Macro Window

	A23		5685				

Branch_Data

	A	B	C	D	E	F	G
1	BRANCH	REGION	LOCATION	RECEIVABLES	MANAGER	NO_EMP	
2	8712	6	GA	$985,632	Tower	9	
3	6731	4	IL	$1,290,000	Clark	18	
4	5612	3	LA	$1,209,875	Brown	12	
5	9430	2	LA	$999,812	Jacobs	14	
6	2214	6	LA	$1,200,975	Black	10	
7	2459	3	LA	$1,178,900	Douglas	12	
8	6652	7	MD	$13,456,332	Yancy	15	
9	3312	4	MD	$980,765	Harris	15	
10	2345	1	MD	$78,999	Myer	15	
11	1235	3	MD	$67,890	Jackson	14	
12	5691	4	MD	$56,900	York	8	
13	3349	8	MI	$865,490	Rogers	7	
14	5609	2	OR	$10,223,469	Stark	20	
15	4435	5	SC	$1,100,673	Jasper	10	
16	5619	6	TX	$1,200,897	Smythe	13	
17	9200	3	TX	$75,908	Ford	11	
18	9311	1	YA	$1,118,500	Woods	15	
19	4328	5	WA	$95,700	Hanson	11	
20	9988	1	MD	$76,000	Bauch	9	

Fig. 5.9. Database records before sorting.

proach is useful in many situations. Having only one specific response that causes the macro to continue greatly decreases the chances of problems from a wrong response.

🍎 File Edit Formula Format Data Options Macro Window

	A12		Sort_by_Branch	

Sort

	A
12	Sort_by_Branch
13	=INPUT("Database records must be selected - Type Y to proceed / N to cancel",2)
14	=IF(A13="Y",GOTO(A16))
15	=ALERT("Records must be selected first",2)+HALT()
16	=SORT(1,"R2C1",1)
17	=SET.NAME("DATABASE",SELECTION())
18	=ROWS(SELECTION())
19	=COLUMNS(SELECTION())
20	=SELECT(INDEX(DATABASE,1,0):INDEX(DATABASE,2,0))
21	=INSERT(2)
22	=SET.NAME("TOP",INDEX(DATABASE,1,0))
23	=SET.NAME("TOP_PRINT",OFFSET(TOP,-1,0))
24	=SELECT(TOP_PRINT:OFFSET(INDEX(DATABASE,DEREF(A18),DEREF(A19)),2,0))
25	=SET.PRINT.AREA()
26	=PRINT(1,,,1,1)
27	=SELECT(OFFSET(TOP_PRINT,1,0):OFFSET(TOP_PRINT,2,0))
28	=EDIT.DELETE(2)
29	=RETURN()
30	
31	

Fig. 5.10. A macro to sort by branch and print a report.

The IF statement in A14 examines the response to the INPUT statement. If the response in A13 is not Y, execution passes to A15. This cell contains the ALERT function with a message indicating that the sort cannot proceed. Following the ALERT function is a plus sign (+), which joins this function with the second function in this cell. The second function, HALT, ends the macro.

Combining two action-taking functions makes debugging more difficult and should be avoided in most situations. On occasion, however, the feature is useful for adding a temporary instruction to a macro during testing without disrupting the existing code arrangement. Adding the temporary function to the end of another function by using the plus sign facilitates deletion when the function is no longer required. In this macro, combining functions is acceptable because if the first instruction fails, the macro will stop anyway.

When the response to the INPUT query is Y, processing moves to the instruction in A16. The SORT function, with arguments specified, performs the sort procedure. The first argument, 1, specifies that the sort is to take place by rows. If this argument were 2, the sort would be a column sort. Every time you run this macro, the same sequence is used. The macro in the next example demonstrates how to build a flexible sort macro that can produce a different sequence each time you use it.

The second argument, R2C1, is the address of the sort key. This argument indicates the first field in the first record of the database. Alternately, you could specify the same field in another database record, and the sort still would be in branch-number sequence. All the records will be sorted numerically according to the branch numbers given in column 1. Another option is to specify the entire first column. This would produce the same branch sequence.

The last argument, 1, indicates ascending order. If you prefer descending order, you can change this argument to 2.

With the sort completed, the next step is to print the sorted records. To spruce up the report, some blank lines are added between the field names and the first data records. After the report is printed, the macro deletes these extra lines from the database.

The SET.NAME and SELECTION functions in A17 store the name DATABASE, a reference to the data cells currently selected. The numbers of rows and columns in this reference are stored in cells A18 and A19, respectively, with the ROWS and COLUMNS functions.

The next step is to select the first two rows of the database. This is accomplished in cell A20 with the SELECT statement and two INDEX functions, which specify the portion of the database you want to select. Rows 1 and 2, respectively, are selected by the second arguments of the INDEX functions. By using zeros for the third arguments, the INDEX functions are set up to reference all the columns of the database.

The INSERT function in A21 adds the two rows selected by the SELECT statement in A20. The argument of 2 causes all rows to be shifted down as the extra rows are added above the selected cells.

This insertion instruction does not affect the range assignment for the database. The database still references cells A2:F12 even though the database records have been moved down. You can deal with this situation in a number of ways. One approach is to print an extra two rows at the bottom of the report to compensate for the blank rows inserted. This is done later in this macro.

The first blank row inserted at the top of the report is labeled TOP by the SET.NAME instruction in cell A22. The row above this inserted row contains the field names; this row is labeled TOP_PRINT by the SET.NAME function in cell A23. The OFFSET function in cell A23 selects a reference of the same size as the selected cells. The *row* and *column* offsets provided as arguments select the particular cells required. In this example, the arguments instruct Excel to select a reference the same size as TOP but one row above it (-1). The column reference stays the same (0).

The statement in A24 is the most complicated in the macro. This statement selects all the cells to be printed. The beginning of the range selected is TOP_PRINT, which contains the field names to be used as headings. The end of the range is two rows beyond what is currently labeled as the last database record. You need to go beyond the defined database because two rows were inserted earlier and no provision was made to adjust the range assignment for the database. For the end of the database range, an offset of two rows beyond the last database record is selected. The database reference for the last row of the database is built using the results of the ROWS and COLUMNS functions. The DEREF function must be used with these to ensure that the contents rather than the addresses of these two references are used.

The SET.PRINT.AREA( ) statement in A25 establishes the selected cells as the print area to be used. When the PRINT instruction is invoked, only those cells are printed.

The PRINT function is the last step in the creation of the report. You may want to add an ALERT message before the PRINT statement to remind the user to turn on the printer. The arguments contained in this example of the PRINT statement specify a range of all, one copy, and continuous forms.

At this point, deleting the blank lines that were inserted for printing purposes may be appropriate. The instructions in cells A27 and A28 accomplish this final task. The top of the print area was named TOP_ PRINT by the statement in A23. The statement in A27 selects the two blank rows below this top line containing headings. After the rows are selected, they are deleted with EDIT.DELETE. The argument, 2, informs Excel that cells should be shifted up to fill the space left by the deletion. The last remaining step at this point is to reselect all the database records in the event the macro is executed again.

This macro may seem like a great deal of work just to handle a simple sort and print operation. However, the advantage of this macro becomes clear when you perform the operation repeatedly. If this is an operation performed daily after records are updated, the time invested is quickly recovered. This approach also offers an advantage to the novice, who may have difficulty remembering the entire sequence of instructions when they are entered from the menus. All the user must remember with this approach is how to execute the macro.

A Macro To Provide Flexibility in the Sort Process

The preceding macro was designed to sort all the records in a database. Also, the sort sequence was fixed and resulted in branch-number sequence. This approach is useful in certain situations but limits the application of the macro. The following sort macro offers more flexibility. This macro lets the user make choices about which database records to sort, which sort sequence to use, and what order to use.

This more flexible sort macro is shown in figure 5.11. The first instruction in the macro, the STEP function, executes the macro one step at a time so that you can check the results of each function. After the macro is working correctly, you can delete this first statement. The statement in A3 selects the cells that will be sorted. This instruction uses the INPUT function. When you run this macro, you can sort the entire database or just some of the rows. The operator's selection is named SORT_RECORDS by the SET.NAME statement in A4.

	A
1	**Sort_Macro**
2	=STEP()
3	=SELECT(INPUT("Select database records only, not field names",8))
4	=SET.NAME("SORT_RECORDS",SELECTION())
5	=SELECT(INPUT("Select field to sort by",8))
6	=SET.NAME("SORT_KEY",SELECTION())
7	=INPUT("Type 1 for ascending / 2 for descending sequence",1)
8	=SELECT(SORT_RECORDS)
9	=SORT(1,SORT_KEY,DEREF(A7))
10	=RETURN()

Fig. 5.11. A sort macro with flexibility.

The next step is the selection of a sort key. Although the Excel package allows as many as three sort keys, only one is selected in this example. In response to the prompt displayed by the INPUT statement in A5, the operator uses the mouse to click a field in one of the database records. The operator's selection is named SORT_KEY by the SET.NAME statement in A6.

The last INPUT statement prompts the operator to select ascending or descending order. A 1 specifies ascending and a 2 descending, as indicated by the prompt displayed by the instruction in cell A7.

After the selections are made, the macro gets ready to perform the sort. First, all the database records again must be selected. The name that was assigned earlier to these cells expedites the selection process. Selecting the required cells is as easy as the SELECT function shown in A8.

The statement in A9 sorts the records. The first argument, 1, indicates a sort by row. The second argument, SORT_KEY, references the sort key entered in A5. The third argument is a 1 or a 2, determined by what was entered in A7.

At this point, the records all should be in the new sequence. The macro ends with the required RETURN statement.

You now have had a chance to look at two macros involving the sort operation. The latter is more flexible, but the choice must be dictated by your particular business needs.

Macros for Finding Information in a Database

You can use Excel commands to view database records that match criteria you establish. For example, you may want to find all the records for Region 1 or find the branch that Mr. Tower is managing. Although you can find records with menu selections, these tasks also can be automated and expedited through a macro.

This section presents two macros:

- A macro to automate the Find process
- A macro to find and replace all matching records

The first macro provides a means for automating the Find operation. By means of a single macro, the database is selected, criteria are created, and a matching record is found. The second macro automates some of the Find process, but the focus is different. Records are selected and criteria established before the macro is executed. Once executed, the macro continues to find matching records and allows you to correct Region codes.

A Macro To Automate the Find Process

Finding a record that meets a specific condition requires a number of steps. First, you have to select the database so that Excel knows where to search for the record. Then you have to establish the criteria for your search. Only then can you execute the Find command to search for the matching record. Because the process requires a number of steps, new users often are confused about the sequence

to be followed. You can create a macro that will perform the required steps and yet provide sufficient flexibility to be useful.

The macro shown in figure 5.12 is called Select _ Record. Like some
other macros in this chapter, Select _ Record has the STEP function
as the first statement so that you can watch your first execution of
the macro step-by-step.

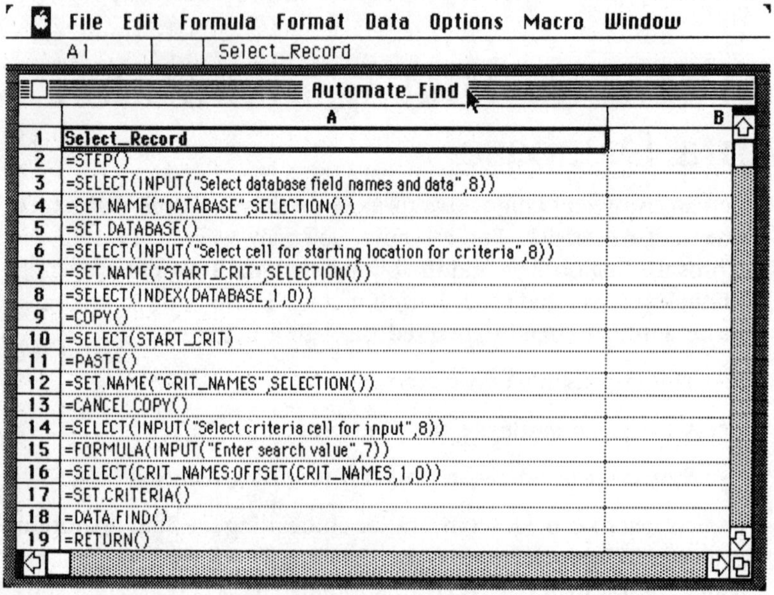

Fig. 5.12. A macro to automate the Find process.

The first action taken by the macro is in cell A3. This entry contains
an INPUT function inside a SELECT statement. This displays a message that prompts the user to select the database and allows the
selection to be made from the keyboard. Once the selection is made,
the SET.NAME statement assigns the selection the name DATABASE.
Then, SET.DATABASE in cell A5 tells Excel where the database is
located.

The second request for user input, in cell A6, also is inside a SELECT
statement; the reference, therefore, can be selected immediately.
This time the macro is expecting one cell. As the prompt message
states, this cell is to be the beginning location for the criteria area.
This cell is given the name START_CRIT by the SET.NAME function
in A7.

After the starting location for the criteria has been established, the
next step is to copy the database field names to the criteria area.

The database field names are selected with the SELECT function in A8. This statement uses the INDEX function to select just the first row of the database. The COPY function is invoked in cell A9.

In A10, the macro selects the PASTE location, START_CRIT. The PASTE function, which follows, copies the field names. With the Step mode, you can watch each action and see the criteria names on the screen at this point. Then the SET.NAME statement in A12 assigns the name CRIT_NAMES to the entire row of criteria names. The entire row is named because the PASTE function selected all these cells even though you specified only the one in the starting location.

The CANCEL.COPY function in A13 is a way of removing the highlighting that sometimes remains around cells after a Copy and Paste operation. In Chapter 4, the approach used was to format the cells. Because formatting isn't required in this instance, the CANCEL.COPY statement is more appropriate.

Before a Find operation can be executed, a criteria value must be entered. A cell under one of the criteria names must be selected to store a criteria value. This is accomplished with an INPUT function in a SELECT statement (A14). An 8 is used for the input *type* so that a cell address can be entered. The user can enter the address, or just click the appropriate cell and let Excel enter the cell address. The FORMULA statement in A15 enters in the selected cell the value the user enters after the prompt. A *type* of 7 is used for this INPUT statement because this option accepts numbers, text, or logical values.

With the criteria value entered, the criteria names and the value just entered are selected. The statement in A16 selects a range beginning with CRIT_NAMES. The end of this range is offset one row from CRIT_NAMES. This selection is established as the criteria range with the SET.CRITERIA function in A17.

The last statement in the macro handles the Find operation. Because only one FIND statement is contained in the macro, only the first matching record is located. If you want, you can add the looping instructions from the next macro in order to perform a complete Find operation.

The Select_Record macro also can serve as the basis for an extract macro. The only difference between the Find and the Extract operations is that you must provide a location for the extracted in-

formation. The beginnings of a Find and an Extract macro are exactly
the same in terms of the database and criteria definition.

A Macro To Find and Replace All Matching Records

The next macro is made more difficult by a "bug" in the current
release of Excel. The program should—but does not—return #N/A
after the program has found the last matching record. The user needs
to know when the program has found this last record so that retrieval
can stop at that point. The current Excel program has no way to
stop the retrieving after the last record has been found. Instead,
Excel continues to "find" the last matching record over and over.

You can overcome this problem, however, if you check the reference
of each matching record against the preceding record found. When
the two references are alike, all matching records have been found.

Assume, for example, that your company undergoes frequent re-
organization. Branches that were in the Mid-Atlantic region may
suddenly start reporting to the New England region. After a reor-
ganization, the codes for the regions must be updated quickly. The
macro for this example does just that (see fig. 5.13).

	A	B	
File Edit Formula Format Data Options Macro Window			
A1	Find_Replace		
1	**Find_Replace**		
2	=STEP()+SET.NAME("HOLD",A1)		
3	=DATA.FIND.NEXT()		
4	=SET.NAME("PLACE",SELECTION())		
5	=IF(NOT(PLACE=HOLD),GOTO(A7))		
6	=ALERT("No more matching records",2)+HALT()		
7	=SELECT(INDEX(SELECTION(),1,2))		
8	=FORMULA(INPUT("Enter new region code",1))		
9	=SET.NAME("HOLD",PLACE)		
10	=GOTO(A3)		
11	=RETURN()		

Fig. 5.13. A macro to find and replace.

Before executing the macro, the user must issue the Data Set Database command so that the selected database records and headings will be recognized by Excel. Next, the criteria should be established in worksheet cells and the location established with Data Set Criteria. If these two preliminary steps are not completed, the macro cannot operate.

You should scrutinize each statement in this macro closely. The first line combines the STEP function with SET.NAME. STEP is added so that you can watch the execution of this macro the first time through. To cancel Step mode, just click the Continue box on any Single Step box. The SET.NAME establishes a name for the immediately preceding record found and holds the reference. Because no preceding record exists at the time the first record is read, the variable HOLD is set to A1.

The next statement is DATA.FIND.NEXT. This function uses the criteria established before the macro is executed to search the database, which is also set before the macro is executed. The DATA.FIND.NEXT function selects the matching record and displays the entire record.

The reference to the selected cells is stored in the variable PLACE by the SET.NAME function in cell A4. This is the second variable name used to store cell references. (HOLD was the first variable.)

As long as the values of PLACE and HOLD are unequal, you know that the last record has not yet been found. In this situation, you want to continue the loop to find additional matching records. The IF statement in A5 checks for the condition of PLACE not being equal to HOLD. This condition is required for processing to continue. When the values are unequal, the macro branches to A7.

The SELECT function in A7 selects the cell in the first row and second column of the record that is currently active. Then the FORMULA function in A8 places a value in this cell. This action requires the combination of both the FORMULA statement to store the new contents in the cell and the INPUT statement that accepts the entry of this new information from the keyboard. Input is restricted to numeric values by the *type* of 1 specified in the INPUT statement.

The contents of PLACE, which contains a reference to the current record, are stored in HOLD by the instruction in A9. This cycling of information from PLACE to HOLD is important. After every Find operation is performed, HOLD always should contain the reference to the record just found. The IF function in A5 is dependent on this transfer of information from one variable to the other. With all these tasks completed, the macro branches to the top of the loop and starts the process again (cell A10).

When the IF statement in A5 shows that the variables PLACE and HOLD contain the same value, the last matching record has been found twice. When this occurs, the functions in A6 are executed. The first function displays an Alert box with a message for the user. The second function, HALT, immediately stops the execution of the macro.

With this macro, you can find all the records matching your criteria. You also can assign a code to each record found. The only limitation of the macro is that at least one record must be found. This makes the macro less than ideal; but if you have a replacement code in mind, you probably are sure that at least one matching record exists. The real advantage of this macro is that it provides a solution for most of the repeated find and replace operations that do not function properly with Excel's regular features.

Error-Processing Macros

Some data entry errors are caught while a macro is processing, but others are noticed only after a significant amount of data has been entered in a database. You can create separate macros to help with error correction if the data volume affected is sufficient to warrant the time investment for creation of the error-correction macro.

You can check for some errors during processing. You can check for errors in cell selections (for example, the operator selected a column, but was instructed to select a row); data values of an incorrect type (for example, the operator entered a number but should have entered text); or values outside the ranges established for the data value (for example, unit prices do not exceed $50, and the operator entered $510). These errors can be intercepted while the macro is processing, and the user can be directed to reenter the faulty data.

Errors in data type are not apparent until a macro has completed execution. If you add error code to check for this particular condition, the macro can intercept these errors during processing. Once the data is entered, you cannot check this set of data and must correct the error after entry is finished.

You can create macros that intercept errors at entry time or macros that correct errors after data has been entered. In this section are both kinds of macros that deal with errors. The macros are

- A macro to intercept data entry errors

- A macro to correct errors in data

A Macro To Intercept Data Entry Errors

The best strategy is to catch errors as they occur. At that time, the operator still has the source document and can make a correction easily. This approach should reduce the number of errors stored in your database.

The next macro is actually part of a larger macro. This macro is a variation of an earlier macro used to demonstrate data entry using input prompts (fig. 5.1). The technique used in this modified macro can be expanded to include checks for all potential errors in each field entered or can be used to check for errors that tend to occur regularly.

A section of the data entry macro is shown in figure 5.14. In cells A11 through A15, a check is performed on the validity of the branch number. The instruction in A11 is the same INPUT function used in the earlier example. An instruction has been added in A12 to determine whether the entered number exceeds the system's allowable maximum, which is 9499. If the number is less than 9500, the macro accepts the value entered in the selected cell as a formula (A15). If the value exceeds 9499, an Alert message appears on the screen (A13). In response to this message, the user must click OK. The macro then branches back up to A11 so that the operator can enter a new branch number in response to the original Input prompt.

You can expand this macro by adding another check, this time for a branch number less than zero. You also can add checks of the Region codes included in the original macro.

If you look at programs used by large organizations, much of the code is for processing exceptions and errors. If you were to check for all potential data errors, your macros would look the same. Mainframe computers have a faster cycle time than personal computers and can handle all the error-processing code without lowering efficiency in performance. At this time, however, personal computers

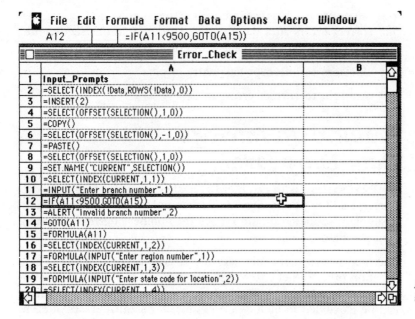

Fig. 5.14. A macro to check the validity of a branch number.

are not that fast, and you will have to weigh the risks of not using a particular error check against the cost of including the check.

A Macro To Correct Errors in Data

Entry of large amounts of data frequently is delegated to individuals with greater typing proficiency than the model designers. After you have designed a model, you may want to have your data entered by someone else on your staff. You may find, however, that your instructions are not always clear. For example, suppose that you requested that only the last name of the branch manager be entered in the database column for MANAGER. You then find that both the first and last names have been entered (see fig. 5.15). Rather than consider this extra information a bonus, you realize that you will not be able to produce a list alphabetized by the branch managers' last names. Records that contain the first name at the beginning of the entry will be sorted by the first name.

You can create a macro that will eliminate the first name from each entry. Like all error-correction macros, the macro must be written to correct the specific error. If only two records are entered incorrectly, editing the records without a macro is preferable. If 500

 File Edit Formula Format Data Options Macro Window

| | E1 | | MANAGER | | | | |

Branch_Data

	A	B	C	D	E	F	G
1	BRANCH	REGION	LOCATION	RECEIVABLES	MANAGER	NO_EMP	
2	8712	6	GA	$985,632	Joe Tower	9	
3	6731	4	IL	$1,290,000	Tom Clark	18	
4	5612	3	LA	$1,209,875	Terry Brown	12	
5	9430	2	LA	$999,812	Paul Jacobs	14	
6	2214	6	LA	$1,200,975	Marion Black	10	
7	2459	3	LA	$1,178,900	Jason Douglas	12	
8	6652	7	MD	$13,456,332	Tim Yancy	15	
9	3312	4	MD	$980,765	Tom Harris	15	
10	2345	1	MD	$78,999	Fred Myer	15	
11	1235	3	MD	$67,890	Jim Jacobs	14	
12	5691	4	MD	$56,900	Carol York	8	
13	3349	8	MI	$865,490	Bob Rogers	7	
14	5609	2	OR	$10,223,469	Tim Stark	20	
15	4435	5	SC	$1,100,673	Mary Brown	10	
16	5619	6	TX	$1,200,897	Carol Smythe	13	
17	9200	3	TX	$75,908	Jane Ford	11	
18	9311	1	VA	$1,118,500	Carol Woods	15	
19	4328	5	WA	$95,700	Bill Hanson	11	
20							

Fig. 5.15. A database with managers' names entered incorrectly.

records are entered incorrectly, the error becomes motivation for a macro.

The Fix _ Names macro eliminates the varying number of characters in the first name in each entry (see fig. 5.16). Before executing the macro, the user selects the range of cells containing the incorrect entries. This selection allows changes to the incorrect records added to the database without disrupting records entered correctly.

The first statement in the macro establishes the name ORIG_ DATA for this selection. The number of rows in this selection is stored in A3.

Because a database normally is entered at the top of the worksheet, the cells below the database entries are assumed to be empty. A section of cells of the same size as the original data chosen is selected immediately below the original cells. This is accomplished with the OFFSET function, which offsets cells from the original data by the number of rows in the original data (A4). The name ALTERED is assigned to this selection of cells (A5).

A counter called LOOP is set up as equal to the number of rows in the selection. This is the maximum iteration count for the processing loop. A second counter called COUNT is also established.

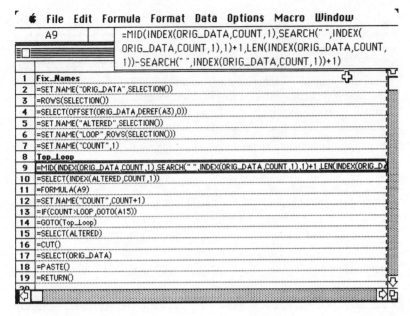

Fig. 5.16. A macro to eliminate first names.

This counter stores the relative number of the record being processed. When COUNT exceeds LOOP, all the records have been processed.

The first statement under Top_Loop is the most complicated in the macro. This instruction must extract the last name and store it temporarily in A9. The long formula meets all the requirements of the task. The statement uses the MID function to obtain the required characters. Each of MID's three arguments is a combination of other functions.

The first argument for MID is the location of the data string. This location is described by the INDEX function, which uses COUNT to access the correct database record. The data, which was selected before the macro started, was named ORIG_DATA in A2. In A9, INDEX accesses the desired cell in this column of names with the statement

    INDEX(ORIG_DATA,COUNT,1)

COUNT determines which cell in the column of names the macro will work on. This cell becomes the first argument for the MID function and so specifies the location of the text that will be manipulated.

The second argument for MID specifies the location of the first character to take from the entry. This location is defined as a blank space plus one, that is, a location that is one position past the space separating first and last names in the cell. To find this position, the macro uses SEARCH and adds 1 to the position of the blank space. The portion of the macro formula that does this is

SEARCH(" ",INDEX(ORIG_DATA,COUNT,1),1)+1

Examine the inner section first. It contains another reference to ORIG_DATA and again uses the INDEX function and COUNT to determine the cell accessed.

The first argument for SEARCH is the character string for which you are searching (in this example, the blank space between the first and last names). The second argument is the data where the search is being conducted. The third argument, a 1 in this example, represents the starting location for the search. The +1 moves the macro one position beyond the blank.

The last argument for MID is the number of characters to extract from the original cell entry. This number is the length of the entire entry less one more position than the location of the blank. LEN and SEARCH pinpoint the number of characters in the last name. First, the length of the entry is determined. From the length, the location of the blank space plus 1 is subtracted. This calculation results in the number of characters in the last name.

As you can see, a number of nested functions are required, but the result of the MID statement is the extraction of the last name from the entry.

The cell where the corrected data is stored is selected by the statement in A10. The FORMULA statement in A11 stores the result of the MID function.

Completing this iteration through the loop, COUNT is increased by one (A12) and compared to LOOP (A13). If COUNT is less than LOOP, control passes to the top of the loop and processing continues (A14).

When COUNT is greater than LOOP, all the incorrect entries have been processed and the last name for each appears in the area named ALTERED. This area is selected (A15), and the CUT function is used. The ORIG_DATA area is selected and the cut entries are pasted over ORIG_DATA (A18). After the macro is executed, the last names appear in the proper place and the first names are removed. The corrected data is shown in figure 5.17.

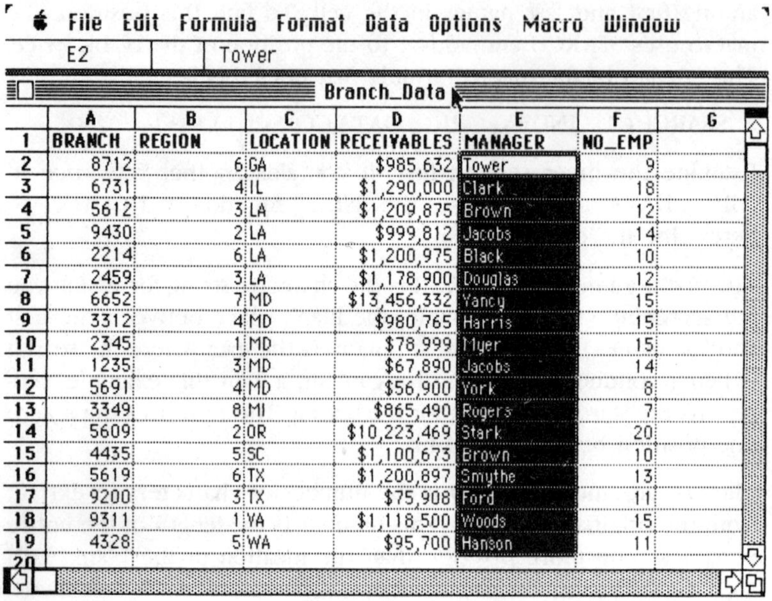

	A	B	C	D	E	F	G
1	BRANCH	REGION	LOCATION	RECEIVABLES	MANAGER	NO_EMP	
2	8712	6	GA	$985,632	Tower	9	
3	6731	4	IL	$1,290,000	Clark	18	
4	5612	3	LA	$1,209,875	Brown	12	
5	9430	2	LA	$999,812	Jacobs	14	
6	2214	6	LA	$1,200,975	Black	10	
7	2459	3	LA	$1,178,900	Douglas	12	
8	6652	7	MD	$13,456,332	Yancy	15	
9	3312	4	MD	$980,765	Harris	15	
10	2345	1	MD	$78,999	Myer	15	
11	1235	3	MD	$67,890	Jacobs	14	
12	5691	4	MD	$56,900	York	8	
13	3349	8	MI	$865,490	Rogers	7	
14	5609	2	OR	$10,223,469	Stark	20	
15	4435	5	SC	$1,100,673	Brown	10	
16	5619	6	TX	$1,200,897	Smythe	13	
17	9200	3	TX	$75,908	Ford	11	
18	9311	1	VA	$1,118,500	Woods	15	
19	4328	5	WA	$95,700	Hanson	11	
20							

Fig. 5.17. A database with managers' names corrected.

You can use adaptations of this macro to add fixed characters to part numbers, reverse first and last name entries, or otherwise alter data that has been entered. Although you can correct data without copying all of it to an ALTERED area, this approach allows you to stop after the ALTERED area is full and review the selections before the original data is destroyed. Errors are never welcome, but macros like this can make error correction almost painless.

Macros for Word-Processing Tasks

Although Excel does not have word-processing capabilities, with macros, the program can handle some word-processing tasks. The macros may take a little effort to set up, but they can be valuable timesaving techniques because they access information already stored on your computer.

In this section, you will see two macros that handle tasks normally done with a word-processing package. You will learn how to create the following macros:

- A macro to create mailing labels

- A macro to create a form letter

A Macro To Create Mailing Labels

To create mailing labels, you need to list several fields from the same database record. These fields must be listed in a vertical sequence of three cells. Then you must skip several cells to allow for the height of the label. In the following example, three spaces are skipped, but you will have to use a number that corresponds to the height of your labels.

The labels are entered in a column of the worksheet. The macro shown in figures 5.18A and 5.18B produces one-up labels; that is, it creates a single column of labels. If you are using two-up or three-up labels, you will want to have two or three labels across the same row. This arrangement takes a little more work because every second or third label goes on a new set of lines. You will have to select a column width that conforms to the width of the labels you use for printing.

	File Edit Formula Format Data Options Macro Window	
	A13	=MID(INDEX(!DATABASE,COUNT,5),DEREF(A12)+2,LEN(INDEX(!DATABASE,COUNT,5))-(DEREF(A12)+1))&" "&MID(INDEX(!DATABASE,COUNT,5),1,DEREF(A12)-1)

1	Create_Labels
2	=SELECT(INPUT("Select top cell in column to be used for label construction",8))
3	=SET.NAME("TOP_ROW",SELECTION())
4	=SELECT(TOP_ROW:OFFSET(TOP_ROW,500,0))
5	=SET.NAME("LABELS",SELECTION())
6	=SELECT(!DATABASE)
7	=SET.NAME("MAXIMUM",ROWS(SELECTION()))
8	=SET.NAME("COUNT",1)
9	=SET.NAME("LABEL_COUNT",1)
10	Top_Loop
11	=SELECT(INDEX(LABELS,LABEL_COUNT,1))
12	=SEARCH(" ",INDEX(!DATABASE,COUNT,5),1)
13	=MID(INDEX(!DATABASE,COUNT,5),DEREF(A12)+2,LEN(INDEX(!DATABASE,COUNT,5))-(D
14	=FORMULA(A13)
15	=SET.NAME("LABEL_COUNT",LABEL_COUNT+1)
16	=SELECT(INDEX(LABELS,LABEL_COUNT,1))
17	=MID(INDEX(!DATABASE,COUNT,6),1,LEN(INDEX(!DATABASE,COUNT,6)))
18	=FORMULA(A17)
19	=SET.NAME("LABEL_COUNT",LABEL_COUNT+1)
20	=SELECT(INDEX(LABELS,LABEL_COUNT,1))

Fig. 5.18A. A macro to create one-up mailing labels.

```
 ⬤  File  Edit  Formula  Format  Data  Options  Macro  Window
         A21              =MID(INDEX(!DATABASE,COUNT,7),1,LEN(INDEX(!
                          DATABASE,COUNT,7)))
                                           A
 21 =MID(INDEX(!DATABASE,COUNT,7),1,LEN(INDEX(!DATABASE,COUNT,7)))
 22 =FORMULA(A21)
 23 =SET.NAME("LABEL_COUNT",LABEL_COUNT+3)
 24 =SET.NAME("COUNT",COUNT+1)
 25 =IF(COUNT>MAXIMUM,GOTO(A27))
 26 =GOTO(Top_Loop)
 27 =SELECT(LABELS)
 28 =RETURN()
 29
 30
 31
 32
 33
 34
 35
 36
 37
 38
 39
 40
```

Fig. 5.18B. A macro to create one-up mailing labels.

The first instruction in this macro combines the SELECT and INPUT functions. The user selects the top cell in the column where the labels will be created. All the labels are constructed on the worksheet and then printed all at the same time.

The instruction in A3 assigns the name TOP_ROW to the selected cell by combining the SET.NAME and SELECTION functions. This name will be used to select enough cells in the column to store all the labels created. If you have more records than will fit in the column, you can add an IF statement. If the range is used up, the macro can print those labels and then begin to fill the column again. In the example, the space requirements do not exceed 500 rows. The SELECT statement in A4 selects 500 cells in the specified column. As its range, the function uses TOP_ROW through an offset of 500 rows from TOP_ROW. The *column* offset is specified as 0 in order to retain the same column as the top cell selected.

When available memory is limited, you may want to consider selecting the database records first. With this approach, you select the exact number of cells required for label storage by multiplying the number of records by the lines reserved for each label.

The cells selected in A4 will be named LABELS to allow for indexing the rows in the selection (A5). A counter keeps track of the processing location in LABELS.

The instruction in A6—SELECT(!DATABASE)—operates on the assumption that the database records are selected and assigned the name DATABASE with a Formula Define Name command before the macro is invoked. The use of the exclamation point (!) with the range name indicates that DATABASE is on the active worksheet. Using this approach, as opposed to entering a document name, allows the macro to function with any worksheet as long as it has the same basic format for data storage.

Figure 5.19 shows a part of the database used to create labels. Notice that the file has an unusual name, *April 17, 1986.* You will see the advantage of using this type of name later in this chapter, when you use this same file for a form letter.

** File Edit Formula Format Data Options Macro Window**

| | E1 | | MANAGER | | |

April 17, 1986

	E	F	G	H
1	MANAGER	STREET ADDRESS	CITY/STATE ZIP	
2	Jacobs, Jim	120 Washer Rd.	Monroe, GA 50132	
3	Myer, Fred	75 Lovely Lane	Stevens, VT 55632	
4	York, Carol	5 Rogers Ave,	Warren, MI 45311	
5	Clark, Tom	16 Elmbank Rd.	Garden, NJ 67891	
6	Hanson, Bill	3214 5th Ave.	Borris, MD 21209	
7	Woods, Carol	67 Tyler Ave.	Towson, MD 21204	
8	Stark, Tom	51 Kurt Ave.	Carver, GA 22167	
9	Tower, Joe	17 North Ave.	Lake City, MO 44512	
10	Brown, Terry	14 Chesaco Ave.	River, OR 32190	
11	Yancy, Tim	16 Oak Branch Way	Vernon, TX 88972	
12	Rogers, John	8 Armour Blvd	York, PA 34217	
13	Symthe, Jim	99 York Rd.	Vine, CA 78642	
14	Harris, Tom	53 Wyler Ave.	Hollow, UT 34217	
15	Brown, Mary	4 Dover Lane	York, PA 34217	
16				

Fig. 5.19. A database used in the creation of mailing labels.

In cell A7 of the macro, a count of the records in the database is taken with MAXIMUM. SET.NAME is used to store in MAXIMUM the number of rows in the database. A second SET.NAME instruction is used to initialize COUNT to a value of 1. COUNT keeps track of the record being used. Because the count for the current database record will not match the current row count in the label storage area, a third SET.NAME function is added. This counter, LABEL _COUNT, keeps track of the current displacement in the area called LABELS. This separate counter is needed because one row of data from the database uses three data rows and two blank rows in the LABELS area.

The label in A10, Top_ -Loop, marks the beginning of iterative processing. After you enter the label in the cell, you must use the Formula Define Name to attach the name to the location. This name provides the capability to branch to this location.

The first instruction in Top_ Loop is the SELECT function, which uses LABEL _COUNT to access the first cell of a label entry. The database entry corresponding to the name field is placed in this cell by the three instructions that follow (cells A11, A12, and A13). The instruction in A11 selects the name field for the current record. The program uses a combination of functions to extract the name from this entry.

The instruction in A12 determines the location of the comma in each name entry. Because the comma is the SEARCH character, names in the database must be entered consistently using a comma between last and first names.

The instruction in A13 reverses the name entry and places the first name at the beginning of the entry. Because a text entry is desired, the MID function is used. It extracts the data found in the database in the fifth field of the record defined by COUNT. The MID function accesses the current record with the INDEX function. The starting location within the string is the location of the comma plus two, DEREF(A12)+2. The number of characters extracted is the length of the string less one more than the location of the comma,

$$LEN(INDEX(!DATABASE,COUNT,5))-(DEREF(A12)+1))$$

This string is joined to a blank space and then to the last name. A similar process extracts the last name.

The entry that is stored in A13 is placed in the selected cell in the LABELS section with the FORMULA(A13) statement in cell A14. The name field is now stored in the LABELS area.

The database count is still correct at this time because additional information is taken from the current database record. LABEL _COUNT must be advanced because each entry prints on a separate line of the label. The SET.NAME function in A15 handles the increment to LABEL_COUNT.

The next cell in the LABELS area is selected with the statement in A16. The address in the current database record is accessed with

the combination of functions in A17, and the text string corresponding to this entry is stored there. The entry stored in A17 is
placed in the selected cell by the FORMULA function in A18, thus
completing the street address section of the label.

The remainder of the first label is completed by the statements in
cells A19 through A22. These add to LABEL _COUNT, select the
next label cell, and place information from the second address line
in the selected cell. This entry completes the label. The counter
used to keep track of the label offset is incremented by three to
allow the required space between label entries. The SET.NAME function in A23 handles the increment.

The COUNT used to monitor progress through the database is now
increased by one, because one record of the database corresponds
to a label (A24). After this COUNT is incremented, the value must
be checked to see whether it exceeds the database length. The statement in A25 handles this by a comparison with MAXIMUM. At the
beginning of this macro, MAXIMUM was set to the number of rows
in the database. If COUNT exceeds MAXIMUM, control branches to
A27 where the iterative processing ends and all the labels are selected in preparation for printing when the macro ends.

When the database count does not exceed the number of rows in
the database, the GOTO statement in A26 makes the macro branch
to Top_ Loop. This begins the iterative process again and creates
the next label from information from the next database record.

Figure 5.20 provides an example of the selected label cells at the
end of this macro. If you want, you can add the printing instructions
to the macro. This macro, however, allows you to review the labels
before issuing the Print command. Regardless of your approach to
printing, you will want to print the labels on continuous forms and
set the top margin to zero.

Although this process may seem lengthy, Excel processes your entries quickly. Whenever the required data is available in database
records, this approach provides an efficient solution for label
production.

If you must produce labels from databases having different formats,
you can add one more enhancement to the macro. At the beginning
of the macro, you can add INPUT statements that allow the selection
of the proper columns. The three statements containing the MID
function then would need to be altered to reference the offsets

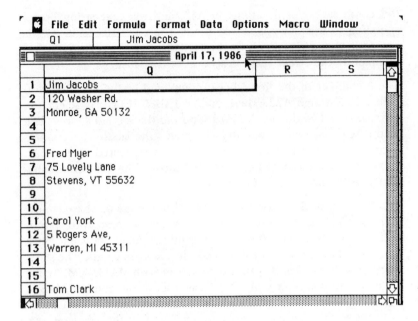

Fig. 5.20. Some of the labels created with the macro.

selected. This enhancement can provide even greater flexibility to your macro.

A Macro To Create a Form Letter

Form letters are a standard feature of word-processing packages. Excel will transfer data to a word-processing package, but you may not want to buy one if your need is only occasional. With macro capability, you can create a form letter with just Excel. The macro takes planning but provides the advantage of easy access to information in Excel's database or spreadsheet.

Creating the letter takes care because the letter must be entered as a series of long labels in a column. Excel has no wordwrap feature or anything similar to provide assistance; but if you proceed slowly, the entry should not present a major problem.

The upper part of the letter for the example is shown in figure 5.21. Note the XXX in the letter wherever variable information will be inserted for the heading and salutation. Also note that the file name is *April 17, 1986*, the date the letter was created. Because Excel automatically centers the file name at the top of each page, you can use this feature to date your letter. When you want to print the letter again next month, the file can be renamed with the current date.

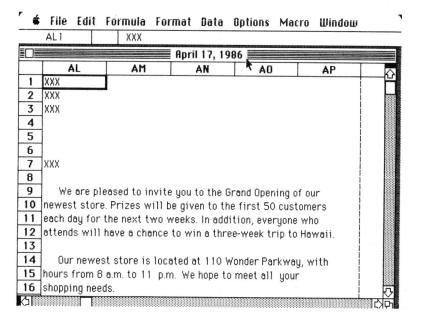

Fig. 5.21. A sample form letter.

Before invoking this macro, the operator selects database records and assigns those records the name DATABASE. The operater must be careful to select only the data. The macro can be altered easily to allow the user to enter the database selection from the macro, as in other examples. You can add INPUT instructions to the macro and assign the selected cells the proper name with the Define Name command.

The macro for creating a form letter is shown in figures 5.22A and 5.22B. This example macro is constructed to find the name field in column 5; the street address in column 6; and the city, state, and ZIP code in column 7. However, the macro can be modified easily for a database that is organized differently.

The first steps are housekeeping functions; the macro establishes a maximum number of database records and a counter. The entry in A2 is actually three instructions joined with plus signs (+). The first instruction assigns the name MAXIMUM to the number of rows selected. The second instruction selects the area where the form letter is stored, and the last instruction sets the print area as the selected

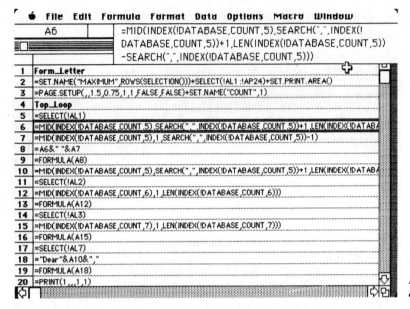

```
 File  Edit  Formula  Format  Data  Options  Macro  Window

   A6            =MID(INDEX(!DATABASE,COUNT,5),SEARCH(",",INDEX(!
                 DATABASE,COUNT,5))+1,LEN(INDEX(!DATABASE,COUNT,5))
                 -SEARCH(",",INDEX(!DATABASE,COUNT,5)))

1  Form_Letter
2  =SET.NAME("MAXIMUM",ROWS(SELECTION()))+SELECT(!AL1:!AP24)+SET.PRINT.AREA()
3  =PAGE.SETUP(,,1.5,0.75,1,1,FALSE,FALSE)+SET.NAME("COUNT",1)
4  Top_Loop
5  =SELECT(!AL1)
6  =MID(INDEX(!DATABASE,COUNT,5),SEARCH(",",INDEX(!DATABASE,COUNT,5))+1,LEN(INDEX(!DATABA
7  =MID(INDEX(!DATABASE,COUNT,5),1,SEARCH(",",INDEX(!DATABASE,COUNT,5))-1)
8  =A6&" "&A7
9  =FORMULA(A8)
10 =MID(INDEX(!DATABASE,COUNT,5),SEARCH(",",INDEX(!DATABASE,COUNT,5))+1,LEN(INDEX(!DATABA
11 =SELECT(!AL2)
12 =MID(INDEX(!DATABASE,COUNT,6),1,LEN(INDEX(!DATABASE,COUNT,6)))
13 =FORMULA(A12)
14 =SELECT(!AL3)
15 =MID(INDEX(!DATABASE,COUNT,7),1,LEN(INDEX(!DATABASE,COUNT,7)))
16 =FORMULA(A15)
17 =SELECT(!AL7)
18 ="Dear "&A10&","
19 =FORMULA(A18)
20 =PRINT(1,,,1,1)
```

Fig. 5.22A. A macro to create and print a form letter.

```
 File  Edit  Formula  Format  Data  Options  Macro  Window

   A10           =MID(INDEX(!DATABASE,COUNT,5),SEARCH(",",INDEX(!
                 DATABASE,COUNT,5))+1,LEN(INDEX(!DATABASE,COUNT,5))
                 -1)

5  =SELECT(!AL1)
6  =MID(INDEX(!DATABASE,COUNT,5),SEARCH(",",INDEX(!DATABASE,COUNT,5))+1,LEN(INDEX(!DATABA
7  =MID(INDEX(!DATABASE,COUNT,5),1,SEARCH(",",INDEX(!DATABASE,COUNT,5))-1)
8  =A6&" "&A7
9  =FORMULA(A8)
10 =MID(INDEX(!DATABASE,COUNT,5),SEARCH(",",INDEX(!DATABASE,COUNT,5))+1,LEN(INDEX(!DATABA
11 =SELECT(!AL2)
12 =MID(INDEX(!DATABASE,COUNT,6),1,LEN(INDEX(!DATABASE,COUNT,6)))
13 =FORMULA(A12)
14 =SELECT(!AL3)
15 =MID(INDEX(!DATABASE,COUNT,7),1,LEN(INDEX(!DATABASE,COUNT,7)))
16 =FORMULA(A15)
17 =SELECT(!AL7)
18 ="Dear "&A10&","
19 =FORMULA(A18)
20 =PRINT(1,,,1,1)
21 =SET.NAME("COUNT",COUNT+1)
22 =IF(COUNT>MAXIMUM,GOTO(A24))
23 =GOTO(Top_Loop)
24 =RETURN()
```

Fig. 5.22B. A macro to create and print a form letter.

cells. In A3, a page setup is established. Margins of 1.5 and 0.75 inches are established for the left and right margins, respectively. (The file containing the letter is formatted at 12 pitch with the Font Option, so these margins work nicely on 8 1/2-by-11-inch paper.) This cell also has a second instruction, which establishes a counter, COUNT, with a value of 1.

The loop for letter creation (Top_ Loop) comes next. Because the letter has a fixed location on the worksheet, specific cell addresses can be used. All the entry cells in the letter (AL1, AL2, AL3, and AL7) are selected by cell address. In A5, the first cell is selected: AL1, the input cell for the recipient's name, which comes from the database.

The MID functions (in A6, A7, A10, A12, and A15) create text values from the current database fields. Corresponding FORMULA functions (A9, A13, A16, and A19) then place in the letter the values in the selected cells.

The names stored in the database are not in the correct format for use in the inside address because they have the last name first: for example, Smith, John. The names must be reversed to normal order: John Smith. Two instructions are used. One handles the first name, and the other handles the last name.

Cell A6 contains the combination of functions that extracts the first name by searching for the comma, adding one for the space, and selecting all the characters that follow. The formula in A7, which extracts the last name, is a little easier to understand because the function starts at the beginning of the entry and proceeds to the comma. The two text results are joined with ampersands, and a space is placed between them (A8). This result is then stored in the current cell with the FORMULA function in cell A9.

In A11, cell AL2 is selected. The street address is extracted in A12, and the statement in A13 places the contents in AL2. Cell AL3 is selected next, and the last line of the address is stored in this cell. This address line is derived by the MID function in A15. The line is stored in the selected cell by the FORMULA statement in A16.

The salutation for the sample letter is created a little differently, by combining the fixed characters *Dear* and the comma (,) with the contents of the cell containing the text value of the first name. Cell A18 references cell A10, which extracts the first name again. This result is used in the salutation of the letter. The completed salutation is stored in AL7 with the instruction in A19.

The PRINT command in A20 executes the printing process. The macro selects the entire letter to prepare for printing. The PRINT statement is invoked, and the first letter is printed. The completed letter is shown in figure 5.23. The macro continues by adding one to COUNT. A check is made to determine whether COUNT exceeds MAXIMUM. If so, the macro ends; if not, the macro branches to Top_ Loop and continues.

April 17, 1986

Jim Jacobs
120 Washer Rd.
Monroe, GA 50132

Dear Jim,

We are pleased to invite you to the Grand Opening of our newest store. Prizes will be given to the first 50 customers each day for the next two weeks. In addition, everyone who attends will have a chance to win a three-week trip to Hawaii.

Our newest store is located at 110 Wonder Parkway, with hours from 8 a.m. to 11 p.m. We hope to meet all your shopping needs.

Sincerely,

Joe Smith
General Manager

Fig. 5.23. Completed form letter.

The macro is a little slower than a word processor but can be the ideal solution for data already stored in Excel. You can find many uses for this technique. For example, until you get that new accounting system installed, you can create client invoices in this way. Perhaps you need to distribute letters on the new incentive program to your sales staff and already have their names and performance data in Excel. Once you ready the printer and get the macro started, you can attend to other tasks while the output is produced.

A Macro To Create a Report from Two Files

Many available database packages cannot produce a single report from two files. Excel provides several ways to handle this task. If the files are in the same sequence, the data from one file can be copied to the other, and a simple print procedure will handle the report. When one file has multiple records for an item or the sequences are different and cannot be changed, however, this method will not work. Instead, you can create a macro that reads information from both files and stores it in the proper format in one of these files or in a separate file.

The Two_ File macro (see fig. 5.24) joins the branch number and name information from one file with receivables information from a second file. Before executing this macro, the user selects the line

	A
1	Two_File
2	=SET.NAME("HEADING_LINE",SELECTION())
3	=SET.NAME("COUNT",1)
4	=SELECT(Names!DATA)
5	=ROWS(SELECTION())
6	=SELECT(OFFSET(HEADING_LINE,1,0):OFFSET(HEADING_LINE,DEREF(A5),0))
7	=SET.NAME("REPORT",SELECTION())
8	Top_Loop
9	=ACTIVATE("Names")
10	=SELECT(INDEX(!DATA,COUNT,1))
11	=COPY()
12	=SELECT(INDEX(REPORT,COUNT,1))
13	=PASTE()
14	=ACTIVATE("Branch_Data")
15	=SELECT(!CRIT)
16	=PASTE()
17	=ACTIVATE("Names")
18	=SELECT(INDEX(!DATA,COUNT,2))
19	=COPY()
20	=SELECT(INDEX(REPORT,COUNT,2))
21	=PASTE()
22	=ACTIVATE("Branch_Data")
23	=DATA.FIND()
24	=SET.NAME("MATCH",SELECTION())
25	=SELECT(INDEX(MATCH,1,4))
26	=COPY()
27	=ACTIVATE("Names")
28	=SELECT(INDEX(REPORT,COUNT,3))
29	=PASTE()
30	=SET.NAME("COUNT",COUNT+1)
31	=IF(COUNT>A5,GOTO(A33))
32	=GOTO(A8)
33	=SELECT(REPORT)
34	=RETURN()

Fig. 5.24. A macro to create a report from two files.

containing the field names in the Names file (see fig. 5.25). This selection defines the area where the report will be written. You also can add instructions so that the operator can make this selection from within the macro. The user also gives the name *DATA* to the database records in both files. These ranges should not include field names.

	A	B	C	D	E
1	BRANCH	BRANCH_NAME			
2	1235	Salsbury, Maryland			
3	2345	Tacoma Park, Maryland			
4	5619	College Park, Maryland			
5	6731	Oak Park, Illinois			
6	4328	Freeland, Washington			
7	9311	Tidewater, Virginia			
8	5609	Portland, Oregon			
9	8712	Norcross, Georgia			
10	5612	New Orleans, Louisiana			
11	6652	Towson, Maryland			
12	3349	South Haven, Michigan			
13	5691	Austin, Texas			
14	3312	Silver Spring, Maryland			
15	4435	Columbia, South Carolina			

Fig. 5.25. Branch and branch name information in the Names file.

The preselected heading line is named HEADING_ LINE (A2). COUNT is established to monitor progress through the controlling database, which is the database that determines the order and content of the report created. The number of rows in Names, the controlling database, is used as a maximum count. This number also is used to select a range for the report, because each line in this database produces one line in the report. SELECT is used with two OFFSET functions to obtain the full report range (A6). This range then is named REPORT (A7). This step ends the preparation phase, and processing moves to the iterative process required to create the body of the report.

The loop is composed of a series of instructions that activate the proper window and copy information to the report. Each record in the Names database provides two fields for the report line, but the third field comes from the Branch _ Data file, where RECEIVABLES information is stored. Because Names and Branch _ Data are not in the same sequence, a DATA.FIND statement is used (A23).

In the example, the database records and the field names in Branch _ Data were selected and set as the database before the macro was executed. Also, the criteria area was established by placing BRANCH in a cell and leaving the cell beneath it blank. The blank cell was assigned the name CRIT. With each record from Branch_Data that is retrieved, the macro will place a new search value in CRIT.

Because quite a few steps are involved in the loop, a "walk" through each step will be valuable. The first step is to activate the Names window. The first line of the database is selected by the statement in A10 because the INDEX function uses the current value of COUNT, which is 1. Only the first field in this database record is accessed because the argument for the column is 1. The COPY function in A11 works on the cell just selected. The first cell in REPORT is selected next by the function in A12. The PASTE function copies the data from the database to this area (A13).

Because this first data field is the branch number that will be used to retrieve the proper record in the Branch _ Data file, the window for Branch _ Data is activated (A14). Remember: This is a completely separate file, not a window on the Names file. The CRIT cell is selected, and the branch number is pasted there. The macro uses the branch number in a DATA.FIND statement later in the macro.

The next task involves the Names file, so the window for that file must be activated (A17). The second field in the first database record is selected and copied to the second field in the report area. This moves the branch name to the output area.

The third field is taken from the Branch _ Data file. You must activate the file again (A22). With the file activated, you are ready for the DATA.FIND function (A23). This function accesses the preselected database and criteria areas and selects the matching record. The name MATCH is assigned to this record so that the macro can access just one field in the record. The fourth field is accessed because it contains the receivables figure for the selected branch. A COPY statement marks the contents of this cell to be copied (A26). The macro will copy the data to the report; but because the report is on the Names file, Names must be activated (A27). The third field of REPORT is selected (A28), and PASTE is invoked to complete the copy. With this statement, the first line of the report is complete.

Before processing loops back to the top, the counter must be incremented and checked. The SET.NAME function adds one to
COUNT (A30), and the IF function that follows handles the check.
If COUNT is less than the number of rows in the Names database,
the macro loops to Top_Loop. If COUNT is greater than the number
of rows, the lines of the report are selected and the macro ends.
Figure 5.26 presents a section of the completed report.

		File	Edit	Formula	Format	Data	Options	Macro	Window		
	G1										

	G	H	I	J	K	
1						
2		Branch Receivables April 1986				
3						
4						
5	BRANCH #	BRANCH NAME	RECEIVABLES			
6	1235	Salsbury, Maryland	$67,890			
7	2345	Tacoma Park, Maryland	$78,999			
8	5619	College Park, Maryland	$1,200,897			
9	6731	Oak Park, Illinois	$1,290,000			
10	4328	Freeland, Washington	$95,700			
11	9311	Tidewater, Virginia	$1,118,500			
12	5609	Portland, Oregon	$10,223,469			
13	8712	Norcross, Georgia	$985,632			
14	5612	New Orleans, Louisiana	$1,209,875			
15	6652	Towson, Maryland	$13,456,332			
16	3349	South Haven, Michigan	$865,490			
17	5691	Austin, Texas	$56,900			
18	3312	Silver Spring, Maryland	$980,765			
19	4435	Columbia, South Carolina	$1,100,673			
20						

Fig. 5.26. A section of the report produced from two files.

This approach allows you to verify visually the report's accuracy
before printing. After testing the macro, you may want to add the
instructions required to print the report immediately.

This macro has many applications. You may have a parts file and an
order file and want to combine price data to prepare invoices. You
may want to prepare project estimates from labor and material rates
stored in different files. This macro allows you to combine into one
report information from a number of files. This feature surpasses
the capabilities of many database packages.

Conclusion

The macros in this chapter are designed specifically to assist you with data management tasks. You have looked at macros that affect many data management tasks. You now have macros that serve as models for formatted data entry, error checking and correction, sorting, reporting, and even creating mailing labels and form letters. The techniques used in the construction of these macros also can be applied to applications outside the data management area.

In the next chapter, you will learn to create macros to assist with the creation and use of Excel's charts.

6

Creating Macros for the Chart Environment

Excel's graphics capabilities are more powerful than the graphics functions found in 1-2-3, Symphony, and other integrated packages. With Excel, you can create a greater variety of graph types. Once you create the graphs, you have many options—such as using arrows, overlay features, and text capabilities—that will enable you to tailor each graph to your exact needs. Unfortunately, all the menu options available in Excel's chart environment have not been duplicated in the macro functions. Still, those available in the Macro Command Language can simplify the creation of graphs significantly. Once a graph is on the screen, you easily can make the necessary changes.

(Note: In keeping with Excel's terminology in the program and the documentation, graphs are referred to as *charts* in this chapter.)

The basic graphics features, such as the selection of a main chart type or an overlay chart type, are available when you use Excel's Macro Command Language. The options offered with all the Gallery commands also are available. In addition, charts can be copied, and legends can be added. But the list of commands not available is long. For instance, commands to add arrows, change the chart patterns, alter the axis presentation, and attach text options all are missing from the macro language.

What all this means is that the basic chart-building process can be handled with a macro, including everything from the selection of cells and a chart type, to the size and placement of the chart window. But after the macro has created the basic chart, the macro will end, and you must use the Chart menu to add "bells and whistles" to the chart.

In this chapter, you will find examples of macros for creating various types of charts. Each macro presented here emphasizes a different option from the Main Chart Type dialog box. The macro that creates pie charts displays a series of four pie charts on the screen. The macro that presents Gallery options for the column chart includes a time-delay subroutine for projecting on the screen the various Gallery options.

The charts created in this chapter follow two basic methods for data selection. In some macros, the operator selects the data while the macros are running; in other macros, the data selections are fixed. Allowing the operator to select the data to be graphed provides flexibility. These macros will transfer to your own data layouts easily. Other macros have the cell selections coded in the macro. In order to run these macros with your own worksheets, you will need to change the cells referenced. Once adapted, these macros will reproduce charts without operator intervention.

As you examine the macros in this chapter, you will learn many techniques that can be applied to the creation of any chart type. The macros discussed in this chapter are the following:

- A macro that creates a scatter chart
- A macro that creates and prints a bar chart
- A macro that creates an area chart with axis titles
- A macro that displays column chart options
- A macro that creates four pie charts on the screen
- A macro that combines data for a line chart
- A macro that creates a combination chart
- A macro that creates an overlay chart
- A macro that presents a slide show

A Macro That Creates a Scatter Chart

If you need to create a whole series of charts, using a basic chart-creation macro can save you time. Just by running such a macro, you easily can have the chart type and format selected for you. If you like, you even can include in the macro the instructions for selecting the worksheet cells to be displayed.

The chart-creation macro in this section creates a scatter chart, with the series points plotted along the x-axis and the y-axis. The macro appears in figure 6.1, and the finished chart, along with the worksheet data that was used, is shown in figure 6.2.

To duplicate this macro and chart, you must first enter into your worksheet the series information. A series is a set of associated data values on your worksheet. The worksheet in figure 6.2 contains two series. Both contain price information organized by date. If more than one series is to be selected for a chart, all the series must be adjacent. In other words, multiple areas cannot be selected at one time for charting. If you need to chart separate areas, you select and chart one group of cells. Then you select another group. This second group is added to the chart with the Copy and Paste Special commands. In the macro in figure 6.1, only one area of cells is selected. In the worksheet in figure 6.2, the selected cells are B2:J4. You will notice that this selection includes the categories as well as the series and category names.

	File Edit Formula Format Data Options Macro Window
A1	Scatter_Diagram

Scatter

	A
1	Scatter_Diagram
2	=SELECT(INPUT("Select a single area to graph",8))
3	=IF(AREAS(SELECTION())=1,GOTO(A6))
4	=ALERT("Cells selected are not contiguous",2)
5	=GOTO(A2)
6	=NEW(2)
7	=LEGEND(TRUE)
8	=MOVE(11,45)
9	=SIZE(494,290)
10	=MAIN.CHART.TYPE(6)
11	=GALLERY.SCATTER(3)
12	=PAGE.SETUP("&F","Page &P",0.75,7,1,9,2)
13	=PRINT(1,,,1,1)
14	=RETURN()
15	
16	
17	
18	
19	

Fig. 6.1. A macro that creates a scatter chart.

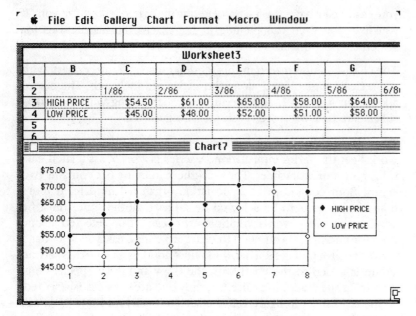

Fig. 6.2. Worksheet data and the scatter chart.

You can enter either the worksheet data or the macro first. For this example, you enter the worksheet data shown at the top of figure 6.2 first. You also must enter the rest of the entries, which are not visible on the screen:

H2: 6/86
H3: 70
H4: 63
I2: 7/86
I3: 75
I4: 68
J2: 8/86
J3: 68
J4: 54

You do not need to be concerned if your worksheet has another name. This macro is designed to reference the current worksheet regardless of its name.

Now that you have supplied data to the worksheet, the macro can handle the rest of the work in creating the scatter chart. For the following discussion of how the macro operates, refer to the macro in figure 6.1.

First, the macro asks you to select the cells to be graphed. As mentioned earlier, you select B2 through J4. Then the macro checks the number of areas in the current selection (A3). If you have selected more than one area, you will see an Alert message (A4), and the macro will let you try again. If you have selected just one area, the macro will proceed by requesting a new chart file (A6). You momentarily will see the selected cells displayed in a column chart, Excel's default chart type.

The instruction in A7 adds a legend to the chart with the TRUE argument. The MOVE instruction in A8 moves the new chart to the upper right corner of the screen. (The location does not match the display in figure 6.2 because the chart was moved down in this figure so that you can see the worksheet data.) The SIZE instruction expands the chart to full screen size.

As the next instruction (A10) executes, the Main Chart Type is changed to a scatter chart. Thus, your screen display will be redrawn using the scatter chart format. In A11, the third format from the Gallery menu's scatter chart options is chosen. The distinguishing feature of this format is the addition of grid lines.

The remaining instructions are the PAGE.SETUP and PRINT instructions in A12 and A13. The important PAGE.SETUP options are the fourth, sixth, and seventh arguments. The fourth argument is the width of the chart, the sixth argument is the chart height, and the last argument is size. The size argument can be 1 for Screen Size and 2 for Fit to Page. The macro ends after creating the chart and printing a copy of it.

You easily can make modifications to the scatter chart macro. For instance, you can provide different arguments in A8 and A9 so that the macro will move the chart window elsewhere or provide a different window size. Or you can change cell A11, which contains the GALLERY.SCATTER function. Although Excel automatically selects the first of 7 available scatter chart formats, you may prefer another format. Format 5, for example, provides both horizontal and vertical grid lines to assist you in interpreting the chart values. If you prefer format 5, you simply can change the format specified in A11 from 3 to 5.

After the macro has completed its work, you can enhance your new scatter chart by accessing some menu commands that aren't available in the Macro Command Language. These commands enable you to embellish the chart with text or arrows, for example.

To present your data in a scatter chart, you had to change the Main Chart Type (A10). This change was necessary because the default chart type, which is set when the package is installed, is a column chart. If you plan to create a series of charts other than column charts, you may want to change the preferred format to a scatter chart or some other format. Then, when the worksheet cells are selected and the new chart window is created, the chart automatically will be a scatter chart.

The Set Preferred Format command, which you use to change the default chart type, is not available in the Macro Command Language. If you want to change the default type, you can initiate this command from the menu after Excel displays the scatter chart created by the macro. Once you have changed the type, subsequent charts can be created more quickly. However, if you plan to use macros to create more than one type of chart, you may want the macro to change the type each time instead of having a separate macro for each type of chart.

Another modification you can make to this basic macro is to add the ECHO function. You can insert *ECHO(FALSE)* at the beginning of the macro in order to prevent the window from being redrawn. A good location for this instruction would be in A6; then you would move everything following down one line. After you make your final selections, you can add *ECHO(TRUE)*, which reinstitutes screen redrawing. This instruction could be placed in A12, after the last change to the chart screen. These extra functions minimize the flicker effect caused by constantly changing windows.

A Macro That Creates and Prints a Bar Chart

Creating and printing a bar chart are typical steps in a month-end closing process. Once you have updated your worksheet data, you may want to print a copy of the worksheet and then create a chart containing the data. If you use a macro to handle the chart building, you will not have to remember the format for last month's chart. The format information, which is recorded in the macro, can be duplicated automatically each month. A sample bar chart is shown in figure 6.3. The macro to create this chart is shown in figure 6.4.

Because the data included in the chart will be in the same worksheet cells each month, you will want to include the cell selection in the

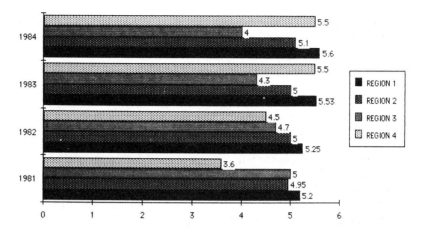

Fig. 6.3. A sample bar chart.

```
  File  Edit  Formula  Format  Data  Options  Macro  Window

      A1                Bar_Chart

                                    Bar
                        A                          B
1   Bar_Chart
2   =SELECT("R2C1:R6C5")
3   =NEW(2)
4   =LEGEND(TRUE)
5   =MOVE(11,45)
6   =SIZE(494,290)
7   =MAIN.CHART.TYPE(2)
8   =GALLERY.BAR(7)
9   =PAGE.SETUP("&F","Page &P",0.75,7,1,9,2)
10  =PRINT(1,,,,1,1)
11  =RETURN()
12
13
14
15
16
17
18
19
20
```

Fig. 6.4. A macro that creates a bar chart.

macro. By including the cells, you won't have to remember to select them before you run the macro. After the macro has selected the cells, it will request a new chart file with the NEW function and a *type* of 2 (A3). The macro then requests a legend with the LEGEND function and a *logical* value of TRUE (A4).

The instruction in A5 moves the chart to the upper left corner of the screen. The next instruction, the SIZE function, expands the size of the chart window to occupy the entire screen, with a width of 494 (from a possible 512) and a height of 290 (from a possible 303).

Because a column chart is the default chart type, the initial display will be in column chart format. The MAIN.CHART.TYPE function in A7 enables you to change the chart type in the active chart window to any of the other types: 1 for Area, 2 for Bar, 3 for Column, 4 for Line, 5 for Pie, and 6 for Scatter.

Seven different formats for bar charts are available. Among the options are grid lines, stacked bars, and overlapping bars. With option 7, a label for the maximum value of each bar is displayed. The bar chart macro in figure 6.4 includes this option in cell A8, which contains the GALLERY.BAR function.

Using the PAGE.SETUP function (A9) is a preliminary step to printing the chart. A special version of this function is used for the chart environment. The function's arguments are *header*, *footer*, *left*, *width*, *top*, *height*, and *size*. Header and footer are specified just as they are for other printing tasks. The left margin in the bar chart macro is set at a value of 0.75, for 3/4 of an inch. The width of the page is set at 7 inches. A top margin of 1 is specified, and a page height of 9 is included. For the last argument, *size*, a value of 2 indicates that the chart should be fit to the size of the page. If 1 had been entered for *size*, the chart would be screen size.

The last macro instruction is the PRINT function. Its arguments are *range*, *from*, *to*, *copies* and *feed*. A *range* of 1, as indicated in figure 6.4, means that all pages should be printed. The arguments *from* and *to* are needed only when the entire file is not being printed. These two options are appropriate for worksheets. In the bar chart macro, *copies* has a value of 1. For the last argument, *feed*, 1 indicates continuous feed. If 2 had been entered for *feed*, the chart would be printed on single sheets.

Although this bar chart macro is not sophisticated, it can be a workhorse in producing your monthly charts. The macro is especially useful if you have 10 or 15 charts to update each month. Once you enter the data, you can use a macro like this one to create a variety of charts. You first may want to create all the charts and then to reactivate them for printing. Or, if you have a large number of charts, you may prefer to create each chart, save it, and then print and close the chart window. If you want titles added to your charts, along with other enhancements, these can be stored in a chart file or

template, and the new data values can be copied to the bar chart
format.

A Macro That Creates
an Area Chart with Axis Titles

Because Excel's Macro Command Language does not allow you to
use all of the program's basic chart features, you cannot automate
the chart process completely. No commands are available in the
Macro Command Language for adding axis titles, arrows, or other
"bells and whistles." There is a solution to this problem, however.
You can create a chart template with the extras included, use it for
your month-end chart, and afterward delete the data values in the
chart by using the Clear command. You then can save the chart
template to disk for later use. Each month, when you want to create
a chart containing your new data and the extra features, you can
use Copy and Paste Special to place your new data on the template.
The extras also will appear on the completed chart.

Now examine the required steps closely. The first step is to create
a chart with data and attach the desired text to the value and category axes. The sample chart is shown in figure 6.5. The label RETAIL
$ has been added for the value axis, and the label BUDGET YEAR
has been added for the category axis.

Now that you have created a chart, you can create a chart template
that you can use to create other charts. To create the template,
choose Select Chart from the Chart menu, then Clear from the Edit
menu. When the dialog box shown in figure 6.6 appears, click Formulas. The result is what appears to be an empty chart window (see
fig. 6.7). You then save this window to your disk, assigning *Trial* as
the name of the window that holds the chart template.

Because you want the macro to open the appropriate chart template,
you must close the blank window so that you can place instructions
in the macro. The macro then can open the window and build the
chart, using the chart template.

With this preliminary work completed, you now can focus on the
macro instructions (see fig. 6.8). If you like, you can use the Recorder to duplicate this macro. This will save you some time and
ensure a functional macro when you finish.

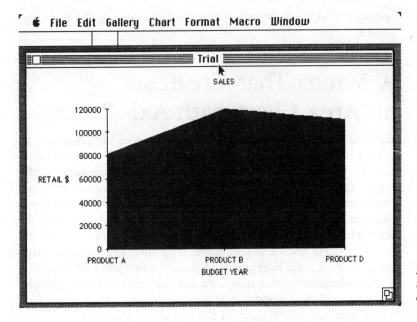

Fig. 6.5. A sample chart with titles, to be used for creating a chart template.

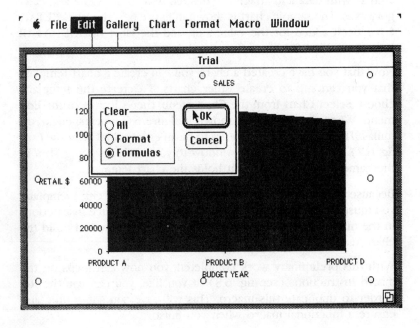

Fig. 6.6. The dialog box for Clear.

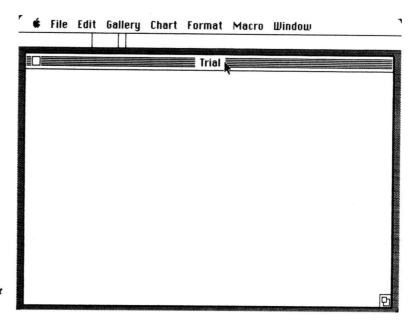

Fig. 6.7. The chart template that appears as a blank window.

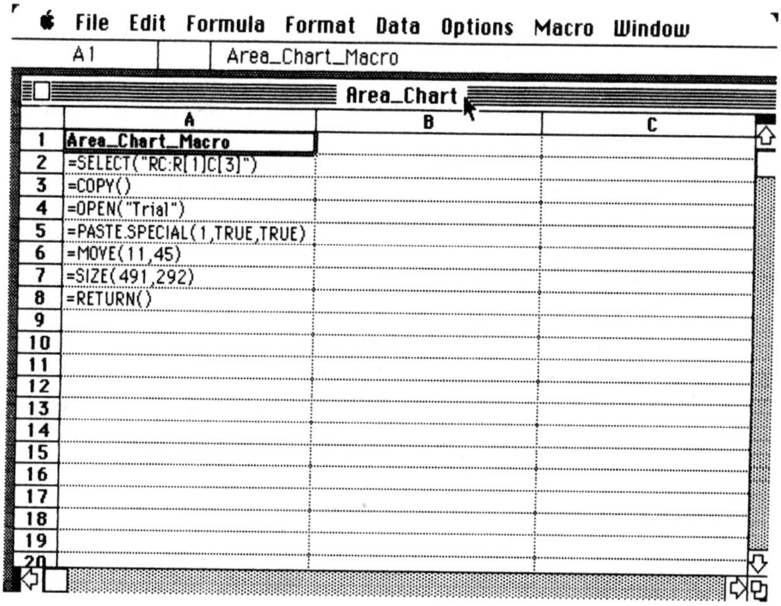

Fig. 6.8. A macro that creates an area chart with axis titles.

Once you have selected the cells containing the current month's data, the cells can be copied. The COPY instruction in A3 will handle this for you. The data shown in figure 6.9 will be copied to the chart template named Trial. Because this template is not currently open, the OPEN function is necessary next. Notice the quotation marks around the file name in A4.

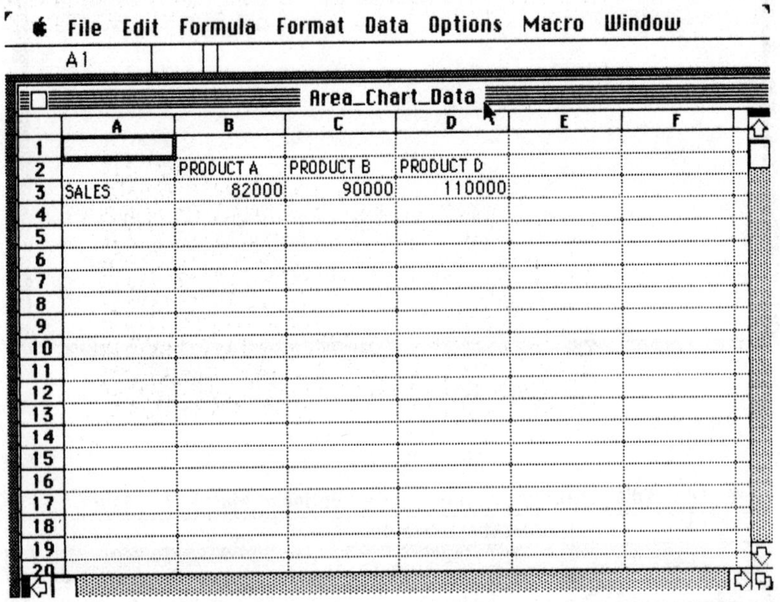

Fig. 6.9. Data for the area chart.

After the template is open and in the active window, the PASTE.SPECIAL function (A5) can complete the chart. The function has three arguments. The first defines the location of the values. The 1 indicates that the values are in rows. (A 2 would indicate that the values are in columns.) If your selection will vary, you should add another INPUT statement to supply this value. Because rows are selected in the sample macro, the arguments that follow (TRUE, TRUE) represent Series Names in First Column and Categories in First Row. Indicating a value of TRUE for either of these options is the same as checking them in the Paste Special dialog box. A value of FALSE would indicate that these options were not checked.

The last steps in the macro are to move the chart window to the upper left corner of the screen and to make the window larger. These two actions are handled by the MOVE and SIZE functions (A6 and A7). By entering these functions with the Recorder, you don't need to calculate the exact x- and y-coordinates. The completed full-screen area chart is shown in figure 6.10. Although the chart displays the new data, the value and category axes titles from the chart you used as a template are represented.

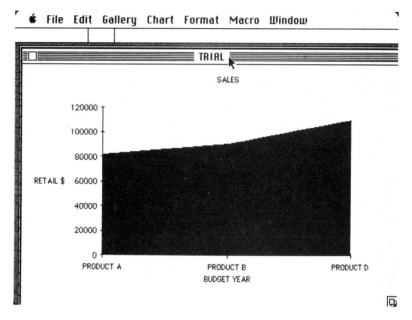

Fig. 6.10. The completed area chart.

A chart template makes it possible to meet monthly charting requirements and create finished quality charts directly from the macro environment. You can create a whole series of chart templates. Because their names will be recorded in a macro, you won't have to remember them. One macro can create all the charts you need and even save and print them as well.

A Macro That Displays Column Chart Options

The Gallery menu offers a graphics display of the various options for each chart type. This feature is helpful because sometimes you need to see your data displayed in several ways before you can decide which option you want.

The data used in this example is presented in figure 6.11. Information on four regional divisions of a company is included. Profit figures for each region are shown by year, and the numbers indicated are in thousands of dollars. The macro shown in figure 6.12 can provide in the chart some of this descriptive information. You will need to add other information later, such as the labels *DIVISION PROFITS* and *THOUSANDS*.

The macro systematically presents a "picture" of the data, using each Gallery option for a chart type—in this case, a column chart. Although you can alter the timing, each sample is left on the screen for approximately 10 seconds before the next sample is provided. A screen message tells you which of the 8 options is being shown.

Notice that the beginning of the Column_Macro (fig. 6.12) does not contain a command for selecting cells for charting. For this particular macro, you must preselect the cells before you begin. Nor does the macro contain code to check the number of areas (ranges) selected. You may want to add these instructions when you duplicate the macro.

As you review the macro, notice the functions in the first few macro lines. The first instruction, ECHO(FALSE), turns off screen updating. Some screen refreshing still will be evident as new windows are requested, but the ECHO function should reduce this problem. Because using an iterative process is better than duplicating the code

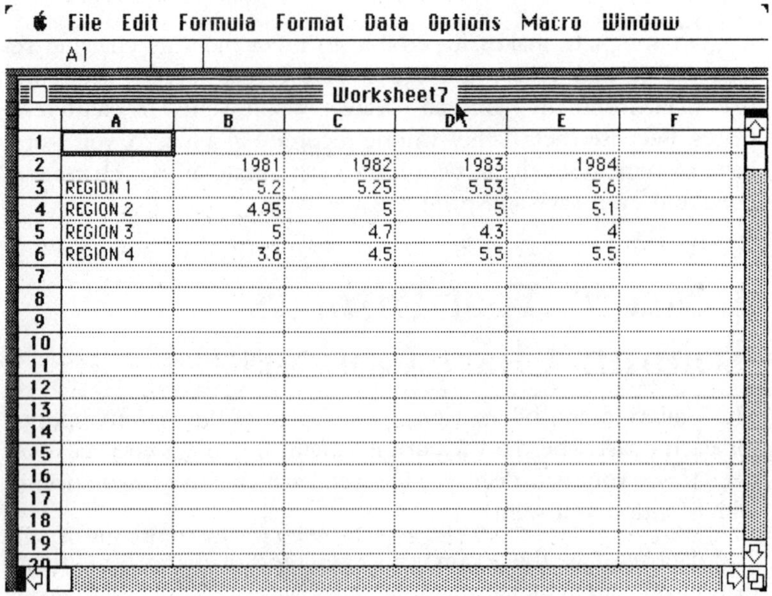

	A	B	C	D	E	F
1						
2		1981	1982	1983	1984	
3	REGION 1	5.2	5.25	5.53	5.6	
4	REGION 2	4.95	5	5	5.1	
5	REGION 3	5	4.7	4.3	4	
6	REGION 4	3.6	4.5	5.5	5.5	

Fig. 6.11. Data for the column chart.

	A
1	**Column_Macro**
2	=ECHO(FALSE)
3	=SET.NAME("COUNT",1)
4	=NEW(2)
5	=MOVE(11,45)
6	=SIZE(491,218)
7	=LEGEND(TRUE)
8	=NEW(1)
9	=SIZE(491,72)
10	=MOVE(13,266)
11	=DISPLAY(FALSE,FALSE,FALSE)
12	=SELECT(!A1:A2)
13	=STYLE(TRUE,FALSE)
14	=SAVE.AS("Message",1)
15	**Top_Loop**
16	=ACTIVATE("Message")
17	=SELECT(!A1)
18	=FORMULA(" This is option "&TEXT(COUNT,"00")&" from the gallery")
19	=SELECT(,"R[1]C")
20	=FORMULA(" of column charts")
21	=C15()
22	=SET.NAME("COUNT",COUNT+1)
23	=IF(COUNT>8,GOTO(Choose))
24	=ACTIVATE("Chart13")
25	=GALLERY.COLUMN(COUNT)
26	=GOTO(Top_Loop)
27	**Choose**
28	=INPUT("What gallery option do you wish to use? Enter the option number. ",1)
29	=ACTIVATE("Col_Chart")
30	=GALLERY.COLUMN(A28)
31	=MOVE(11,42)
32	=SIZE(490,293)
33	=RETURN()

Fig. 6.12. The Gallery column chart options macro.

for each option, a counter is initialized to 1 in A3. In A4, a new chart window is selected with the NEW function; a *type* of 2 tells Excel to select a chart window.

This new chart window will be in the traditional location, a little below the active window. And the chart window will be much smaller than the screen. If you plan to display your data in a full-sized window, then the Gallery column chart options should be used with a full-sized display.

When you are not using a macro, you create a full-sized display by moving the upper left corner of the window and dragging the title bar. With a macro, however, you can use the MOVE function to specify the upper left corner of the window and the SIZE function to specify the size of the window.

When you use the MOVE function in a macro, you must specify the exact location for the upper left corner of the window. In cell A5 of the Column_Macro, the first argument for the MOVE function indicates that the window's upper left corner will be in position 11 from the left edge of the screen. (There are a total of 512 horizontal positions, and the distance from top to bottom is 342 positions.) The second argument for MOVE specifies position 45 from the top of the screen. If you create your macro by using the Recorder, you can focus on where you want the window without having to calculate a numeric location.

Like window placement, window size can be established through the macro. If you use the Recorder, you can establish the window's size by pulling or pushing on the size boxes at the lower right corner of the window. If you don't use the Recorder, you need to specify the exact size of the window with the SIZE function. Like MOVE, SIZE operates with exact x- and y-coordinates. SIZE does not affect the placement of the window, only its total width and height. From edge to edge, the total width cannot exceed 512, just as for window placement. Because the Column_Macro does not place the upper left corner of the window in position 1, position 512, for example, would be impractical for the width of the window because the right edge of the screen would be out of view. In this macro, then, the choice for width is 491 (A6). For the sample macro, this number (which may appear to be a somewhat random choice) was entered with the Recorder, based on the movement of the size boxes for the window.

The height of the screen can never be the full window height of 342. The formula bar at the top of the screen takes up 39 positions, leaving just 303 positions from below the formula bar to the bottom of the screen. Because the upper left corner of the window began at position 45 (a few positions below the formula bar), a position of 303 would put the bottom of the window out of view. In this macro, therefore, the choice for height is 218 (A6). This number is smaller than the limit allowed, thus saving room for a message area at the bottom of the screen.

If you plan to use a legend with your final selection, you should add a legend to each display so that you can get the full effect of each Gallery column chart option. In the macro, a legend is requested with LEGEND(TRUE) in A7. The *logical* value of TRUE indicates that you want a legend, whereas FALSE means that you do not want a legend.

A message window keeps track of which Gallery column chart option is being displayed. This window is a small worksheet window, placed at the bottom of the screen, without column headings and grid lines.

To create the message window, you use the NEW function, as indicated in A8. A *type* of 1 specifies a worksheet window. In this example, the message window is given the same width (491) as that of the chart window. The height of the message window is 72. If you add the height of the message window (72) and the height of the chart window (218), you can see that 290 positions of a possible 303 are used.

The message window will begin in position 11 (horizontally), which is the same position in which the left side of the chart window begins. The message window will begin 266 positions from the top so that it will appear at the bottom of the screen.

Any new worksheet window automatically displays column headings and grid lines. In the message window, the presence of such extraneous information may be confusing to users of the macro. To change these options, you include the DISPLAY function (A11). This function has three arguments, all of which are FALSE in this macro. The first one controls the display of formulas or their results. FALSE indicates that formulas will not be displayed. The second argument controls the display of grid lines. FALSE removes grid lines. The last argument determines whether column headings will be present in the display. FALSE eliminates the column headings.

The message will be placed in cells A1 and A2 of the new window. Even though the length of the message will cause the display to extend across other cells, the characteristics of the cells in which the message is entered (A1 and A2) will control the display. In the Column_Macro, the two cells to contain the message are selected in A12 with the SELECT function. The STYLE function in A13 controls the style. You can highlight the message at the bottom of the screen by using the bold style. The two arguments of the STYLE function are *bold* and *italic*. Because *bold* is the first argument, TRUE indicates that the text entered will be in boldface. FALSE for the second option indicates that italic will not be used.

The next macro instruction deals with Excel's use of a different name whenever a new file is requested. When you run the macro, for example, the message window may indicate Worksheet7. At another time, the window may indicate Worksheet1 or Worksheet20. You cannot solve this problem by using the Next (Command-N) and Previous (Shift-Command-M) window options, however, because this would mean that you would need to alternate between the chart and worksheet windows, and you may still have other opened windows on the screen.

The solution is always to assign the same names to your windows (that is, your files). You can delete these file names, if you like, when you have finished using the macro. This way, the file names will not be present when the macro is used again. Be sure to assign names you will not be using for other files you create. The message window will be saved under the name Message. Notice that this name must be enclosed in quotation marks in the SAVE.AS function in A14. In this example, the *type* is 1 for Normal. A *type* of 2 here would indicate the SYLK format; a *type* of 3, text; and a *type* of 4, WKS.

To prevent the duplication of instructions for each Gallery column chart option, the iterative instructions are grouped together in the macro. Because Column is the default chart type, the first Gallery column chart option is selected automatically, and the first column chart is created before the beginning of the loop. The other column chart options, however, must be placed inside the loop.

The label Top_Loop appears in cell A15. The first instruction in the loop is the ACTIVATE function (A16). The name Message is used because the message window is where the description of the Gallery column chart option will appear. Although on this first iteration, this window is already the active window, on subsequent iterations, that won't be the case, and the instruction in A16 will be required. The presence of this instruction on the first pass does not cause any difficulty—only the execution of an instruction that does not accomplish anything.

In A17 of the loop, the SELECT function selects the first cell in the message window. The FORMULA function that follows places a message in that cell. This message consists of a fixed portion and a variable portion. The fixed portion of the message has two parts: *This is option* and *from the gallery*. The variable portion of the message is the column chart option to be shown. This option value is stored in the loop counter, COUNT. Because the option is a numeric value, it must be used with the TEXT function before the option value can be combined with the two fixed text variables. The next cell is then selected (A19), and the rest of the message is placed on the second line of the message window. The FORMULA function in A20 will enter the rest of the fixed message: *of column charts*. This second line can be entered as a text value because it won't be combined with numeric data.

Cell A21 contains a subroutine call, and the subroutine to be executed begins in cell C15. The instructions for the subroutine are shown in figure 6.13. In any subroutine, instructions are executed, in order, until a RETURN function is encountered. This function then causes control to be given to the calling macro (specifically, to the statement following the call). In the macro in figure 6.12, control is returned to cell A22.

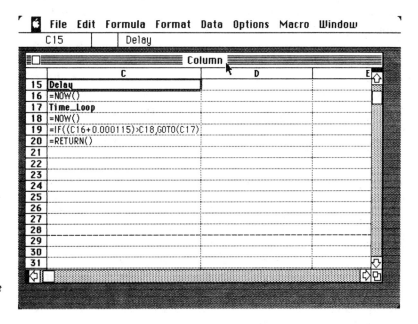

Fig. 6.13. A subroutine that creates a time delay.

A subroutine call differs from a branch with a GOTO because with a call, control is returned automatically. The concept of a subroutine call, discussed in Chapter 2, is used often in macros. One advantage of a subroutine call is that many macros can share the same subroutine. If a GOTO were used, the returning branch would have to be to one particular location. With a subroutine call, Excel keeps track of where control is returned after the macro code executes.

As the subroutine's label (C15) indicates, the purpose of the subroutine is to create a delay. Without the delay, each of the eight column chart options would flash on the screen so fast that you wouldn't have a chance to see them. Suppose that you want the subroutine to generate a 10-second delay before control returns to the calling macro and another column chart option is placed on the screen. In generating the 10-second delay, the subroutine first obtains the current date and time with the NOW function (C16). Although you are interested in only the decimal portion of the number, you don't need to separate the two components. Cell C17 begins the loop, which will be executed until the required amount of time has elapsed.

If you think about how Excel stores time, you will see how any amount of time can be represented. The number 1 represents 24 hours. Therefore, .5 is 12 hours, and .25 is 6 hours. As you continue to divide, you will find that 1 second can be represented by .0000115, and 10 seconds by .000115. You can determine any amount of time you want by calculating its decimal representation. For example, suppose that the date is April 25, 1986, and the time is 2:17:57 p.m. If you place =NOW( ) in a cell at this time, Excel will display 30065.595798611. The whole number portion of the number represents the date, and the decimal portion represents the time. By selecting either a Date or a Time format, you can determine whether the whole or decimal portion of the number controls the display.

The Delay subroutine obtains the time twice with each pass through the loop. The IF function in cell C19 sets up a condition. The second time, which is stored in C18, will be compared to the time in C16, and .000115 will be added to the time in C18. If the time in C16 plus 10 seconds is greater than the time in C18, then the loop will continue. As soon as the time in C16 is not greater, the required delay has elapsed, and the RETURN function in C20 will be executed. The RETURN ends only the called macro (the Delay subroutine), not the calling macro (the Column_Macro). Control is then returned to A22 in the calling macro.

After the delay has elapsed, the next column chart option can be placed on the screen. For this step, the counter will be incremented. COUNT is increased with the SET.NAME function in A22. The IF function in A23 will check to see whether COUNT has exceeded the limit of 8. If COUNT has exceeded 8, control is passed to the Choose subroutine in A27. But if COUNT is still within the acceptable range, the chart window will be activated. The next column chart option is then requested in A25 with the GALLERY.COLUMN function and a *type* specified by COUNT.

Control is then passed to the top of the loop (A26). A new message, which describes the current column chart option, is displayed in the lower window. The Delay subroutine is again called, and each option is allowed equal time on the screen.

If you decide which column chart option is most appropriate for your data before you finish viewing all the options, you can interrupt the macro by pressing the Command key and holding it while pressing the period (.) key. (You can use the Command-period sequence to stop any macro.) Then you can use the Gallery menu to make your selection by choosing the option you want.

If you allow the macro to display all eight options, it will ask you to select the one you want after you have seen all the possibilities. The number you supply will be used for the last GALLERY.COLUMN function. Based on your choice, a new column chart will be created.

You can close the Message and preview windows and delete these files from the disk until the macro runs again. This cleanup process is required if you are going to use the same macro again. Otherwise, the file names will remain on your disk, and the opened windows from the last execution may remain on the screen. A second execution of the macro therefore will fail.

Before executing your macro, you will want to remember to name the macro with Define Name. The section names Top_Loop and Choose also should be named, but you will not have to check the Command option for them. You must use the Formula Define Name command to place the range name Top_Loop in the proper cell, which allows branching to this location.

You can alter the Column_Macro by including reminders to add a title or other enhancements. Although the macro cannot actually add the enhancements, a reminder on the screen can help you remember to add them before the chart is printed.

You also might want to change the macro so that it can handle a Gallery preview for all types of charts. You include at the beginning of the macro an INPUT function, allowing for the selection of the chart type. Depending on the type you select, you could set a maximum value for COUNT. In this way, one macro can provide a quick preview of your data, using all 42 types of charts.

A Macro That Creates
Four Pie Charts on the Screen

Excel's chart environment is flexible enough to allow you to create a number of charts on the screen at once. You may want to present, through a series of pie charts, "snapshots" of business operations. Creating several of these charts on the screen lets you provide a glimpse of the company's results and also minimize the number of screens or pages each manager must review. The macro in this section will create four pie charts on the screen. Each chart will show the profits for one of four regions during the preceding four years. By putting all four charts on the screen at once, you can make quick comparisons. The data for the pie charts is the same data shown in figure 6.11. The data will be copied to create category names for each series.

The next macro will select the updated data for each chart and copy category names into each chart. Without the copy process, only the first pie chart would contain category names because the names are located only in the row above the information for Region 1. Because the same format will be used for data storage year after year, the Recorder is useful in creating this macro quickly. You should select the Absolute Record command from the Macro menu before you begin recording.

The Pie_Charts macro is long because of many copying, pasting, sizing, and moving instructions required to create four separate charts. If you were to work out an equation for the SIZE and MOVE functions, you could use an iterative loop for part of the macro, but using the Recorder is easier and simpler. The macro is shown in figures 6.14A and 6.14B. Refer to these figures as you read the following discussion of how the macro works.

The macro begins by selecting the cells for the first pie chart (A2). A new chart window is then selected (A3), and the data in the cells is initially displayed in a column chart. The next instruction, in A4, changes the chart type to a pie chart. Then a legend is added with the LEGEND function and an argument of TRUE (A5). The sixth pie chart option is selected in A6. This option adds a percentage for each pie slice. The chart window is moved and sized appropriately (A7 and A8) so that it will occupy the upper left quadrant on the screen.

At this point, the worksheet containing the data for the charts is no longer active. The worksheet must be reactivated (A9) for the selection of the second data series. So that the macro can use the category names to create the second and subsequent charts, these names and the data values must be copied into contiguous rows. First, the categories in row 2 are copied (A10 through A13) and then the values below them (A14 through A17). After the COPY and PASTE operations are completed, the macro requests a second chart file with the NEW function (A19). Because the earlier macro instructions affected only the first chart window, the chart type must be specified again (A20) and a legend added (A21). The sixth pie chart option is selected again (A22). This second chart is moved to the upper right quadrant of the screen. Half the macro's work is now completed.

The Pie_Charts macro will create the remaining two chart windows in the same manner. First, the COPY and PASTE operations are per-

	A
1	Pie_Charts
2	=SELECT("R2C1:R3C5")
3	=NEW(2)
4	=MAIN.CHART.TYPE(5)
5	=LEGEND(TRUE)
6	=GALLERY.PIE(6)
7	=MOVE(9,43)
8	=SIZE(249,161)
9	=ACTIVATE("Worksheet7")
10	=SELECT("R2C1:R2C5")
11	=COPY()
12	=SELECT("R8C1")
13	=PASTE()
14	=SELECT("R4C1:R4C5")
15	=COPY()
16	=SELECT("R9C1")
17	=PASTE()
18	=SELECT("R8C1:R9C5")
19	=NEW(2)
20	=MAIN.CHART.TYPE(5)
21	=LEGEND(TRUE)
22	=GALLERY.PIE(6)
23	=MOVE(191,45)
24	=SIZE(241,160)
25	=MOVE(259,44)
26	=ACTIVATE("Worksheet7")
27	=SELECT("R2C1:R2C5")
28	=COPY()
29	=SELECT("R11C1")
30	=PASTE()
31	=SELECT("R5C1:R5C5")
32	=COPY()
33	=SELECT("R12C1")
34	=PASTE()
35	=SELECT("R11C1:R12C5")
36	=NEW(2)
37	=MAIN.CHART.TYPE(5)
38	=LEGEND(TRUE)
39	=GALLERY.PIE(6)
40	=MOVE(9,43)
41	=SIZE(249,167)
42	=MOVE(10,174)
43	=SIZE(254,147)
44	=MOVE(10,196)
45	=SIZE(246,142)
46	=ACTIVATE("Worksheet7")
47	=SELECT("R2C1:R2C5")
48	=COPY()

Fig. 6.14A. A macro that creates four pie charts on the screen.

	A
49	=SELECT("R14C1")
50	=PASTE()
51	=SELECT("R6C1:R6C5")
52	=COPY()
53	=SELECT("R15C1")
54	=PASTE()
55	=SELECT("R14C1:R15C5")
56	=NEW(2)
57	=MAIN.CHART.TYPE(5)
58	=LEGEND(TRUE)
59	=GALLERY.PIE(6)
60	=MOVE(11,43)
61	=SIZE(246,159)
62	=MOVE(258,177)
63	=SIZE(245,150)
64	=MOVE(259,189)
65	=ACTIVATE("Chart1")
66	=ACTIVATE("Chart2")
67	=ACTIVATE("Chart3")
68	=RETURN()

Fig. 6.14B. A macro that creates four pie charts on the screen.

formed. Then the adjacent cells containing categories and values are selected before a new chart file is requested (A36 and A56). Once each chart file is available, format changes can be made in terms of the type, style, and legend. The third chart is moved to the third quadrant of the screen, and the fourth chart is moved to the fourth quadrant.

After all four charts have been created, the last one will be on the screen, overlaying Worksheet7, which contains the data for the charts. The other three charts are activated one at a time (A65 through A67). The final result shows all four pie charts on the screen. A screen dump will produce an image of the four charts, as shown in figure 6.15. Just press the Caps Lock key and then Shift-Command-4.

The Pie_Charts macro uses Chart1, Chart2, Chart3, and Chart4 for file names. These names always are the first four chart file names generated by Excel during a session. If you run this macro a second time during a session, this feature will be a limitation because Excel will generate files with the names Chart5 through Chart8. The macro for a combination chart, which is given later in this chapter, provides a method for overcoming this limitation by saving the charts under predetermined names.

Without the Pie_Charts macro, the process of creating and displaying four charts would be quite tedious to duplicate. Using the macro, you can produce multichart screens with just one key sequence. By expanding this idea, you can create a series of charts of some other

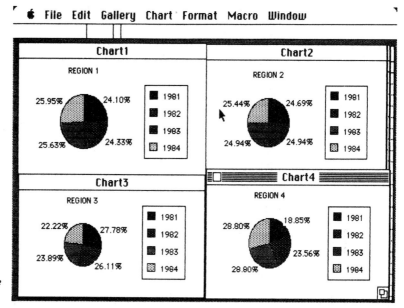

Fig. 6.15. The result of the Pie_Charts macro.

type that may be more appropriate in recapping your monthly results. Whatever chart type you choose, a macro can help provide a
quick look at the pulse of your organization.

A Macro That Combines Data for a Line Chart

At times, you may not want to separate your data into a series of
charts on your worksheet. You may prefer to group several sets of
numbers and present one chart summarizing the results. Perhaps
you already have the summary totals on your worksheet, or you may
need to calculate them. You can create a macro that will calculate
the totals, if needed, and produce a line chart showing the results.
For this example, the worksheet data appears at the top of figure
6.16. Figure 6.17 contains the Add_Lines macro, which produced
the line chart (at the bottom of fig. 6.16) showing combined
monthly total sales for three regions.

Because this macro is designed for a specific worksheet, you will
want to select Absolute Record from the Macro menu and record
the macro by using Set and Start Recorder. Using the Recorder will
save you some time in creating the macro.

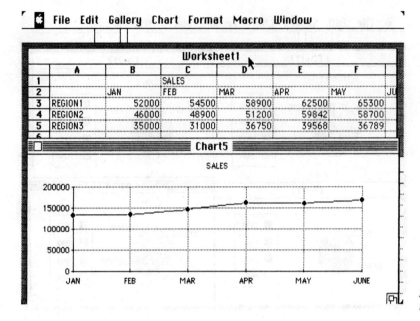

Fig. 6.16. Worksheet data and the completed line chart.

	A
1	Add_Lines
2	=SELECT("R2C2:R2C7")
3	=COPY()
4	=SELECT("R7C2")
5	=PASTE()
6	=SELECT("R1C3")
7	=COPY()
8	=SELECT("R8C2")
9	=PASTE()
10	=SELECT("R8C3")
11	=FORMULA("=SUM(R[-5]C:R[-3]C)")
12	=COPY()
13	=SELECT("R8C3:R8C7")
14	=PASTE()
15	=SELECT("R7C2:R8C7")
16	=NEW(2)
17	=MAIN.CHART.TYPE(4)
18	=GALLERY.LINE(5)
19	=MOVE(11,42)
20	=SIZE(490,293)
21	=RETURN()

Fig. 6.17. A macro that combines data values and creates a line chart.

Now examine the macro in figure 6.17. First, the instructions in A2 through A7 copy the category names to a cell so that they will be adjacent to the summary figures to be added. If you want to include additional series in your chart, you can copy the data for Region 1 to this area, in front of the totals. This way, you will be able to include a legend if you later add more series to the chart. The functions in A6 through A9 handle this copy process.

Next, the macro adds all the sales totals. In A10, R8C2 is the cell selected for the first total. The formula is entered with the FORMULA function in A11. This formula then is copied to the other cells in row 8 where the formula will be used again.

The row containing the results and the preceding row containing the category names are selected in A15. A new chart file is requested (A16), and a line chart option is selected (A17). Cell A18 requests a Gallery line chart with the fifth format option. The line chart is then moved to the upper left corner (A19) and enlarged to fill the screen (A20).

Although the line chart is similar to other charts discussed in the chapter, this chart and the macro used to create it illustrate how you can combine worksheet features into a macro in order to create a chart. The preliminary worksheet steps that combine the data are an integral part of creating the chart, but they are not part of Excel's chart environment commands because they copy and combine data on the worksheet.

A Macro That Creates a Combination Chart

Excel offers a chart type called Combination, which combines two different chart formats on one chart. You need at least two data series for a combination chart. The first series is shown in the first chart, the second in the overlay chart. The basic combinations available are the following: (1) and (2) column charts with line chart overlays (the first option is in reverse video), (3) two line charts with interdependent scales, and (4) an area chart with a column chart overlay. You can obtain any of these combinations by selecting Gallery Combination and then choosing a combination chart option between 1 and 4, corresponding to the particular format you want.

Figure 6.18 contains a macro that presents worksheet data in a combination chart. The data used to create this chart is shown in figure 6.19. The completed chart is shown in figure 6.20. Refer to these figures for the discussion that follows.

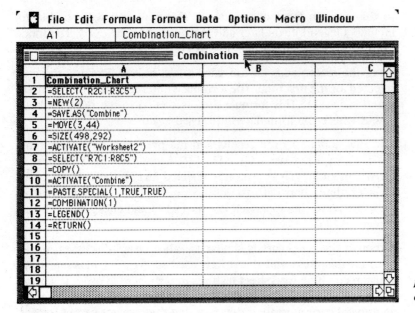

```
 ** File  Edit  Formula  Format  Data  Options  Macro  Window
    A1                   Combination_Chart

 ═══════════════════════════ Combination ═══════════════════════
            A                         B                    C
 1  Combination_Chart
 2  =SELECT("R2C1:R3C5")
 3  =NEW(2)
 4  =SAVE.AS("Combine")
 5  =MOVE(3,44)
 6  =SIZE(498,292)
 7  =ACTIVATE("Worksheet2")
 8  =SELECT("R7C1:R8C5")
 9  =COPY()
 10 =ACTIVATE("Combine")
 11 =PASTE.SPECIAL(1,TRUE,TRUE)
 12 =COMBINATION(1)
 13 =LEGEND()
 14 =RETURN()
 15
 16
 17
 18
 19
```

Fig. 6.18. A macro that creates a combination chart.

```
 ** File  Edit  Formula  Format  Data  Options  Macro  Window
    A1

 ═══════════════════════════ Worksheet2 ════════════════════════
            A             B          C          D          E
 1
 2                      1986       1987       1988       1989
 3  PRODUCT 1 SALES    $3,500     $3,815     $3,900     $4,200
 4
 5
 6
 7                      1986       1987       1988       1989
 8  PROD 1 DIRECT SALES $1,800     $2,100     $2,200     $2,800
 9
 10
 11
 12
 13
 14
 15
 16
 17
 18
 19
```

Fig. 6.19. Data for the combination chart.

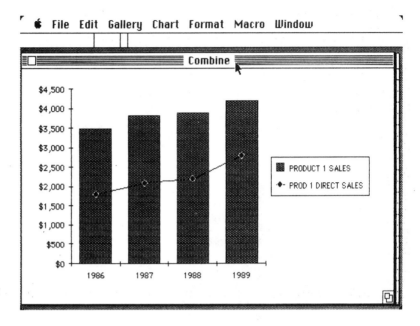

Fig. 6.20. The completed combination chart.

Because the data series used for the chart are not adjacent in the worksheet, they must be selected separately. The first data series is selected in cell A2 of the macro, and a new chart file is requested in A3. The chart file is saved as Combine (A4). The functions in A5 and A6 enlarge the chart to screen size. Next, because the chart file is on the screen, the worksheet is reactivated (A7). The second data series is then selected in A8 and copied to the activated chart file with COPY (A9) and PASTE.SPECIAL (A11). Both data series are shown as column charts, Excel's default, until you change the layout option. Finally, in A12, the COMBINATION function with a *type* of 1 specified causes the first data series to remain in column format, but the second data series to appear as a line chart overlay.

A Macro That Creates an Overlay Chart

Although Excel provides four combination chart options, you can alter the overlay chart so that the resulting combination will be different from any of the options provided. You can create a macro that uses the MAIN.CHART.TYPE and OVERLAY.CHART.TYPE functions to produce an overlay chart to your exact specifications.

Suppose that you want a combination chart consisting of an area chart and a line chart overlay. Figure 6.21 shows an example of this combination, and figure 6.22 presents one macro strategy for creating the chart. This macro is similar to the one in the previous section.

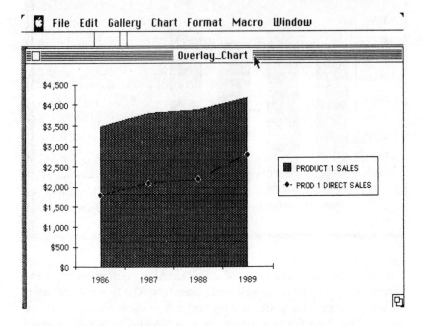

Fig. 6.21. The overlay chart.

```
 File  Edit  Formula  Format  Data  Options  Macro  Window
        A1              Overlay_Chart
                             Overlay
                         A                    B
 1   Overlay_Chart
 2   =SELECT("R2C1:R3C5")
 3   =NEW(2)
 4   =SAVE.AS("Overlay_Chart")
 5   =MAIN.CHART.TYPE(1)
 6   =ACTIVATE("Worksheet2")
 7   =SELECT("R7C1:R8C5")
 8   =COPY()
 9   =ACTIVATE("Overlay_Chart")
10   =PASTE.SPECIAL(1,TRUE,TRUE)
11   =OVERLAY.CHART.TYPE(5)
12   =SIZE(495,296)
13   =LEGEND()
14   =RETURN()
15
16
17
18
19
20
```

Fig. 6.22. A macro that creates an overlay chart.

The first data series is selected in cell A2, and a new chart file is requested in A3. The chart is saved as Overlay_Chart (A4) in order to prevent the problem of Excel's using a new chart name each time the macro is executed. An area chart is then selected with the MAIN.CHART.TYPE function and a *type* of 1 (A5). The worksheet is reactivated (A6) just as it was for the combination macro. Next, a second data series is selected (A7) and copied into the chart with PASTE.SPECIAL (A8 through A10). At this point, both series are displayed as area charts. The second series is converted to a line chart with the OVERLAY.CHART.TYPE function and a *type* of 5 (A11). The SIZE function in A12 makes the window larger in order to display the chart in full screen size. A LEGEND function is found in A13.

As you can see, this approach is almost identical to using the COM-BINATION function except that here you have more flexibility. With either approach, the data series will be split evenly between the two charts. If you have an odd number of data series, the first, or main, chart will show the extra series.

A Macro That Presents
a Slide Show

The charts created by Excel are of professional quality. If you have access to some extra monitors or a large projection device, you may want to consider using Excel charts to present a "slide show" for your next management meeting. While you are making your pre-sentation, you won't want to be concerned with the logistics of the slide display. You can create an Excel macro that will automatically display the slides at fixed intervals.

A macro that can handle this task is shown in figures 6.23A and 6.23B. The macro enables you to select the chart files you want to use each time you use the macro. This approach is flexible but re-quires that you reselect the chart files each time the macro is run.

Two counters are required for the Slide_Show macro. One counter will be incremented each time a slide is selected. The other counter will be incremented each time a slide is displayed. The two counters will ensure that you do not attempt to display more slides than you have selected. The counter for the slides selected is named COUNT, and the counter for the slides displayed is named CHART. These counters are initialized in A2 and A3.

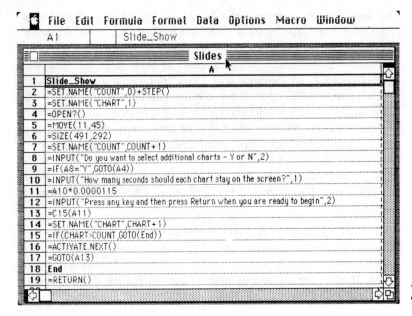

Fig. 6.23A. A macro that creates
a slide-show presentation.

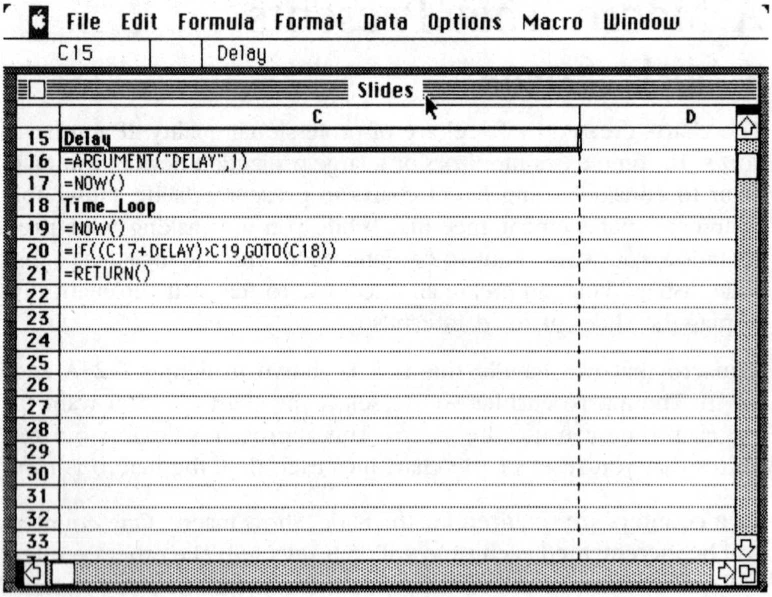

Fig. 6.23B. A macro that creates
a slide-show presentation.

Because the macro allows a new slide selection with each running,
the OPEN?( ) function is used in A4. This form of the function will
display the dialog box that enables you to make your selection. You

can eject a disk or switch drives just as you can by using the Open command from the File menu.

After each file is opened, it will be moved (A5) and sized (A6). Because each chart file is moved to the upper left corner of the screen, a full-sized screen can be specified.

Next, the counter for the number of charts opened is incremented by 1 (A7). Because this counter was initialized at zero, the counter will contain 1 after the first chart is selected.

Beginning in line A8, the macro uses an INPUT statement to determine whether you want to select additional charts. The INPUT prompt requests that you indicate your preference by entering either Y or N. The IF statement in A9 checks for a value of Y. If Y was supplied, control passes to the OPEN function in A4. Because you could respond with Y and then cancel the request to select additional charts, you may want to include additional macro instructions to check for a FALSE in A4 and to skip over the instructions for processing a selection.

After all the charts have been selected, control will pass to the INPUT function in A10. The prompt requests that you supply a time that will determine how long each chart will remain on the screen. The number you enter will be stored as seconds in A10. This number then will be multiplied by Excel's decimal representation for 1 second. Carried to 7 decimal places, this number is .0000115. For a 10-second delay, you would enter *10*, and the multiplication in A11 would generate an appropriate number. For a 30-second delay, you would enter *30*.

The INPUT function in A12 enables you to have everything prepared but not started until you give the signal. You press any key and then press the Return key to start the slide show.

The macro's first step in handling the actual slide presentation is a call to the Delay subroutine (shown in fig. 6.23B). This is the same subroutine used in the Column_Macro, except for one difference. The delay time was fixed in the Column_Macro; in the Slide_Show macro, the operator can select a delay time. Whenever the Slide_Show macro is executed, the statement in A13 passes to the Delay subroutine (C15) the value stored in A11. Because A11 stores Excel's representation of the delay time, the macro can calculate a different delay time whenever the Slide_Show macro is run.

The argument passed to the Delay macro contains the delay time, which is computed in A11 of the calling macro. The time is obtained in C17 and again in C19 of the Delay macro. The macro will keep looping, obtaining the time until it is finally greater than the first time stored in C17 plus the delay time. The macro then proceeds to the RETURN function in C21, which passes control back to A14 of the calling macro.

In A14, the value of the CHART counter is incremented by 1. If CHART exceeds COUNT, the macro will end. If CHART does not exceed COUNT, the next window will be activated, and the macro will branch to A13 for another execution of the delay instruction. This looping will continue until all the charts opened have been displayed the specified number of seconds.

You can modify the Slide_Show macro by using a fixed set of charts in the macro. To do this, you include an OPEN function for each chart you use in the macro. This fixed approach will save time, but you must make a change to the macro whenever you want to add a new slide. This method offers one other advantage. You more easily can control the order of the slide presentation. In other words, you consider the order only once, not each time the selections are made for the macro.

You also might want to consider making two other modifications. You can modify the macro so that multiple charts can be displayed on the screen at once. Also, you can create a small window at the bottom of the screen and use an INPUT function to control when the next chart will be displayed. But even without any additional enhancements, you have a macro that enables you to showcase your charts without printing copies of them for all the meeting participants.

Conclusion

In this chapter, you have learned how to use macros to create many types of charts. You have seen the capabilities of Excel's macro functions at work in the chart environment. And you have learned how to use chart templates to overcome some of the limitations of Excel's Macro Command Language. Now you have the necessary tools for creating any type of chart, or even a slide show, for your next management meeting.

This is the last chapter that covers a specific Excel environment. In the final chapter of this book, you will look at some applications that integrate techniques from all of Excel's environments.

7

Automating Applications

Each of the preceding chapters has focused on one specific aspect of macro use. Individual chapters have concentrated on function macros, macros for worksheet applications, macros for data management, and charting applications with macros. These chapters have introduced you to the basic tools you need to make macros handle all your Excel tasks.

You now are ready to learn how to use macros in complete applications. By studying the examples in this chapter, you will learn techniques and structure that you can use to automate your own applications. This chapter explains how to use macros in four business applications:

- A personnel system
- A security system
- A trend-reporting system
- A budget system

The macros presented here cover all aspects of these four applications, so, in a sense, this chapter is the capstone of the book. The material in this chapter will show you how to integrate the concepts you learned in the other chapters.

sing macros to automate certain applications enables you to delegate Excel tasks to users who are not familiar with Excel's features. With the menu screens and documentation you create for your applications, even novice users can consolidate budgets, print reports, and update data files. Also, operators can perform these tasks without damaging worksheets or the data they contain.

The macros in this chapter have such broad applicability in the business environment that you may have to modify them only slightly before you can use them. But even if your needs differ significantly from those addressed here, you will learn how to accommodate them by using the approaches described in the examples.

A Personnel System

Whether you have 10 employees or 500, you have to maintain and manage information on them. The kind of information you keep depends on your company structure, the number of employee classifications, and the kinds of reports you want to produce. But no matter what kind of information you need, you can create a macro to automate each task you perform. For example, most personnel record-keeping systems add and delete records, sort data, and produce month-end reports. The personnel system you will build in this section performs all 4 of these tasks. To make the system easy to use, you will create menus from which operators can select the tasks they want to perform.

The personnel system created in the examples here has three main components: the Employees database, the Personnel System Menu, and the Personnel_System macro. The Employees database, stored on a worksheet, holds various types of information about the employees in a company. The Personnel System Menu is the menu displayed during the macro's execution to allow the operator to select specific tasks. The Personnel_System macro is designed according to the modular construction method. This method keeps each section of macro code manageable and segregates the macro-processing instructions by functions.

The Personnel_System macro is made up of six subroutines: Menu, Error_Routine, Add_Record, Adjust_Range_For_New_Record, Delete_Record, Sort, and Month_End_Reports. You will see the design and function of each of these subroutines in the sections that follow.

Getting Started

Before entering any macro instructions, you should map out the task you want to accomplish and ensure that you have an acceptable structure for your personnel database. After you determine what database field names you want to use, type them in your worksheet file. You may want to type a record or two into the file at this time to ensure that the layout you have chosen suits your specific needs.

In this example, the worksheet file is called Employees, and the database records and field names have the range name DATA. Figure 7.1 shows part of the Employees file.

	A	B	C	D	E	F	G	H	I
		EMPLOYEE NAME			JOB		DATE OF		DATE OF
2	SS#	LAST	FIRST	LOCATION	CODE	SALARY	HIRE	SEX	LAST EVAL
3	231-99-1237	Harper	Jill	Dallas	18	$42,800	11/28/81	F	2/12/85
4	555-84-8821	Larkins	Jack	Dallas	5	$49,650	1/11/82	M	4/3/85
5	567-78-9983	Henry	Tim	Boston	21	$21,500	8/13/78	M	6/3/85
6	222-98-6641	Bruder	John	Chicago	18	$45,600	9/30/80	M	7/18/85
7	231-71-1269	Reese	Jim	Chicago	4	$12,400	4/24/79	M	11/12/85
8	341-89-7653	Ford	Alice	Boston	5	$48,750	2/5/82	F	11/12/85
9	214-78-6753	Greene	Mary	Dallas	21	$23,450	2/13/85	F	2/1/86
10	198-11-6543	Worth	Paul	Atlanta	21	$19,800	7/19/72	M	2/6/86
11	564-87-3442	Mason	Sue	Atlanta	18	$38,900	12/12/75	F	2/15/86
12	328-65-7892	Perkins	Pete	Chicago	23	$15,600	1/7/86	M	3/14/86

Fig. 7.1. A portion of the Employees database.

The second step is creating the Personnel System Menu screen, which you enter in a worksheet file called Emp _ Menu (see fig. 7.2). This menu will be displayed for the operator when the macro is executed. Displayed along with the menu will be an Input box that the operator will use to select the menu option (see fig. 7.3).

When you create the menu, you will want to be sure to enter the menu options at the top of the screen. This is because the macro will cause the Input box to appear near the center of the screen, and the Input box therefore may cover part or all of the menu. If you place the menu at the top of the screen, the Input box may hide part of the menu options, but will not cover the menu completely. The operator at least will be able to tell that a menu is there and may have to drag the box down in order to display the complete menu.

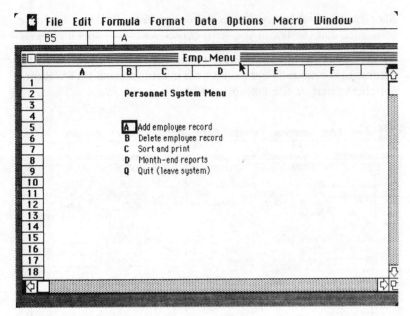

Fig. 7.2. The Personnel System Menu.

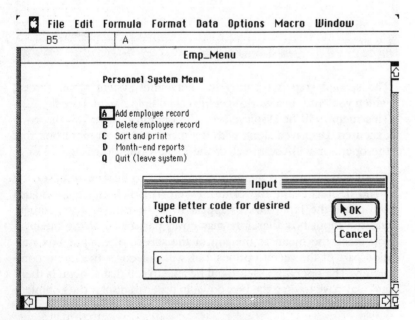

Fig. 7.3. The Personnel System Menu with the Input box overlay.

Processing the Menu Selection

The macro is called Personnel_System. You type this name in cell A1 of the macro sheet and then issue the Formula Define Name command to define the name. The macro is modular in construction, with each section labeled separately. Because the macro is long and is used one routine at a time, each section is discussed separately.

The first section is labeled Menu, which refers to the menu-processing instructions the section contains (see figs. 7.4A and 7.4B). The first instruction in this section activates the Emp_Menu window (A3). ACTIVATE assumes that the document is currently open. If you want, you can add an instruction that opens the file before the ACTIVATE statement.

	A	B
1	Personnel_System	
2	Menu	
3	=ACTIVATE("Emp_Menu")	Display menu
4	=INPUT("Type letter code for desired action",2)	Accept menu choice
5	=IF(A4="A",A18())	Call Add_Record
6	=IF(A4="B",A40())	Call Delete_Record
7	=IF(A4="C",A55())	Call Sort
8	=IF(A4="D",A63())	Call Month_End_Reports
9	=IF(A4="Q",GOTO(A13))	Go to Closing_Routine
10	=IF(A4="Match",GOTO(A3))	Check whether already processed
11	=C10("Invalid menu selection")	Call Error_Routine
12	=GOTO(A4)	Branch to top for next request

Fig. 7.4A. The Personnel_System Menu subroutine.

	A	B
13	Closing_Routine	
14	=ACTIVATE("Employees")	Activate Employees
15	=SAVE.AS("Employees",1)	Save file
16	=RETURN()	

Fig. 7.4B. The Personnel_System Menu subroutine.

After the Personnel System Menu appears, the INPUT statement in cell A4 displays the Input box that gives the operator instructions and accepts input. The instructions prompt the operator to enter the menu letter code. The macro's INPUT statement specifies a *type* of 2, which means that the input must be text. The operator's input is stored in cell A4.

A series of logical IF statements examines the result of the INPUT instruction. If an A is stored in A4, the subroutine Add_Record, which begins in A18, is called. If the value B is stored in A4, the subroutine Delete_Record, which begins in A40, is called. If a C is stored in A4, the subroutine Sort, which begins in A55, is called. If a D is stored in A4, control passes to the subroutine beginning in cell A63. That subroutine produces the month-end reports.

The last valid menu option is Q for Quit. If A4 contains this value, the macro branches to a closing routine. With the other options, calls to subroutines rather than branches are used. In this way, the operator can select additional menu options.

When the macro reaches the instruction in A10, one of two conditions exists. Either the macro has processed the selection of one of the values A through D, or the operator has entered an invalid value. Altering the value of A4 to *Match* in each of the subroutines tells the program that a match already has been found. If A4 contains Match, the macro branches to A3. Emp_Menu is reactivated, and additional input is requested. The macro then continues processing menu selections until the operator presses Q to stop the macro.

Processing Errors

If the operator enters an invalid menu selection (A4 is not equal to Match), the macro executes the instruction in A11. This instruction calls a subroutine that begins in C10 and passes the argument "Invalid menu selection" to that subroutine (see fig. 7.5). In cell C11, the ARGUMENT statement assigns this argument the label *Message* and indicates that the value must be text (a *type* of 2). The ALERT function in C12 displays an Alert box containing the text stored in Message, thereby warning the operator that the option selected is unacceptable.

	C
10	Error_Routine
11	=ARGUMENT("Message",2)
12	=ALERT(Message,2)
13	=RETURN()

Fig. 7.5. The Error_Routine subroutine.

The last instruction in Error_Routine is a RETURN statement. This returns control to the original macro, to the instruction following the macro call (cell A12).

An advantage of the Error_Routine in cells C10 through C13 is that it can be used for all errors, regardless of their type. While any of the subroutines in the macro can display a message tailored to the specific error, the error-processing code in Error_Routine can stay the same and does not have to be duplicated throughout the macro. Another advantage is that by using a macro call (such as the one in A11) to call the Error_Routine, you don't have to use a GOTO in order to branch back to the macro. Excel keeps track of the location to return to, sparing you this housekeeping chore.

Now that you have examined what happens if the operator makes an invalid menu selection, you can look more closely at subroutines for the valid menu selections. The following sections examine the subroutines that process the options listed on the Personnel System Menu.

Adding Records

Figure 7.6 shows a subroutine named Add_Record, which contains instructions that prompt the operator to enter values. Because the method for entering data is the same for each field, only one example of inputting data is provided. To add data for other fields of your records, you use this method as many times as necessary.

	A	B
18	Add_Record	
19	=A30()	Call routine to adjust range
20	=INPUT("Enter last name",2)	
21	=IF(LEN(A20)<21,GOTO(A24))	
22	=C10("Entry for last name is too long")	Call error routine
23	=GOTO(A20)	
24	=SELECT(INDEX(SELECTION(),1,2))	Select last name field
25	=FORMULA(A20)	
26	=SET.VALUE(A4,"Match")	
27	=RETURN()	

Fig. 7.6. The Add_Record subroutine.

Adjusting the Range

The first task that Add_Record does is call the subroutine shown in figure 7.7. This subroutine adjusts the range assigned to the database records in order to accommodate the new record. As explained in Chapter 5, if the range is not shifted, new records added at the end are not included in the defined range of the database.

This subroutine's label, Adjust_Range_For_New_Record, is in cell A29. Excel does not process the contents of this cell; the label merely acts as documentation. The actual instructions begin in A30.

	A
29	Adjust_Range_For_New_Record
30	=ACTIVATE("Employees")
31	=SELECT(INDEX(!DATA,ROWS(!DATA),0))
32	=INSERT(2)
33	=SELECT(OFFSET(SELECTION(),1,0))
34	=COPY()
35	=SELECT(OFFSET(SELECTION(),-1,0))
36	=PASTE()
37	=SELECT(OFFSET(SELECTION(),1,0))
38	=RETURN()

Fig. 7.7. The subroutine that adjusts the database range for adding a new record.

The first instruction (A30) activates the Employees document. Before you can select a cell for data entry, this document must be active.

The SELECT function in A31 selects the last row of the database. To accomplish this task, SELECT uses two other functions—INDEX and ROWS. INDEX, which has three arguments, references the last row. INDEX's first argument is !DATA, a reference to the range name on the current worksheet. INDEX's second argument is ROWS(!DATA), which selects the row. The row you want is DATA's highest-numbered row because it represents the number of rows that DATA contains. INDEX's third argument is 0, which selects all columns.

A blank row is inserted (A32) while the cells are shifted down to make space for the extra row. The INSERT function's argument, 2, defines the direction of the shift. The last database record is now preceded by a blank row.

Next, the three functions in A33 select the row below the newly inserted row. The SELECT function defines the current selection. Currently, this function references a blank row. The OFFSET function indicates the location of the new selection when compared to the existing one. The first argument of the OFFSET function is the SELECTION function, which provides the reference for the cells currently selected. The second and third arguments for the OFFSET function are for row and column offset. A row offset of 1 specifies one row below the current selection. A column offset of 0 indicates that the same columns referenced in the old selection should be used. Once the row below the newly inserted row is selected, the COPY function in A34 marks the new selection for the copy operation.

The combination of SELECT, OFFSET, and SELECTION in cell A35 specifies the area in which the copied information is placed. This instruction indicates that the columns selected should remain the same, but that the rows selected should be one row above the current selection. PASTE completes the copying process.

Once the last record in the database is copied, the macro selects the record below the current record (A37). You can erase this record if you want, because it is a duplicate of the one above it. Because the copied record will hold the new record, you may decide to leave the existing information and just overwrite this duplicated record with new information. The RETURN that concludes this subroutine returns the macro to the cell following the calling location, cell A20 in Add_Record.

Entering the Data Elements

Once the range has been adjusted to accommodate the new record, the operator can enter individual data elements. Each piece of data is entered separately. Excel checks each entry for validity, then stores it in the appropriate cell. Although the subroutine in figure 7.6 shows instructions for entering only one element, you can repeat the process for each element you want to enter.

Whenever a macro is going to accept an entry from the operator, you first must include an INPUT statement. The *type* you specify can help you screen the values entered. If the *type* is 1, only numeric data is accepted; if the *type* is 2, only text is accepted. By specifying other types, you can flag the entry as valid for arrays, cell addresses, or logical values.

After the INPUT statement, you can add as many error checks as you want. You may want the macro to check the length of the operator's entry. Or, if the entry is coded input, you may want the macro to look up in a lookup table the value entered; in this way, you can check for a valid code or perform a substitution based on the code entered. For example, the operator may enter a 10, which might cause *Accounting Department* to be substituted in the record. If only a few codes are required, the operator easily can learn the appropriate codes. Using codes for data entry can save the operator a significant number of keystrokes.

The Add_Record subroutine prompts the operator to enter a piece of data—in this case, a last name (A20). The statement in cell A21 checks the length of the entry. Any name that does not exceed 20 characters is acceptable. If a name has more than 20 characters, an error occurs; and the code in cell A22, which calls the error subroutine, is executed. (This is the same subroutine that processes menu selection errors.) Then a message appears indicating that the name's length is unacceptable.

After processing the subroutine and displaying the error message, the macro branches back to the INPUT statement and asks the operator to reenter the data. If the entry is acceptable, the FORMULA statement places the data in the active cell.

You can use a similar sequence—INPUT statement, error check, and error processing—to allow the operator to select the next cell and enter the next element. You can enter this sequence for each data element that you want the operator to enter. After those instructions, the macro sets cell A4 to a value of Match, which indicates correct menu selection and processing.

Deleting Records

The record-deleting subroutine, called Delete_Record, begins in cell A40 (see fig. 7.8). This subroutine deletes the record that contains the Social Security number that the operator enters. Although each Social Security number is unique, mistyping or transposing digits is possible. Therefore, the macro takes the precautionary step of displaying the record before deleting it.

	A
40	Delete_Record
41	=INPUT("SS# of record to delete? ",2)
42	=ACTIVATE("Employees")
43	=SELECT(!M1)
44	=FORMULA("SS#")
45	=SELECT(!M2)
46	=FORMULA(A41)
47	=SELECT(!M1:M2)+SET.CRITERIA()
48	=SELECT(!DATABASE)+SET.DATABASE()
49	=DATA.FIND()
50	=INPUT("Delete this record? - Y or N",2)
51	=IF(A50="N",GOTO(A54))
52	=DATA.DELETE()
53	=SET.VALUE(A4,"Match")
54	=RETURN()

Fig. 7.8. The Delete_Record subroutine.

The INPUT statement in A41 stores the Social Security number of the record that the operator wants to delete. Because the number entered by the operator includes hyphens, it is considered text. Therefore, the *type* specified is 2, for text.

The subroutine does not check for errors when the Social Security number is entered. However, you could add a length check similar to the one used in cell A21 of the Add_Record subroutine (see fig. 7.6). After the operator enters the number, the instruction in A42 activates the worksheet that contains the database.

The criteria area is established next. Although part of this work could be done before executing the macro, the criteria area for this example is established within the macro. By including these instructions within the macro, you can allow for your application's particular requirements for search criteria. These applications, for instance, might require a larger criteria area, which you might want to set up permanently in another area of the worksheet. Because this example specifies one specific criterion, the criteria area could be preestablished and only the new criteria value placed into the area with each deletion.

The statement in A43 selects cell M1 of the worksheet to store the field name for the criteria selection. The FORMULA function in cell A44 of the macro enters the field name SS# (for Social Security number) into this worksheet cell. Another FORMULA statement (A46 of the macro) places in M2 of the worksheet the current SS# value entered by the operator. The macro selects both these cells and issues the SET.CRITERIA function to mark them as criteria (A47). Next, the macro selects the database, with its assigned name of DATABASE. This selection is placed in A48 along with the SET.DATABASE command in order to inform Excel of the database's location.

Although deleting the record could be the next step, a DATA.FIND statement has been included first. That statement will display the matching record and ask the operator whether the deletion should be made (A50). This procedure gives the operator a chance to cancel the delete request after viewing the record. Because DATA.FIND slows down the process a little, you will have to consider the trade-off between speed and accuracy in your particular application.

Depending on what answer the operator gives, the macro either continues with or stops the delete operation. If the operator wants to stop, the only step left is to set A4 to Match. If the operator wants to continue, a delete is executed with DATA.DELETE (A52). The criteria and database settings already have been established, so all that is required is the execution of the DELETE function. In both cases, control returns to cell A7 in the Menu section after A4 is set to Match.

Sorting Records

After adding records to a file, the operator may want to print a new copy of the records. Any sequence established for the records before the addition no longer exists because the new records have not been added in sequence. They have been added at the end of the file. Selecting C from the Personnel System menu calls the Sort subroutine and enables the operator to select the sort sequence desired. The operator can print the report in a new sequence each time C is selected from the menu.

Figure 7.9 shows the Sort subroutine. It begins by selecting the preestablished range DATA, which includes data but not field names. Because of the procedure used for adding records, the range DATA expands with each record addition. After this range is selected, the SET.DATABASE function (A57) is executed; this function tells Excel what database range has been chosen.

	A
55	Sort
56	=SELECT(!DATA)
57	=SET.DATABASE()
58	=SORT?()
59	=PRINT(1,,1,1)
60	=SET.VALUE(A4,"Match")
61	=RETURN()

Fig. 7.9. The Sort subroutine.

You make an open-ended sort request by using the question-mark (?) form of the SORT function (A58). A dialog box appears on the screen, which enables the operator to tailor a request to immediate needs. The operator can select one sort-key or several. The macro then prints the sorted records (A59).

As in the other subroutines, the value of A4 is set to Match in order to indicate that a valid menu selection was processed. Control then returns to the Menu subroutine.

Creating Month-End Reports

Creating reports on a monthly basis may involve printing parts of the database, printing the complete database in a fixed sequence, or extracting records according to a specific set of criteria and printing those records. By recording a certain sequence of instructions in a macro, you can ensure that you do not forget a part of the process, such as requesting a sort, before printing. This arrangement also prevents you from making an incorrect selection for a print range. You store the information concerning your monthly report requirements in a macro, which, when executed, follows your specific directions month after month.

Figure 7.10 shows a subroutine that produces month-end reports. The first statement (A64) activates the Employees document. The range DATA is selected (A65), and the database is set to these cells (A66). Because the same sequence of events is required month after month, you do not want to make the operator select the sort sequence. That procedure would introduce an unnecessary margin of error in this particular situation. Therefore, rather than use the question-mark form of SORT described in the preceding section, you include the sort parameters with the instruction (A67).

	A
63	Month_End_Reports
64	=ACTIVATE("Employees")
65	=SELECT(!DATA)
66	=SET.DATABASE()
67	=SORT(1,"R13C9",1)
68	=ROWS(!DATA)
69	=COLUMNS(!DATA)
70	=SELECT(!A1:INDEX(!DATA,A68,A69))
71	=SET.PRINT.AREA()
72	=PAGE.SETUP("EVALUATION DATES","Page &P",0.75,0.75,1,1,TRUE,TRUE)
73	=PRINT(1,,,1,1)
74	=SET.VALUE(A4,"Match")
75	=RETURN()

Fig. 7.10. The subroutine for printing month-end reports.

After the sort, the operator will want to print the newly sequenced report. But first, the print area must be set. This process involves several steps.

First, the macro must specify the end of the report. The ROWS and COLUMNS functions determine the size of the complete database area, which is selected by the SELECT statement in A70. This information is used for setting the print area (A71).

The SELECT statement in A70 of the macro accesses the worksheet data from A1 to the last row and column in DATA. SET.PRINT.AREA (A71) restricts printing to these cells. The PAGE.SETUP command in cell A72 supplies header and footer information as well as margin specifications. And the PRINT function (A73) prints the report.

The macro ends by setting the value in A4 to Match so that, when returning to the calling macro, the macro responds as if a valid menu selection had been processed. When you create your own macro, you will want to duplicate the code from A67 through A73 for the number of reports you plan to create from this document. Naturally, each report may use different columns and sort parameters. When the macro ends, all the month-end reports should be available for the operator's review.

A Security System

An application often encompasses a wide variety of tasks, and you may want to control who performs what tasks. For instance, you may want all system users to be able to perform some tasks, but you may want to permit only one or two individuals to carry out other tasks.

Take the example of a personnel system, which stores information on a firm's employees. You may want to allow all department heads to add all fields to records except salary. Only the head of the Personnel Department should be able to enter or edit the salary.

After records have been added, you may want only Personnel Department employees to be able to make changes to those records, except, again, the salary field. To handle this task, you will have to check the authority of each individual using the system and make available to them only the appropriate capabilities.

The focus of the macro in this section is on a security system. Therefore, the instructions cover the system's security aspects only. A shell for updating salaries, changing records, and adding names of new employees is provided, along with comment instructions.

The first step is establishing a menu (see fig. 7.11). Four levels of menu security appear next to the options. Using Excel's password capability, you can give each of these four levels a specific password. As a user of this protected system, if you can't supply the correct password, you can't access particular menu options.

The menu-processing procedures in this macro differ from those in the last macro. Branching instructions are used rather than subroutine calls. You should use branching instructions rather than subroutine calls if operators will use the application to make only single selections. With this method, after branching to the appropriate subroutine and executing its instructions, the macro ends without branching back to the menu-processing segment.

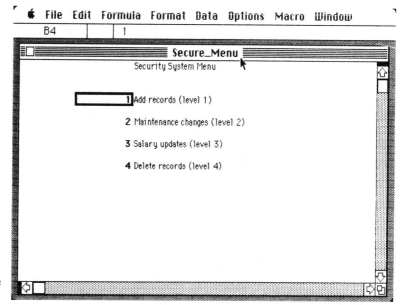

Fig. 7.11. The Security System
Menu.

The four menu options in the macro branch to Add _ Records (A14),
Maintenance (C1), Salary _ Update (C9), and Delete (C17). Figure
7.12 shows the menu-processing instructions that pass control to
these subroutines. An INPUT statement (A3) accepts the menu selection, and one of four IF statements makes the appropriate branch.
If none of the branches is taken, the ALERT function in A8 tells the
operator that an invalid selection was made, and the macro branches
back to cell A3 to request another entry (A9).

*Fig. 7.12. The subroutine that
processes the Security System
Menu selections.*

	A
1	**Process_Menu**
2	=ACTIVATE("Secure_Menu")
3	=INPUT("Enter number of menu option",1)
4	=IF(A3=1,GOTO(A14))
5	=IF(A3=2,GOTO(C1))
6	=IF(A3=3,GOTO(C9))
7	=IF(A3=4,GOTO(C17))
8	=ALERT("Invalid option number - reselect",2)
9	=GOTO(A3)
10	=RETURN()

Adding Records

When this system was designed, a decision was made not to require
that an operator have special authorization to use the record addition

features. Therefore, anyone who uses this system can add records. Although no special authorization is needed, you can think of this function as a level 1 authorization. The features can be accessed by everyone.

The Add_Records subroutine begins in A14, but no code is provided for this particular example (see fig. 7.13). However, the preceding macro model and others throughout the book have addressed record addition, so you can "plug" the code from one of those macros into this system. In this example, Add_Records establishes the shell for the complete application by displaying an Alert message to let you know the code has been executed.

	A
14	Add_Records
15	Macro instructions to add records
16	would be placed at this location.
17	=ALERT("Add routine",1)
18	=RETURN()

Fig. 7.13. The Add_ Records subroutine (with incomplete code).

Maintaining Records

When you use Excel's password features, you need to use separate macros for each authorization level and connect each macro to a particular document. If you want the authorization level to vary from one menu option to another, you need to use a number of Excel macros to allow for the unique passwords. This procedure provides a measure of safety in the event that an individual does not give the correct access code. The file that an individual wants to work with will not appear on the screen until the correct password is given. If the file was allowed to appear, the user could use the Command-period option and access the data outside the control of the macro.

Figure 7.14 shows part of the macro code for the Maintenance subroutine. Maintenance activities require a level 2 password. The Maintenance subroutine uses ECHO(FALSE) to turn off the screen-update capability (C2), then opens the macro sheet named Mac_Main (C3). This sheet contains the macro that changes fields in the personnel database. Because Mac_Main is a separate macro file, you can assign a unique password to this file. The instruction in cell C4 requests that the Change macro in Mac_Main be run. The code for the Change macro begins in A1 in figure 7.15.

	C
1	**Maintenance**
2	=ECHO(FALSE)
3	=OPEN("Mac_Main")
4	=RUN("Mac_Main!Change")
5	=ACTIVATE("Mac_Main")
6	=CLOSE()
7	=RETURN()

Fig. 7.14. The macro code for the Maintenance subroutine.

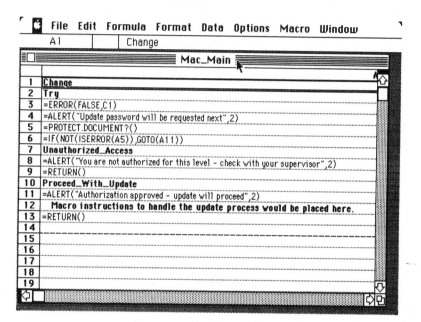

Fig. 7.15. The macro code for checking authorization to make changes.

The Change macro tries to unprotect the worksheet in an effort to verify the operator's security level. If this process fails, the macro ends in an error, with the macro still on the screen. Because you want to retain control and reject the operator's attempted access, you will want to disable Excel's error-checking capability. The instruction in A3 does just that with an ERROR statement that specifies a logical of FALSE. The second argument of the ERROR statement, C1, specifies the location for an error-processing routine if you want to include one. If no error-processing is required, the macro moves to the instruction following the ERROR statement.

If an operator enters an incorrect password, Excel does not stop the macro. (Remember that you turned off Excel's error-checking capability.) Rather, the macro branches to C1, then returns to the statement that follows the branch instruction.

An ALERT instruction is next (A4). This prompts the operator to provide the update password. Because the password structure is organized by menu option rather than operator, the operator must give the appropriate password for each menu task. This mechanism is the only one for informing the operator of the specific password required in this application.

The instruction in A5 is the PROTECT.DOCUMENT function. Because the worksheet is protected, this statement unprotects the document.

When an incorrect password is entered, the error is noted, and the instruction in A6 is executed. If an error exists, this statement proceeds to A7. Cell A7 contains a label, so the next instruction executed is the one in A8. The ALERT statement displays a message telling the operator that the password is invalid, and ends the macro. Control returns to Maintenance, which activates Mac_Main and closes the current sheet.

If the operator enters a correct password, the macro proceeds to A11. A message appears indicating that the update can proceed, and the operator can select a record. To complete the macro, you need to add a section here that opens the file to be updated, handles the update process, and saves and closes the file at the end. (Refer to the Update macro in Chapter 5 as a model for these instructions.)

You should make the update capability menu driven. This method enables you to prevent the salary field from being changed. You don't make the salary update one of the menu options.

The one failure of Excel's password process becomes evident as this macro concludes. The operator must enter a password to reprotect the worksheet. If the operator enters the wrong password, the next operator cannot access the worksheet, even if that operator gives the correct password. Because you must use the question-mark form of the PROTECT.DOCUMENT function in the update section, the only solution is to create your own password-processing routines and not use Excel's capabilities. This issue is discussed further in the section, "Another Approach to Security."

At the end of the Change macro, control returns to Maintenance. That subroutine's last step is to close the macro file.

Updating Salaries

Changing the salary field requires a higher security level than adding records or changing the name or address fields. Initially, if the operator chooses option 3 on the menu, Excel accesses the Salary_Update macro, which begins in cell A9 of figure 7.16. This macro is organized so that the macro for changing the salary field is stored not in Salary_Update, but in a separate macro sheet. Before retrieving this other macro sheet, the Salary_Update macro uses ECHO to turn off the screen-updating feature (C10).

	C
9	Salary_Update
10	=ECHO(FALSE)
11	=OPEN("Mac_Sal")
12	=RUN("Mac_Sal!Updsal")
13	=ACTIVATE("Mac_Sal")
14	=CLOSE()
15	=RETURN()

Fig. 7.16. The Salary_Update subroutine.

Then Salary_Update opens the macro sheet named Mac_Sal (see fig. 7.17). The Updsal macro, which updates salaries, is a duplicate of the Change macro, except that the salary update password, as well as the messages displayed in the Alert boxes, are different.

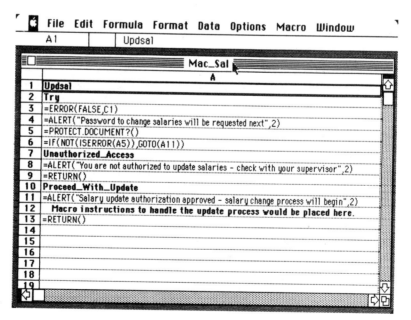

Fig. 7.17. The macro code for checking authorization to change values in the salary field.

Following the ALERT statement (A11), which tells the operator to proceed with the update, you need to add macro instructions that ask the operator to enter the Social Security number of the record to be updated. You can use the FIND technique described in Chapter 5 and copy one of those macro examples into this macro. You will have to alter the instructions to conform to your current file structure.

Just as in the Change macro, after the operator enters the salary update password and completes the update, the macro must remind the operator to enter a password to reprotect the worksheet. In addition, you will want to include macro instructions that save the updated copy of the file and close it.

Deleting Records

Record deletions require the highest security code. This task can be very destructive if made available to the wrong individuals, so you will want to limit its use to one or two people.

Again, the coding requirements parallel those of Maintenance and Salary_Update. After the operator selects the fourth menu option, control passes to the Delete subroutine (see fig. 7.18). Like the other subroutines, this one turns off the screen-updating capability and opens the appropriate macro file. In this example, that file is named Mac_Del and is shown in figure 7.19.

The macro accessed in this file is named Delrec. Before beginning the deletion process, the macro checks the operator's password. If the check fails, the macro ends. The same message and error-checking logic used in Change and Updsal work in this macro. The only difference is that this macro sheet was stored with a different password.

If the operator gives the correct password, the macro continues with the Proceed_With_Update instructions (A10). To complete this

	C
17	Delete
18	=ECHO(FALSE)
19	=OPEN("Mac_Del")
20	=RUN("Mac_Del!Delrec")
21	=ACTIVATE("Mac_Del")
22	=CLOSE()
23	=RETURN()

Fig. 7.18. The Delete subroutine.

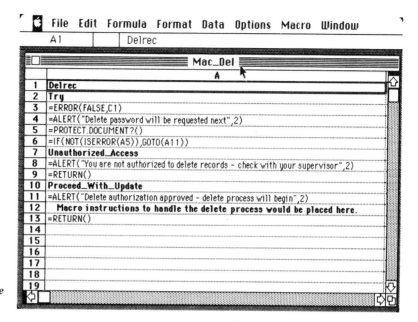

File   Edit   Formula   Format   Data   Options   Macro   Window

| A1 | | Delrec |

Mac_Del

	A
1	Delrec
2	Try
3	=ERROR(FALSE,C1)
4	=ALERT("Delete password will be requested next",2)
5	=PROTECT.DOCUMENT?()
6	=IF(NOT(ISERROR(A5)),GOTO(A11))
7	Unauthorized_Access
8	=ALERT("You are not authorized to delete records - check with your supervisor",2)
9	=RETURN()
10	Proceed_With_Update
11	=ALERT("Delete authorization approved - delete process will begin",2)
12	Macro instructions to handle the delete process would be placed here.
13	=RETURN()
14	
15	
16	
17	
18	
19	

Fig. 7.19. The macro code for checking authorization to delete records.

macro, you need to add instructions here that prompt the operator to enter the Social Security number of the record to be deleted. For this macro, you can use Social Security numbers to find the records, then use those numbers to delete the records. You can use the same code used in earlier examples in this chapter.

The code that processes incorrect passwords in this macro (cells A3 through A9) is the same as that of the other macros in this chapter. The macro's housekeeping instructions also should be the same. Therefore, to save yourself some time, you can use COPY and PASTE to transfer the code from one macro sheet to another. Then you can edit the entries to make any needed alterations.

A Security Precaution

Another technique you can use with this macro and others is to display macro values rather than formulas. This technique prevents the operator from reading the macro, determining what files it accesses, or learning other details about the macro's operation. Figure 7.20 shows an example of a macro protected in this way. The entries TRUE, FALSE, and #VALUE! represent the results of evaluating each macro statement. Alone, these words are meaningless because hundreds of macros could have created this display. Displaying the macro in this way protects the macro by preventing the user from viewing and accessing the macro instructions.

File	Edit	Formula	Format	Data	Options	Macro	Window

A1   Change

Mac_Main

A

1	Change
2	Try
3	TRUE
4	FALSE
5	#VALUE!
6	FALSE
7	Unauthorized_Access
8	FALSE
9	TRUE
10	Proceed_With_Update
11	FALSE
12	Macro instructions to handle the update process would be placed here.
13	TRUE
14	
15	
16	
17	
18	
19	

Fig. 7.20. Macro with formulas hidden.

To protect the macro, choose Options Display and click Formulas so that it is unchecked. Then use the Cell Protection command from the Format menu to set the format of the macro cells as Hidden. Then, if you password-protect the macro by using Options Protect Document, the operator won't be able to see the formulas, even if the operator points to them with the cursor.

Another Approach to Security

The approach used here to design a security system capitalizes on Excel's features. This approach works if security levels control both file updates and access to pieces of information. When an individual tries to access information, the security code on the macro sheet easily can determine whether the individual is authorized and present only the information that the operator is allowed to see. When the inquiry process is finished, the file can be closed. Because the files are not changed, no need exists to save the file back to disk. No danger exists that the operator will enter a different password.

However, when an operator is updating files, that danger does exist. The operator accidentally or deliberately can reprotect the file by using a new password. If this happens, the old password no longer unlocks the worksheet. You can try to prevent this problem by displaying an Alert box that prompts the operator for the correct password. If formulas are hidden, unauthorized users can't detect the password by reading the macro instruction, because the screen displays only values.

Another way to prevent a password from being replaced with erroneous values is not to use passwords to reprotect the file. You may wonder how a security system can operate if these passwords aren't used. The key is not to display formulas on the macro sheet. The operator is asked to enter a password, and it is checked against a password stored in a macro cell.

However, because macro cells still will display values, you have to be careful here too. You can use text formulas to construct the value, and before the macro ends, you can change the value of the cell in which the value appears. For example, suppose that you choose the value SECURE as your password. You can use a formula to reference the cells in a macro sheet that contain those individual alphabetical characters; the formula would store SECURE in a cell.

To make the deception total, you could list on the macro sheet all the letters of the alphabet and create a text formula that concatenates the letters required to equal SECURE. Then, when the operator enters a password, the system would check the password against the value constructed in the macro. If the passwords are not identical, the system would reject the operator.

To simulate further a response typical of a mainframe system, you can borrow the time delay macro from Chapter 6. This delay loop can discourage repeated attempts to get at a password.

Both the security system and the outline of the system just described enable you to safeguard stored information. You cannot wait until you have a problem to consider adding these features to your applications. The time to include these capabilities is at the beginning, while you can build them into the macro structure.

A Trend-Reporting System

Although reporting current financial figures is valuable in itself, you can make this information even more useful by also reporting some earlier figures. In this way, you can compare today's performance with past results. This process always has been a challenge in spreadsheet applications because it necessitates "rolling off" figures that are outdated to make room for additional current data. Often, too many or too few months are removed. This can result in lost data or reports that do not contain all the correct data.

Macros can solve this problem for you. They enable you to specify how to remove and add data, and they can perform this function at your command. An example is the trend macro described in this section. Figure 7.21 shows a portion of the 13 months of data stored in a worksheet file. A period of 13 months was selected so that the current month's figures, the figures for each of the previous months, and the figures from the same month in the previous year could be shown. Perhaps less data would suffice for your needs. However, whenever seasonal fluctuations are involved, being able to compare figures for this month with figures for the same month last year is helpful.

 É File Edit Formula Format Data Options Macro Window

R37C1

Trend

	1	2	3	4	5	6	7
37							
38							
39		PRODUCT A		PRODUCT B		PRODUCT C	
40		$	UNITS	$	UNITS	$	UNITS
41	Oct-85	$25,641	1100	$27,800	980	$32,000	500
42	Nov-85	$28,462	1188	$30,302	1147	$35,840	570
43	Dec-85	$31,592	1283	$33,029	1342	$40,141	650
44	Jan-86	$35,067	1386	$36,002	1570	$44,958	741
45	Feb-86	$42,000	1750	$47,690	2540	$92,300	999
46	Mar-86	$45,000	1890	$48,000	2600	$103,376	1139
47	Apr-86	$49,950	1950	$52,320	3042	$115,781	1298
48	May-86	$55,445	2106	$57,029	3559	$129,675	1480
49	Jun-86	$61,543	2274	$62,161	4164	$145,236	1687
50	Jul-86	$68,313	2456	$67,756	4872	$102,000	1923
51	Aug-86	$75,828	2653	$73,854	5700	$114,240	2193
52	Sep-86	$84,169	2865	$80,501	6669	$127,949	2500
53	Oct-86	$86,500	2810	$85,600	7200	$154,500	2900
54							
55							

Fig. 7.21. Storage area for Trend data.

Cells in another location in the worksheet reference the data. These cells are laid out in an attractive report format (shown at the top of fig. 7.22). Each month, the macro "rolls" the history area (shown at the bottom of the figure) so that the earliest month is eliminated and a new month is added. Each month the macro rebuilds the data at the top of the screen.

File Edit Formula Format Data Options Macro Window

R54C7

	1	2	3	4	5	6	7
				Trend			
3							
4		SALES PRODUCT A		SALES PRODUCT B		SALES PRODUCT C	
5		$	UNITS	$	UNITS	$	UNITS
6	Oct-86	$86,500	2810	$85,600	7200	$154,500	2900
7	Sep-86	$84,169	2865	$80,501	6669	$127,949	2500
8	Aug-86	$75,828	2653	$73,854	5700	$114,240	2193
9	Jul-86	$68,313	2456	$67,756	4872	$102,000	1923
10	Oct-85	$25,641	1188	$30,302	1147	$35,840	570
43	Dec-85	$31,592	1283	$33,029	1342	$40,141	650
44	Jan-86	$35,067	1386	$36,002	1570	$44,958	741
45	Feb-86	$42,000	1750	$47,690	2540	$92,300	999
46	Mar-86	$45,000	1890	$48,000	2600	$103,376	1139
47	Apr-86	$49,950	1950	$52,320	3042	$115,781	1298
48	May-86	$55,445	2106	$57,029	3559	$129,675	1480
49	Jun-86	$61,543	2274	$62,161	4164	$145,236	1687
50	Jul-86	$68,313	2456	$67,756	4872	$102,000	1923
51	Aug-86	$75,827	2653	$73,854	5700	$114,240	2193
52	Sep-86	$84,169	2865	$80,501	6669	$127,949	2500
53	Oct-86	$86,500	2810	$85,600	7200	$154,500	2900

Fig. 7.22. Trend report area (top) and trend history area (bottom).

You will notice that the macro for this example uses the R1C1 style (discussed in Chapter 1). This example is presented in this style in order to illustrate how the R1C1 and A1 styles differ. After completing the macro, if you want to convert it to A1 style, all you have to do is select Options A1 from the Options menu. You can choose either R1C1 or A1 style for any of your macros depending on your preferences.

Warning Users about Data Loss

Each month, the earliest month in the report is rolled off automatically, and operators should be alerted to this fact. You can display a message that tells the operator that if the macro continues executing, it will delete the history for a particular period of time.

Before the macro begins executing, both the Trend_Rpt macro sheet and Trend data file should be open. Opening these files allows the macro to access the value of the earliest date on the Trend data sheet. The date is stored in row 41, column 1 of Trend. Row 2 of figure 7.23 shows the formula that stores the date's value as text.

	1
1	Trend_Rpt
2	=TEXT(Trend!R41C1,"MMMM YY")
3	="History data for "&R[-1]C&" will be lost - Type Y to proceed / N to stop"
4	=INPUT(R[-1]C,2)
5	=IF(R[-1]C="Y",GOTO(R[3]C))
6	=ALERT("Trend update is cancelled",2)
7	=HALT()
8	=Trend!R53C1+30
9	=DATE(YEAR(R[-1]C),MONTH(R[-1]C),15)
10	=ACTIVATE("Trend")+STEP()
11	=SELECT(Trend!R[31]C:R[42]C[7])
12	=CUT()
13	=SELECT(Trend!R41C1)
14	=PASTE()
15	=SELECT(Trend!R53C1)
16	=FORMULA(R[-7]C)
17	=FORMAT.NUMBER("MMM-YY")
18	=SELECT(Trend!R53C2)
19	=FORMULA(INPUT("Enter sales $ for product A",1))
20	**Remaining input instructions would be placed here.**
21	=SELECT(Trend!R6C1:R35C10)
22	=FORMULA("=R[47]C")
23	=SELECT(,"RC[1]")
24	=FORMULA("=R[47]C")
25	=SELECT(,"R[1]C")
26	=FORMULA("=R[45]C")
27	**Remaining formulas for report would be placed here.**
28	=SELECT(Trend!R6C1)
29	=FORMAT.NUMBER("MMM-YY")
30	**Remaining formatting instructions would be placed here.**
31	=RETURN()

Fig. 7.23. The macro code for the trend report.

The converted date value, stored in row 2 of the Trend_Rpt macro, represents the month of the earliest data in the data file. This month, which corresponds to the data that will be removed if the macro proceeds, is displayed in an Input box along with a message about the data the macro will delete (row 3). The message asks the operator to press Y in order to proceed or N in order to stop. If the operator presses anything other than Y, the update is canceled. If the operator presses Y, the macro continues with the update process.

Updating the Database

After the operator approves the update, the first task the macro performs is generating the date for the new month. The existing dates all are stored under the 15th of each month, so the date for the next month can be generated by adding 30 days to the date for the previous month. The instruction in row 8 of the macro generates this serial date. The month and year in this date can be changed, but the day always must be entered as 15. (Because a month-year format is used to display the date, the fact that the 15th is used is not evident.)

Next, the macro activates the Trend document (row 10) and selects the history area (with the exception of the earliest month). CUT is invoked to mark this selection for relocation (row 12). The macro selects the first cell in the earliest month (row 13). Then PASTE moves the selected area up one row (row 14). This process deletes the earliest month's data and shifts all the more recent data up one line.

Next, the date area in the most recent month's figures (row 53 of the Trend file) is selected, and the newly created date is placed in this cell. The date has a format of MMM-YY (row 17 of the macro).

Now the macro records each data element for the current month. An INPUT statement and its associated prompt (row 19 of the macro) enter each field in the current month row. Using a combination of FORMULA and INPUT is the best method for entering the data directly. An alternative method is to use the approach described in the section in this chapter about the Personnel System. If you use this alternate approach, you must use additional instructions; but these added instructions enable you to store the value, check it for errors, and manipulate it before using FORMULA to store the value. You can add range checks, code validity checks, and any other kind of processing before accepting the data.

In this macro, only one data element is entered. Expanding the entry process, however, is easy. You use additional SELECT and FORMULA INPUT statements for each field to be entered. Although this procedure is a little slower than allowing the operator to move across the data while entering, it can help protect the integrity of your data.

The last step is to place the information from the reshuffled history area into the cells in the report area. Like the section that contains the instructions for inputting the data, this section requires many macro instructions. Each element must be transferred from the history area to the report area. The process is not difficult, just a little time-consuming. The instructions in rows 21 through 26 of the macro show the values for three entries being moved to the top of the report area.

An alternate way to transfer the data to the top of the report area is to enter a macro formula that moves the data to the first section in each segment of the report. Then you make the macro copy these formulas across the row. Whether this option is viable depends on whether blank columns have been added for aesthetic purposes. Although the blank columns improve the readability of the report, they preclude copying, unless the history area has the same spacing.

A Budget System

Most budget systems perform more than one task, and menus are the ideal way to display the names of those tasks. Operators do not have to memorize the names of the various macros that perform the tasks. Only one name needs to be familiar: the name of the macro that displays the menu. That macro "remembers" the names of all the other macros that may be needed in the application.

The Budget macro in this example performs three primary operations: updating the budget for a particular region, producing a budget consolidation, and printing a consolidated budget report. You already have seen numerous examples of printing, so the focus here is on the first two tasks.

The Budget Menu

The Budget_Menu (see fig. 7.24) and the Budget macro (see fig. 7.25) are similar to others presented in this chapter. In the macro, Excel activates the menu window and displays an Input box that prompts the operator to select an option. Four IF statements check the option selected. Each of the three menu selections calls a macro subroutine: Budget_Update (C1), Consolidate (E1), or Print_Consolidated (G1).

The Budget macro uses cell B1 as an indicator that a valid selection was made. This cell is initialized with a value of N. When the operator makes a valid selection, the macro places an S in B1. The subroutine calls return to the Budget macro in the instruction immediately after the call, so you need to know whether a match was found or whether an invalid value was input. If a match is found, the macro branches to A11; if not, the macro displays the error message in A9. If B1 still contains an N, no match occurred. If B1 contains an S, a match did occur.

The instruction in row 8 checks the value of B1 and initiates the appropriate action. A loop enables the operator to continue selecting menu options. Each time the loop executes, B1 is set to N so that

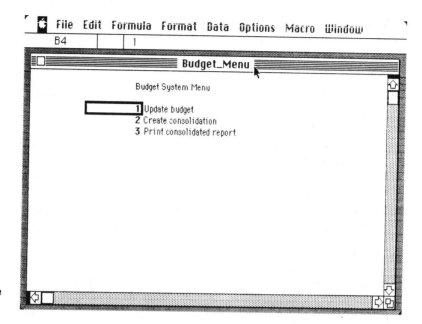

Fig. 7.24. The Budget System Menu.

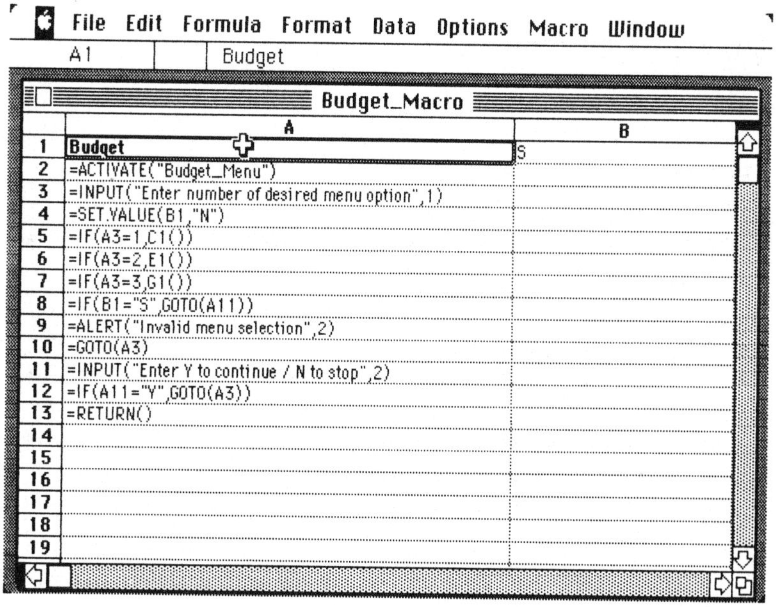

Fig. 7.25. The Budget macro.

each selection can be verified. If the operator presses N in response to the prompt about continuing (row 11), the macro ends.

Updating a Region Budget

Figure 7.26 shows the Budget_Update macro. This subroutine, which updates the budgets for several regions, contains some unique code that dynamically alters the file opened by the macro. The approach used in this macro requires that the file names of the regions' budgets be standardized. In this example, the budget files are named Region1, Region2, and so on.

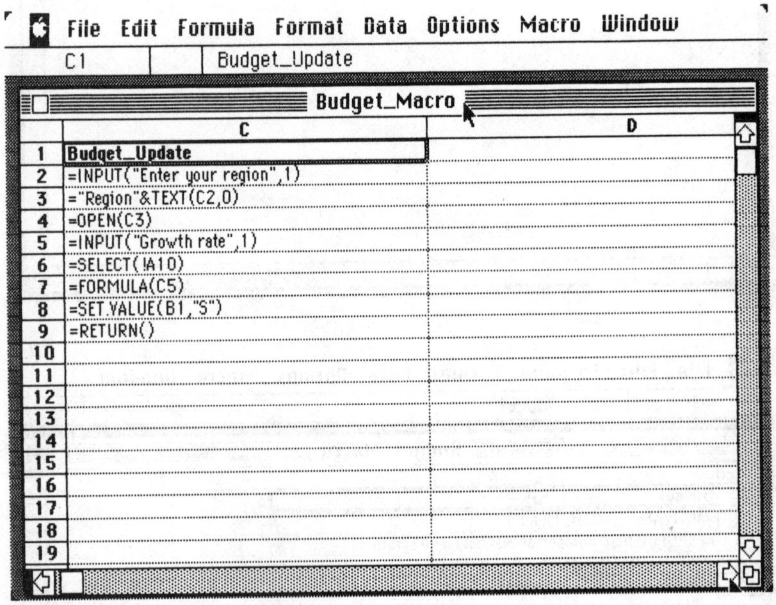

```
 File  Edit  Formula  Format  Data  Options  Macro  Window

   C1              Budget_Update

                        Budget_Macro
                   C                          D
1  Budget_Update
2  =INPUT("Enter your region",1)
3  ="Region"&TEXT(C2,0)
4  =OPEN(C3)
5  =INPUT("Growth rate",1)
6  =SELECT(!A10)
7  =FORMULA(C5)
8  =SET.VALUE(B1,"S")
9  =RETURN()
10
11
12
13
14
15
16
17
18
19
```

Fig. 7.26. The Budget_Update subroutine.

The operator selects a file name by entering a number, as requested in the INPUT statement in C2. A *type* of 1 acts as an error checker and ensures that only a numeric value is accepted. The formula in C3 combines the constant *Region* with the text equivalent of the number the user entered in C2. And the result of this formula is used in C4 to open the appropriate file.

Figure 7.27 shows the file for Region1. This example is designed to allow a change in the growth rate in the budget selected. The operator enters the new rate (C5 in the Budget_Update macro). Because all the regional budgets are standardized, cell A10 of each regional budget file can be selected to store this value. The FORMULA statement in C7 enters this value into the selected cell. Before returning, the macro places the value S in cell B1. You can expand this macro to change many budget figures. Use this example as a model to develop macro code for updating as many fields as you like.

	A	B	C	D	E	F
1						
2						
3		SALES	$670,900			
4		SALARIES	$100,500			
5		TELEPHONE	$12,300			
6		UTILITIES	$32,000			
7		RENT EXPENSE	$45,000			
8		CONSULTING	$112,000			
9		POSTAGE	$600			
10		FREIGHT	$750			
11		TRANSPORTN.	$121,780			
12		TRAVEL	$54,000			
13		AUTO LEASE	$31,500			
14		MISC.	$600			
15		INS.	$900			
16						
17						
18						
19						

Fig. 7.27. The budget file for Region1.

Creating Budget Consolidations

If your company has more than one region or division, you probably will want to consolidate the values in each individual budget to produce a total company figure. Using a macro to accomplish this task is a good idea. You don't have to worry about omitting one of the regions or using one region twice. After you have entered and tested this macro, you can rely on its continued, accurate performance.

The macro that consolidates the budgets has four separate sections (see fig. 7.28). The first section opens the document named Total and selects cells C3 through C15 as the area of the document in which the consolidated information will be entered. The last statement in the first section establishes an initial value for COUNT, which controls the opening of the required region files.

Loop is the name of the next section. The first instruction creates the file name by combining *Region* with the current text value of

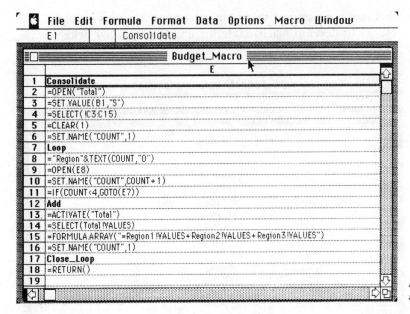

Fig. 7.28. The consolidation
subroutines.

COUNT. The instruction in E9 opens the file, and the next instruction increments COUNT. Only three regions exist, so the loop stops
after all three region files have been opened.

The Add section is next. Now that all three files are open, the operator can reactivate the Total file. The section of that file from C3
through C15 has been prenamed Total!VALUES and is selected at
this time. The Add subroutine uses a FORMULA.ARRAY statement
to enter an array formula into the selected cells. This statement
simulates the use of the Option key when entering a formula. The
formula is

   =Region1!VALUES+Region2!VALUES+Region3!VALUES

This formula adds the values in all three files and stores the result
in the Total worksheet, shown in figure 7.29.

In this example, the macro shows only a RETURN instruction in the
last section, Close_Loop. However, you probably will want to modify
this section to include instructions to activate, then close each of
the Region files.

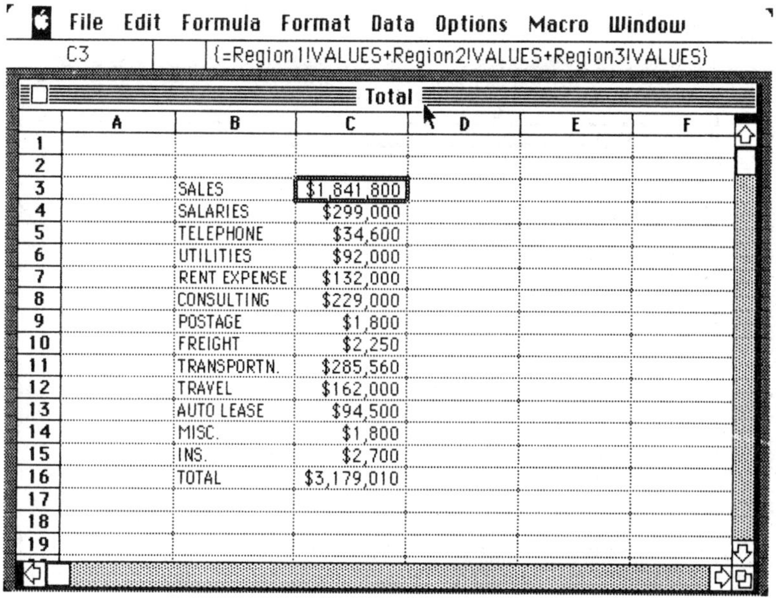

| | File | Edit | Formula | Format | Data | Options | Macro | Window |

| C3 | | {=Region1!VALUES+Region2!VALUES+Region3!VALUES} |

Total

	A	B	C	D	E	F
1						
2						
3		SALES	$1,841,800			
4		SALARIES	$299,000			
5		TELEPHONE	$34,600			
6		UTILITIES	$92,000			
7		RENT EXPENSE	$132,000			
8		CONSULTING	$229,000			
9		POSTAGE	$1,800			
10		FREIGHT	$2,250			
11		TRANSPORTN.	$285,560			
12		TRAVEL	$162,000			
13		AUTO LEASE	$94,500			
14		MISC.	$1,800			
15		INS.	$2,700			
16		TOTAL	$3,179,010			
17						
18						
19						

Fig. 7.29. The Total document with consolidated figures displayed.

Printing the Consolidated Report

You also need to create a routine for printing the consolidated report. Figure 7.30 shows one option for printing consolidations. The macro assumes that the Total file is open and ensures that the file is active in A2. The PAGE.SETUP statement in A3 changes the left margin. This statement also eliminates the printing of grid lines and headings with the two FALSE arguments. The three arguments for the PRINT command in A4 specify High Quality, 1 Copy, and Cut Sheet as the paper-feed method. You easily can make modifications to print the consolidations in any format you desire.

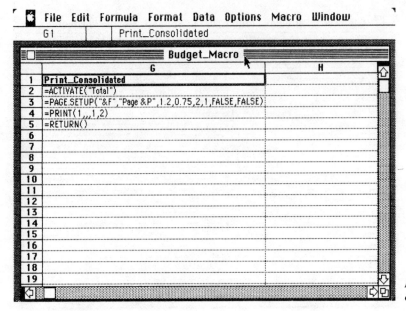

Fig. 7.30. Macro for printing
consolidated reports.

Conclusion

In this chapter, you have learned techniques for combining a variety
of macro subroutines into an automated application. You have seen
how to link the various components of a system by using menus,
calls to subroutines, and branching logic.

The four applications in this chapter have wide applicability in the
business environment. But even more important, you can use the
techniques presented here to construct hundreds of other business
applications.

Glossary of
Macro Functions

This appendix contains a comprehensive list of Excel's Macro Command Language functions. The commands are organized according to the Excel menu command structure, which they parallel. The commands are described generally here. For fuller descriptions of particular commands, refer to Chapters 4, 5, and 6 of this book. The commands that don't have menu parallels are listed in separate categories.

As you review the macro commands, pay particular attention to their syntax. It must be followed exactly. Especially important are the use of commas to separate arguments; the use of periods rather than spaces to separate parts of a macro name; and the use of quotation marks to enclose most text arguments, such as window and document names.

File Menu Commands

NEW?( )
NEW(type)

The first form of this function causes the dialog box for the File New command to appear. You then can click Worksheet, Chart, or Macro Sheet, depending on the kind of file you want to create. Using this form can make a macro more flexible by enabling you to pick a kind of file rather than specify a particular kind in the macro. If the macro requires a specific kind of new file, you should use the second form of the function.

In the second form, you must use one of the following numbers for *type*: 1 for a worksheet window, 2 for a chart window, or 3 for a macro sheet. For example, to create a chart window, you type =NEW(2).

OPEN?( )
OPEN(document,update)

The first version, OPEN?( ), displays the dialog box for the Open command. You then can click a file name on the list in the dialog box or scroll through the list. You also can change the drive, eject the current disk, cancel the request, or select the highlighted file name.

When you use the second version, Excel opens the document specified. If Excel does not find the document on your disk, a dialog box appears prompting you to insert the disk that contains that document. An example of this function is =OPEN("Chart5").

The *update* argument is used only if the specified *document* contains external references. *Update* should contain your directions for updating these references. The *update* argument must be a logical value: TRUE indicates update, and FALSE specifies no update. If you don't use *update*, Excel uses the default value TRUE.

OPEN.LINKS?( )
OPEN.LINKS(documents-1,documents-2,...)

The first version of this function displays the dialog box for the Open Links command. You can select as many of the linked documents from this dialog box as you want. Then you click Open or Cancel.

The second version enables you to enter from 1 to 14 document names in the form of text. The function opens all the documents specified and updates all external references. An example is =OPEN.LINKS("Region1","Region2","Region3").

The LINKS function generates a text array of linked documents that you can open with OPEN.LINKS. For instance, you could use LINKS with OPEN.LINKS to open all the documents linked to Total _ Company. To do so, type =OPEN.LINKS(LINKS("Sales")).

SAVE( )

This function duplicates the File Save command. SAVE( ) resaves the active document under the name you last used to save the document.

SAVE.AS?( )
SAVE.AS(document,type)

The first version displays the dialog box for the Save As command. You then can type a document name and save the document in Normal, SYLK, Text, or WKS format. If you need to change drives, click Drive. If the appropriate disk is not in the drive, click Eject and insert the disk you need. You also have the option of clicking Save or Cancel after you make other changes.

In the second form, *document* is a document name in text format. The *type* argument does not apply when the active window is a chart. At other times, a *type* of 1 indicates Normal format; 2, SYLK; 3, Text; and 4, WKS. An example is =SAVE.AS("Budget1",4). This saves the contents of the current window as Budget1 in a worksheet file. The default drive is used with the second version of SAVE.AS unless you specify otherwise. To change the drive or current disk, use the first form of the function.

FILE.DELETE?( )
FILE.DELETE(document)

This command is equivalent to the worksheet File Delete command, which deletes files from a disk. The first version, FILE.DELETE?( ), displays the dialog box for File Delete, listing the file names on your disk. You can scroll through the various file names and click the one you want to delete. After selecting the file to delete, you click the Delete box. You also can select Eject to change the disk, Drive to switch drives, or Cancel to end the command.

In the second form, *document* must be a text entry that represents a document name. An example is =FILE.DELETE("Budget"). If Excel can't find the specified document on the disk, a dialog box appears and prompts you to insert the appropriate disk.

PAGE.SETUP?( )
PAGE.SETUP(header,footer,left,width,top,length,headings,message)
PAGE.SETUP(header,footer,left,right,top,bottom,headings,gridlines)
PAGE.SETUP(header,footer,left,width,top,height,size)

This function has four versions. The first generates a dialog box with which you can make selections that affect the active window. This is the same dialog box you see if you select Page Setup from the File menu.

The second version of PAGE.SETUP is the equivalent of the Page etup command when the active window is a worksheet and the printer is TTY. You specify a *header* and/or *footer* in the form of text. For header and footer entries, you can specify instructions such as &F to print the name of the document and &T to print the current time. For a TTY printer, Excel uses the numbers you specify as character spaces rather than inches. Therefore, the numbers you specify for the *left* and *top* margins as well as for print *width* and *length* should be in characters rather than inches. For *headings*, you specify whether you want to print row and column headings. You use TRUE if you want them printed; FALSE, if you want them omitted. For *message*, you can type text to send setup messages to your printer in order to activate special printer features.

You use the third version of PAGE.SETUP with a worksheet and a Macintosh™ printer. You use the arguments *header*, *footer*, and *headings* the same way you used them in the second version. Margins for a Macintosh printer are measured in inches, so you specify the numbers used for the *right*, *left*, *top*, and *bottom* margins in inches. *Gridlines* is a logical value. TRUE specifies that you want gridlines printed; FALSE, that you do not want them printed.

You use the last version when you print charts. The arguments *width* and *height* specify the area in inches in which you want to print the chart. The arguments *left* and *top* are the indentation, in inches, from the top and side of the page. For *size*, you use 1 to indicate Screen Size; 2, to specify Fit to Page. An example is =PAGE.SETUP("&F","Page &P",0.75,7,1,9,2).

PRINT?( )
PRINT( )
PRINT(range,from,to,copies,feed)

The first version, PRINT?( ), displays the File Print dialog box, which is appropriate for an ImageWriter™ or TTY printer. With the ImageWriter, you can check options such as Quality, Page Range, Number of Copies, Screen Preview, and From and To range. With TTY, your options are Page Range, Copies, From and To Range, and Continuous or Single Feed Paper. After choosing the desired options, click OK to make the macro proceed.

You use the second version, PRINT( ), when Macintosh is specified in Printer Setup and your printer is not an ImageWriter, ImageWriter 2, or LaserWriter™. You cannot specify any arguments; the current settings are used.

You use the third version when TTY is specified or when Macintosh is specified with an ImageWriter, ImageWriter 2, or LaserWriter. All five arguments must be numbers. A *range* of 1 indicates that you want to print all pages; 2, that you want to print only a section. If you specify 2 for *range*, you must use the *from* and *to* arguments to specify which pages to print. You indicate how many copies you want with the *copies* argument. For *feed*, you can type 1 for continuous or 2 for cut sheets. An example of this version is =PAGE(1,,,1,1), which indicates that you want to print one copy of all pages on continuous-feed paper.

PRINTER.SETUP?( )
PRINTER.SETUP(printer,port,baud)

The first form displays the dialog box for Printer Setup. In this dialog box, you choose a Macintosh or TTY printer and the appropriate device speed.

For the second version, you enter your choices as arguments. For *printer*, you type either 1 for Macintosh or 2 for TTY. For *port*, you type either 1 for printer or 2 for modem. The baud argument is a number that represents the transmission rate. You type 1 for 300, 2 for 600, 3 for 1200, 4 for 2400, 5 for 4800, or 6 for 9600. Although these PRINTER.SETUP commands are among the macro functions, you will find that you use these less frequently than the PRINT and PAGE.SETUP commands.

Edit Menu Commands

UNDO( )

This function, which is the equivalent of Undo on the Edit menu, undoes the last editing operation. UNDO must be the next command after the edit. If another command is issued first, UNDO doesn't work.

CUT( )

CUT is the equivalent of the Cut command on the Edit menu. You use CUT with PASTE to move the current cell selection. If you use CUT in a macro, Excel assumes that you already have preselected cells, either with another macro instruction or before executing the macro.

COPY( )

This function duplicates the Copy command on the Edit menu. Like CUT, COPY assumes that you have preselected cells. When you use COPY with PASTE, the cells remain in their original location as well as appear in a new location. After being pasted, the cells remain highlighted. To remove the highlighting, you either can use CANCEL.COPY in the macro or select an option such as Format Number.

COPY.CHART?( )
COPY.CHART(as-shown)

The first version displays the dialog box for the Copy Chart command on the Edit menu. You can click As Shown on Screen or As Shown when Printed. These options control the size of the image placed on the Clipboard. After you select an option, click OK to proceed.

The second version has a number argument, *as-shown*. If it is 1, the result will be As Shown on Screen. If *as-shown* is 2, the result will be As Shown when Printed. When you want the Clipboard image to be screen size, you use =COPY.CHART(1).

COPY.PICTURE( )

COPY.PICTURE( ) is equivalent to pressing the Shift key while selecting Copy from the Edit menu. Excel copies the chart to the Clipboard as a picture.

PASTE( )

This function duplicates the Paste command on the Edit menu. PASTE( ) inserts copied or cut cells into cells that are currently selected. You can specify a fixed selection of cells you want to paste, for example, =SELECT("R2C1:R6C3"); or you can make the selection more flexible with a statement such as =SELECT(INPUT("Select cells in Paste location",8)).

CLEAR?( )
CLEAR(parts)

The first version displays the Edit Clear dialog box and waits for your response. You can click All, Formats, or Formulas. Click OK to proceed, or click Cancel to negate the command.

In the second version of CLEAR, *parts* specifies how many of the selected cells you want to clear. The *parts* argument is a number that controls CLEAR's action. To clear all cells, you use a 1; to clear formats, a 2; and to clear only formulas, a 3. Using =CLEAR(1) in a macro clears everything from the selected cells.

PASTE.SPECIAL?( )
PASTE.SPECIAL(parts,operation)
PASTE.SPECIAL(values-in,series-names,categories)
PASTE.SPECIAL(parts)

PASTE.SPECIAL copies only the parts of cells defined with the Copy command. The first version of this function displays the dialog box for Paste Special on the Edit menu. Before displaying the appropriate dialog box, Excel assesses your last action. Which dialog box is displayed depends on whether your last action was to copy a chart or a worksheet and whether the active window is a chart or a worksheet window. If you use the first version, the function waits while you fill in your choices in the dialog box. If you use the other versions of PASTE.SPECIAL, you must specify that information as arguments in the function.

You use the second version of PASTE.SPECIAL when you have copied a worksheet selection and the active window contains a worksheet document. The *parts* and *operation* arguments are numbers. The *parts* argument specifies what part you want to copy to the worksheet you are pasting to. You use 1 for All, 2 for Formulas, 3 for Values, or 4 for Formats. The *operation* argument specifies the operation to be performed with the selected parts as they are combined with the worksheet to which you are pasting. You use 1 for None, 2 for Add, 3 for Subtract, 4 for Multiply, or 5 for Divide.

You use the third version of PASTE.SPECIAL when you have copied a worksheet selection, and a chart is the document in the active window. The *values-in* argument is numeric: 1 indicates rows, and 2 specifies columns. *Series-names* and *categories* are logicals. TRUE represents checked; FALSE, unchecked. Depending on what you specify for *values-in*, these represent Series Names in the First Column or Row, and Category Names in the First Column or Row.

You use the fourth version of PASTE.SPECIAL when the copied selection is from a chart, and the active window contains a chart. For *parts*, you use 1 for All, 2 for Formats, or 3 for Formulas.

You can use the third and fourth versions of the function to compensate for some of the missing Chart commands in the macro environment. You can store chart templates, which can contain some extras such as axes labels. And you can copy your data to the chart templates, creating a finished product without leaving the macro environment.

EDIT.DELETE?( )
EDIT.DELETE(direction)

EDIT.DELETE deletes worksheet cells in the same way the Edit Delete command does in the worksheet environment. The cells to be deleted must be preselected. You can select them before executing the macro or by using a macro instruction that is executed before EDIT.DELETE.

The first version of EDIT.DELETE displays Edit Delete's dialog box and waits for your entry. You can shift cells up or to the left. After you make your selection, you make the macro continue by clicking OK.

The second form has a *direction* argument. If you use 1, Excel shifts cells left. If you use 2, Excel shifts cells up.

INSERT?( )
INSERT(direction)

INSERT( ) displays the dialog box for the Insert command on the Edit menu. In the dialog box, you specify whether Excel should shift cells down or to the right as cells are inserted.

If you use the second version, a *direction* of 1 shifts cells right; 2, shifts cells down.

FILL.DOWN( )
FILL.RIGHT( )

These functions duplicate the Fill Down and Fill Right commands on the Edit menu. No arguments are required. With FILL.RIGHT, the leftmost column of the selection is copied to the remaining rows in the selection. With FILL.DOWN, the top row is copied down to the remaining rows.

Formula Menu Commands

DEFINE.NAME?( )
DEFINE.NAME(name,refers-to,type,key)

The first version, DEFINE.NAME?( ), displays the dialog box for the Formula Define Name command and waits for you to respond. You can type a name up to 255 characters long; it must not have any spaces, and the first character must be a letter. Excel displays the current selection in the "Refers to" box. You can click the box and change it to a cell reference, value, or formula. Then, you can click OK or Cancel. The dialog box also provides a Delete option. To use it, you select an existing name by clicking, then click Delete. If the command is executed while the macro sheet is in the active window, the dialog box also will contain a box that enables you to check the type of macro. If you check Command, Excel highlights the Option key box to permit you to assign a letter code to the macro.

If you use the second version of DEFINE.NAME, you must provide arguments for names, references, values, and formulas. The *name* argument must be text. The *refers-to* argument can be text, a number, a logical value, or a formula in the form of text. If you omit *refers-to*, the function refers to cells in the selection. These cells could have been selected either with the mouse before executing the macro or with a macro instruction. If *refers-to* contains text, a number, or a logical value, *name* refers to that value. If *refers-to* is a formula, the references it contains must be in the R1C1 style. If *refers-to* is an external reference, *name* refers to those cells. Two examples of this function are =DEFINE.NAME("Salary_ Expense") and =DEFINE.NAME("Total","=R[2]C").

The *type* and *key* arguments are used only with macro sheets. The *type* argument is numeric: 1 indicates a function, and 2 represents a command macro. The argument *Key* must be a single that indicates the Command-key option for command macro execution.

DELETE.NAME(name)

DELETE.NAME has the same capabilities as the Delete option under the Formula Define Name command. The *name* argument must be text.

CREATE.NAMES?( )
CREATE.NAMES(top-row,left-column)

The CREATE.NAMES( ) function, which displays the dialog box for Create Names on the Formula menu, enables you to assign names to many cells quickly. The macro waits while you make your selection of Top Row or Left Column from the dialog box. The macro takes the names at this location and assigns them to adjacent cells.

The second version of CREATE.NAMES expects two logical values, *top-row* and *left-column*. TRUE has the same result as checking the equivalent boxes in the dialog box, and FALSE is the same as not checking the boxes is =CREATE.NAMES(TRUE,FALSE) an example of this function.

FORMULA.GOTO?( )
FORMULA.GOTO(ref)

The first version displays the dialog box for the Formula Goto command. You use this dialog box to select a name from a list, type a cell reference, or type a name. FORMULA.GOTO?( ) finds this reference on your worksheet immediately.

In the second version, *ref* can be either an external reference (such as !$G$1 or Budget!$F$2) or a text entry containing an R1C1 format (such as R2C4). Both forms are the equivalent of the Formula Goto command. For instance, to go to cell B10, you could use =FORMULA.GOTO(!$B$10) or =FORMULA.GOTO("R10C2"). If B10 were defined as Profit, you also could use =FOR-MULA.GOTO(!Profit) or =FORMULA.GOTO("Profit") could be used also.

FORMULA.FIND?( )
FORMULA.FIND(findtext,look-in,look-at,look-by,direction)

FORMULA.FIND, which is equivalent to the Find command on the Formula menu, looks for specified text. The first version displays the dialog box for Formula Find. If you want to change the defaults, you can enter the text you want to search for and check the appropriate options in the dialog box. You can look in values or formulas for your entry. And you can look at the whole entry or only part of the entry. You can also look by rows or columns.

The second version contains all the required arguments. The *find-text* argument contains the information you are looking for. The last three arguments are numbers. The *look-in* argument can be 1 for Formulas or 2 for Values. The *look-at* argument can be 1 for Whole and 2 for Part. For *look-by*, you specify 1 for Rows or 2 for Columns. For *direction*, you indicate whether you want the next or previous match: 1 is the default and implies next; 2 requests the previous match. Following is an example of this function: =FORMULA.FIND("BUDG",1,2,1).

SELECT.LAST.CELL( )

This function duplicates the Formula Last Cell command, selecting the last cell used or referenced in the worksheet.

SHOW.ACTIVE.CELL( )

This function is identical to the Formula menu's Show Active Cell command. SHOW.ACTIVE.CELL( ) scrolls the worksheet until the active cell is visible and provides a quick way of returning to the place where you were working.

Format Menu Commands

FORMAT.NUMBER?( )
FORMAT.NUMBER(format)

FORMAT.NUMBER?( ) displays the dialog box for the Format Number command. You can scroll through the options and click the one you want. Or you can create your own options in the format area at the bottom of the dialog box. You can select Delete on the dialog box to eliminate a format you have created.

In the second version, you provide the desired format as text. For example, you might enter =FORMAT.NUMBER("000,000"). Any valid format characters that can be used with the worksheet Format Number command can be used with this macro function.

DELETE.FORMAT(format)

This command is the equivalent of deleting a format with the Format Number command. DELETE.FORMAT deletes the format you specify. The *format* argument must be text—for instance, =DELETE.FORMAT("###-##-####"). Only formats that you have created can be deleted, just as with the menu command. If you try to delete a nonexistent format, an error message appears.

ALIGNMENT?( )
ALIGNMENT(type)

The first form of this function displays the dialog box for the Format Alignment command and pauses to enable you to make selections and click OK. The options you can select are General, Left, Center, Right, and Fill.

If you use the second form of the function, *type* indicates your alignment selection. *Type* can have one of five values: 1 for General, 2 for Left, 3 for Center, 4 for Right, or 5 for Fill. An example is =ALIGNMENT(3).

STYLE?( )
STYLE(bold,italic)

With this function, you can access the Bold and Italic options under the Format Style command. Both arguments are logical values, with TRUE representing checked and FALSE indicating unchecked.

BORDER?( )
BORDER(outline,left,right,top,bottom)

BORDER provides the same options as the Border command on the Format menu. The first version displays the dialog box for Format Borders.

The second version contains a series of logical values. TRUE indicates that the corresponding dialog box was checked; FALSE indicates unchecked. The arguments *outline*, *left*, *right*, *top*, and *bottom* correspond to the option on the dialog box. An example of this function is =BORDER(TRUE,FALSE,FALSE,FALSE,TRUE).

CELL.PROTECTION?( )
CELL.PROTECTION(locked,hidden)

The first version displays the dialog box for Format Cell Protection and waits for your response. You can click either Locked or Hidden to change the status of either setting. The changes you make affect the cells that are currently selected. If you choose Locked, you can't edit the selected cells. If you choose Hidden, Excel doesn't display the formulas for these cells.

The second version requires logical values for *locked* and *hidden* TRUE represents a check in the dialog box, and FALSE indicates that the option is unchecked. The following macro instruction locks and hides the cells selected: =CELL.PROTECTION(TRUE,TRUE).

COLUMN.WIDTH?( )
COLUMN.WIDTH(width)
COLUMN.WIDTH(width,ref)

The first form displays the dialog box for Format Column Width and pauses for your input. You can enter a column width or click Standard.

The second form is the equivalent of the menu command for width adjustment. The argument *width* specifies the new column width for the column or column selected. The selection process can be handled by a macro instruction or can be handled before the macro is executed.

The last version is equivalent to dragging the border of the column. The *ref* argument is an external reference to a specified cell or column or to an R1C1 text reference. The column width is changed according to the location of *ref*. For example, =COLUMN.WIDTH(20,"C[1]:C[2]") changes the column width of columns B and C to a width of 20 if the active cell is in column A when the instruction is executed. Cells B and C are selected because C[1] refers to a column one column to the right (that is, the beginning of the selection), and C[2] refers to a column two columns to the right (that is, the end of the range of columns whose widths are to be changed).

Data Menu Commands

DATA.FIND(logical)

If *logical* is TRUE, DATA.FIND carries out the Data Find command. If *logical* is FALSE, the Exit Find instruction is executed.

EXTRACT?( )
EXTRACT(unique)

EXTRACT?( ) displays the Data Extract dialog box. You can click Unique Records Only, or you can click OK to proceed.

The second version tells Excel that you want the Unique option from the Extract dialog box. TRUE indicates that the Unique option is checked; FALSE, that Unique is unchecked.

Before you use either version of this command, you should enter and set the criteria, and set the database. You also should have copied the field names for your extraction to an area and selected them. The area below these field names is used for the extracted information.

DATA.DELETE( )

Using DATA.DELETE in a macro has the same effect as selecting the Delete command from the Data menu. Records matching the criteria are removed permanently from your database.

SET.DATABASE( )

This function duplicates the Data Set Database command and enables you to define the current selection as the range of cells comprising the database.

SET.CRITERIA( )

This function is the same as the Set Criteria command on the Data menu. The current range of cells selected is defined as the criteria range.

SORT?( )
SORT(sort-by,1st-key,order,2nd-key,order,3rd-key,order)

The first version of this function displays the dialog box for Data Sort for you to complete. You can decide whether to sort by rows or columns. You also can enter as many as three sort keys and specify an ascending or descending sequence.

The second form of this function duplicates the capabilities of the Data Sort command. The first argument, *sort-by*, indicates row or column orientation, with 1 indicating rows and 2 columns. The *order* argument can appear as many as three times in the function. In each case, *order* tells Excel whether you want the sort on the key specified to be ascending or descending. A 1 indicates ascending; a 2, descending. You can specify from one to three sort keys, using either a text form for R1C1 references or external references to the active worksheet. As you record a macro, your specifications are recorded as A1 style text references that will be converted to R1C1 style. In the dialog box, you can indicate your reference type. If you choose this approach, you enter relative references in the dialog box, and your selection is recorded relative to the active cell. Enter absolute references if you want absolute references.

An example of the second form of this function is SORT(1,!$D:$D,2). The 1 in the first argument indicates a row orientation for the sort.

The second argument specifies column D as the sort key. And the third argument, 2, specifies descending order for the sort.

DATA.SERIES?( )
DATA.SERIES(series-in,type,unit,step,stop)

DATA.SERIES?( ) displays the dialog box for the Data Series option on the Data menu. In the second version, the arguments are all numbers. For *series-in*, you specify a 1 if the series is in Rows or a 2 if the series is in Columns. For *type*, you use 1 for Linear, 2 for Growth, or 3 for Date. For *unit*, you use 1 for Date, 2 for Weekday, 3 for Month, or 4 for Year. The *step* argument indicates the distance between series values, and *stop* is the ending value for the series.

TABLE?( )
TABLE(row-input,column-input)

The first version, TABLE?( ), displays the dialog box for the Data Table command. The second version enables you to include your specifications in the macro. The arguments *row-input* and *column-input* can be external references to single cells in the active worksheet or R1C1 references in text format. As you record your macro, your input cells are recorded as text, and A1 style is converted to R1C1 style. If you want relative or absolute references, you record them that way in the dialog box. For instance, to use cells B1 and D10 as input cells and create a table in the cells you selected before executing this macro instruction, you could use TABLE(!$B$1,!$D$10).

Option Menu Commands

SET.PRINT.AREA( )

This function, which duplicates the Option menu's Set Print Area command, allows you to print a specified area on the worksheet. Before including this function in your macro, you should make sure that a prior instruction has selected the appropriate range of cells.

SET.PRINT.TITLES( )

SET.PRINT.TITLES( ), which is the equivalent of the Set Print Titles command on the Option menu, enables you to print a set of titles on each page of your output. Prior to executing this command, you can select rows or columns anywhere on the worksheet.

SET.PAGE.BREAK( )

This command is the equivalent of the Set Page Break command on the Options menu. SET.PAGE.BREAK( ) inserts a page break above and to the left of the active cell.

REMOVE.PAGE.BREAK( )

This function is the equivalent of the Remove Page Break command on the Options menu. The active cell should be below or to the right of the page break to be removed.

FONT?( )
FONT(name,size)

The first version, FONT?( ), displays the Options Font dialog box, with which you can select such fonts as Chicago, Geneva, and London. The dialog box also presents several size options for most of these fonts.

In the second version, you type the name of a font and the size you want—for example, =FONT("Geneva",12).

DISPLAY?( )
DISPLAY(formulas,gridlines,headings)

The first form of this function displays the dialog box for the Options Display command. The dialog box contains Display options for Formulas, Gridlines, and Row and Column Headings. An x in the box indicates that the feature will be displayed. Clicking these options has the same effect as a toggle. That is, if the box contains an x, the click removes the x. If the box doesn't have an x, the click adds an x.

In the second version of DISPLAY, *formulas*, *gridlines*, and *headings* are logical values. TRUE indicates that the item is checked in the dialog box; FALSE, unchecked. To display all three options, you would use =DISPLAY(TRUE,TRUE,TRUE) in a macro.

PROTECT.DOCUMENT?( )
PROTECT.DOCUMENT(logical)

This function duplicates the Options Protect and Unprotect commands. The first version displays the dialog box, in which you can use a password to protect a document. If you are unprotecting a document, you must enter the password. This form is the only version of the macro function that works with password protection.

With the second version, you can specify your choice in the function. TRUE indicates Protect; FALSE, Unprotect. If a password has been used to protect the document, you must use the first version.

PRECISION(logical)

This function lets you choose between Full Precision and Precision As Displayed. TRUE indicates Full Precision; FALSE, Precision As Displayed. Full Precision uses the full internal accuracy of Excel, and the maximum number of decimal places is retained. Precision As Displayed limits internal accuracy to the number of displayed decimal places. With the Precision As Displayed option, numbers are rounded internally to the required number of decimal places.

A1.R1C1(logical)

When *logical* is TRUE, this command is the equivalent of the A1 command on the Options menu. When *logical* is FALSE, the R1C1 command is executed.

CALCULATE.NOW( )

This function is the same as the Options Calculate Now command.

CALCULATION?( )
CALCULATION(type,iteration,number-of,change)

CALCULATION?( ) displays the dialog box for Options Calculation and pauses to allow you to respond. Your choices are Automatic, Manual, and Automatic Except Tables. Clicking Iteration enables you

to calculate multiple times. You can specify the number of calculation iterations Excel will perform and the acceptable difference
between iterations.

The second version has four arguments. Of the four, *iteration* is a
logical value; the rest are numbers. For *type*, you use 1 for Automatic,
2 for Automatic Except Tables, or 3 for Manual calculation. For
iteration, FALSE indicates that the option is unchecked; TRUE, that
the option is checked. You use the *number-of* argument to specify
the number of iterations. For *change*, you indicate the maximum
change you want to allow between iterations.

Window Menu Commands

SHOW.CLIPBOARD( )

This function is the equivalent of the Window Show Clipboard command. SHOW.CLIPBOARD( ) opens the Clipboard and displays its
contents.

NEW.WINDOW( )

This function duplicates the New Window command on the Window
menu. NEW.WINDOW( ) creates an additional window for the active document.

Gallery Menu Commands

GALLERY.AREA?( )
GALLERY.AREA(type)

These two versions of the GALLERY function are the prototypes for
the other five Gallery chart types. Although AREA is replaced with
other graph types, such as SCATTER, BAR, COLUMN, PIE, or LINE,
the functions performed are the same. The first version displays the
dialog box containing the options available for a particular kind of
graph. You click the option you want.

In the second version, *type* specifies the number of an option on
the Gallery menu. For example, to choose the third area chart option,
you use =GALLERY.AREA(3).

COMBINATION?( )
COMBINATION(type)

The first version displays the dialog box for the Combination command on the Gallery menu. This box contains the combination chart options. You click the option you want.

In the second version, *type* must be a number that corresponds to a Gallery Combination chart option.

PREFERRED( )

This function duplicates the Gallery Preferred command. PREFERRED( ) changes the format of the active chart to the format defined with the Set Preferred command.

Chart Menu Commands

MAIN.CHART.TYPE?( )
MAIN.CHART.TYPE(type)

The first form, MAIN.CHART.TYPE?( ), displays the dialog box for Main Chart Type on the Chart menu. You then choose the kind of chart you want to use.

When you use the second form, *type* must be a number from 1 to 6. You use 1 for Area, 2 for Bar, 3 for Column, 4 for Line, 5 for Pie, or 6 for Scatter.

OVERLAY.CHART.TYPE?( )
OVERLAY.CHART.TYPE(type)

This function is similar to MAIN.CHART.TYPE, except for two differences. First, the selections refer to the overlay chart. And second, one more *type* code is available: 0 for None (no overlay chart desired).

LEGEND(logical)

This function has the capabilities of Add Legends and Delete Legends on the Chart menu. If *logical* is TRUE, a legend is added. If *logical* is FALSE, a legend is deleted.

SELECT.CHART( )

SELECT.CHART( ) is the equivalent of the Select Chart command on the Chart menu.

Macro Menu Commands

RUN?( )
RUN(ref)

The first version of RUN displays the dialog box for the Run command from the Macro menu. In the second version, you specify the macro you want to execute. The argument *ref* can be an external reference to a macro sheet or an external R1C1 reference in text format.

Action Commands

ACTIVATE(window)

The ACTIVATE(window) function changes the active window to the one specified. You can specify the *window* in two ways. You can put the window name in text format, as in "Budget" (or "Budget:5" if you have more than one window for the document). Or you can substitute the document name for *window*, but then the function always opens the first window of the document.

ACTIVATE.NEXT( )
ACTIVATE.PREV( )

The equivalents of Command-M and Command-Shift-M, respectively, these functions enable you to browse through a list of windows. No arguments are required.

CLOSE( )

This function closes the active window.

DATA.FIND.NEXT( )
DATA.FIND.PREV( )

These functions are the equivalent of pressing Command-F to find the next record and Command-Shift-F to find the previous record, respectively.

FORMULA(formula-text)

This function enters a formula in a cell. The *formula-text* argument can be a formula in text format that is entered in the active cell. Or *formula-text* can be a number, text, or a logical value that is entered as a constant. If the argument is a reference, it must have the R1C1 format. An example is =FORMULA("Now( )"), which places the DATE function in the selected cell on the worksheet.

FORMULA.ARRAY(formula-text)

You use this function to simulate pushing the Command key while entering an array formula. The *formula-text* argument can be either a formula in text format or a number, text, or logical value entered as a constant. Cell references in the array formula must be in the R1C1 format.

FORMULA.FILL(formula-text)

This function is the equivalent of pressing the Option key while entering a formula. FORMULA.FILL enters *formula-text* in the entire selection.

FORMULA.FIND.NEXT( )
FORMULA.FIND.PREV( )

The FORMULA.FIND.NEXT( ) and FORMULA.FIND.PREV( ) functions, which are equivalent to their counterpart instructions in the worksheet environment, find the next or previous record that matches the specified search text. FORMULA.FIND.NEXT is the equivalent of Command-H, and FORMULA.FIND.PREV is the same as Command-Shift-H. For these instructions to work, the macro must have executed the FORMULA.FIND function previously. These commands use the specifications in FORMULA.FIND to find the next and previous worksheet cells.

FULL(logical)

This function changes the active window's size. If *logical* is TRUE, Excel makes the window full size, just as you can do by double-clicking the title bar in the worksheet environment. If *logical* is FALSE, the window returns to its former size.

HLINE(number)
VLINE(number)

These functions affect the scrolling of your screen. They have the same effect on the active window as clicking the scroll arrow. If *number* is a positive integer, Excel scrolls the screen to the right or down by the number of lines specified. If *number* is a negative integer, Excel scrolls the screen to the left and up.

HPAGE(number)
VPAGE(number)

Clicking in the gray area of the scroll bar causes Excel to scroll a windowful of information at a time. These two functions have the same effect. HPAGE scrolls horizontally, and VPAGE scrolls vertically. If the *number* is positive, Excel scrolls the screen to the right or down the number of windows indicated. If the *number* is negative, Excel scrolls the screen to the left or up.

HSCROLL(column-number)
VSCROLL(row-number)

These commands are equivalent to dragging the scroll box in order to move the window horizontally or vertically. For *column-number* or *row-number*, you specify the row or column number of your destination in the sheet.

MOVE(x-number,y-number,window)

You use this function to move a window, just as you do by dragging the title bar when working in the worksheet environment. The argument *x-number* is the distance in pixels from the left edge of the screen; *y-number*, the distance in pixels from the top edge of the screen. Restrictions apply to the values you can give the arguments. The *x-number* argument cannot exceed the width of the screen,

512 pixels. And *y-number* must be greater than 40 but no greater than 342.

The *window* argument must be a window name in the form of text. To move the active window, you can omit the window name—for example, MOVE(100,100). If you want to display a window halfway or a third of the way down the screen, you can approximate a location. MOVE does not change a window's size or make a window active. MOVE's sole function is to control the location of windows.

SELECT(selection-ref,active-cell-ref)

With this function, you select cells or change the active worksheet cell. All the cells included in *selection-ref* are selected, and *active-cell-ref* becomes the active cell. If you use *active-cell-ref*, the active cell must be within the selection area. If you omit this argument, the active cell is the upper leftmost cell in the selection area. If you omit *selection-ref*, the selected area doesn't change.

The argument *selection-ref* must be either an R1C1 reference in the form of text or a reference to the active worksheet (for instance, !Total or Budget!Total). If you use the R1C1 style, the selection is relative to the current active cell in the worksheet. The argument *active-cell-ref* also can use both reference styles but refers to a single cell—for instance, !Z2 or "R[-2]C[3]".

When you record a macro with Relative Record On, the R1C1 style is used to record selections. With Absolute Record On, the selection is recorded as an absolute reference. For example, to select cell A10, you use SELECT(!A10). To select an entire range of cells, you specify the range and the cell you want to be active. SELECT(!A1:D8,!B5) is an example of selecting a range.

SIZE(x-number,y-number,window)

If you are working in the worksheet or chart environment, you can change the size of a window by dragging the size box. With the SIZE function, you can accomplish this same task from within a macro. (SIZE, however, doesn't alter the window's location; the upper left corner of the window stays the same.) You use *x-number* and *y-number* to specify the window's width and height, respectively. The maximum width is 542 positions of a window, and the maximum height is 342. The height number you specify cannot be greater than 303—the distance from the formula bar to the bottom of the screen. The *window* argument must be a window name in text form. If you omit the name, Excel uses the name of the active window.

Macro Calculation, Arguments, and User Interface Commands

ALERT(text,type)

This function controls the display of error and warning messages. You can display three kinds of Alert boxes, specified by the *type* argument: 1 for Note, 2 for Caution, and 3 for Stop. The *text* argument contains the message that appears in the box.

ARGUMENT(name,type,ref)
ARGUMENT(name,type)

The ARGUMENT function passes arguments to macros called from a worksheet function or from another macro. For each argument passed to the called macro, the called macro must contain one AR-GUMENT function. If you omit an ARGUMENT function, the called macro uses the error value #N/A. You put ARGUMENT functions at the beginning of a macro. The only function you can use before them is RESULT.

The arguments are *name*, which is defined in the macro sheet and permits the use of names in formulas; *type*, which defines acceptable values for the argument; and *ref*, which represents a cell reference. For *type*, you use 1 for Number, 2 for Text, 4 for Logical, 8 for Reference, 16 for Error, or 64 for Array. If you want to accept more than one type, you use the sum of the valid types. For example, to accept numbers and text, you use a *type* of 3. If you omit *type*, 7 is assumed, which indicates that a number, text, or logical value is acceptable. If the value passed is not of the type specified, the error value #VALUE! is returned.

In the version of ARGUMENT that includes the argument *ref*, the cell that *ref* refers to contains a constant of the type specified in *type*. When *type* is 8, you can't use this version of the function. Because *ref* is itself a cell, *ref* can't contain a cell address.

=ARGUMENT("Rate",1,A14) an example of the ARGUMENT function. The *name* is "Rate", and the *type* is 1, which indicates a numeric value. The value for *ref* is A14, indicating that Excel will assign the contents of that address to "Rate".

BEEP( )

This function sounds the Macintosh's bell. You can control the volume of the bell with the control panel settings. In automated applications, this function is useful for asking the operator for additional input or telling the operator that an error has occurred.

ECHO(logical)

This function controls screen updating while a macro is executing. When logical is FALSE, screen updating is turned off. In other words, the display remains constant. When logical is TRUE, screen updating is turned on. Every macro instruction that changes the screen causes the display to flicker. Turning off updating improves the speed of command macro execution. When a macro is completed, the screen is always updated, regardless of the setting.

ERROR(logical,ref)

With this function, you turn error checking on and off. A *logical* of TRUE turns on error checking and branches to the upper left corner of *ref*. If you don't use *ref*, a dialog box appears, displaying the error's cell address. You then can continue, stop, or switch to executing the macro a step at a time. When *logical* is FALSE, error checking is turned off, and errors are ignored.

GOTO(ref)

This function changes the flow of execution. The next instruction executed is contained in the upper leftmost cell in *ref*. The *ref* can be an external one, but the worksheet should be open; otherwise, the Alert box appears.

HALT( )

This function stops the running of all macros, including nested macros.

INPUT(prompt,type,title)

This function, which is one of the most powerful in Excel's Macro Command Language, enables you to create prompt messages for users. The input that a user provides is the result that INPUT returns. Both *prompt* and *title* must be text. Excel creates a dialog box for the prompt, using the *title* you specify and the text in *prompt*. If you omit *title*, the word *Input* appears at the top of the dialog box. When the user provides input, OK and Cancel boxes are available. Also, when the user is entering input, all the editing commands in the formula bar are available. Therefore, Paste Name and Paste Function can be used to create the function. If the user chooses Cancel or presses Command-period, INPUT returns the value FALSE.

The *type* argument specifies what input is acceptable and also tells Excel how to return the value entered. The acceptable types are 0 for Formula, 1 for Number, 2 for Text, 4 for Logical, 8 for Reference, 16 for Error, and 64 for Array. If the user enters the wrong type of input, Excel tries to convert the value. If Excel can't convert the value, the program displays an Alert box.

MESSAGE(logical,text)

You can use this function to keep users informed during time-consuming macros. When *logical* is TRUE, the message in *text* appears above the formula bar. When *logical* is FALSE, the message is not displayed. To display no message, you can use TRUE for the *logical* value and make *text* a null string (*""*).

RESULT(type)

This function controls the type of result a function macro returns. In a function macro that returns single values, RESULT is optional. In a function macro that returns cell references or arrays, RESULT is required and must be the first argument in the macro. For *type*, you use 1 for Number, 2 for Text, 4 for Logical, 8 for Reference, 16 for Error, and 64 for Array. If you want to allow more than one type of result, you can sum the numbers that represent the types. For instance, to allow either a number or text, you use a *type* of 3.

RETURN( )
RETURN(values)

This function stops the execution of the current macro. If the macro was executed with the Run command or the Option-Command-key sequence, control returns to the user.

In the second version of the function, if the macro was called by another macro or a function in a worksheet, control returns to the formula that called the macro. In that situation, *values* contains the text, logical value, error value, array, or reference. You can specify the type of this returned value with the RESULT function.

SET.NAME(name,value)

This function assigns a value to a name in the macro sheet. You use SET.NAME to store constants or intermediate values during a macro calculation. The *name* argument must be text, but *value* can be any kind of value, including an array or reference. If *value* is a cell reference, *name* refers to that reference. For example, SET.NAME("Rate",.12) establishes the name Rate in the macro sheet and gives Rate a value of .12. SET.NAME("Rate",A2) establishes the name Rate and defines it as a reference to A2.

If you want *name* to refer to the value of the reference rather than the reference itself, you use SET.NAME with the DEREF function. For instance, in the statement SET.NAME("Rate",DEREF(A2)), if A2 contains .14, Rate is assigned the value .14.

SET.VALUE(ref,values)

This function initializes cells in macros. The *ref* argument points to cells in the macro sheet, and SET.VALUE converts those cells to the value in *values*. If the area is a range of cells, *values* should be an array of values of the same size as *ref*. SET.VALUE does not destroy any formulas that may be in cells.

STEP( )

STEP( ) invokes Step mode, which executes instructions one at a time and therefore is useful for debugging macros. STEP( ) displays a dialog box with Step, Halt, and Continue options. You can click Step to execute the next instruction, Halt to stop the macro, or Continue to end Step mode. While a macro is running, you can turn the Step mode option off and on by pressing Command-period. This function requires no arguments.

Miscellaneous Commands

ABSREF(ref-text,ref)

Using the upper left corner of *ref*, this function applies the relative reference directions in *ref-text* and returns an absolute cell address. For example, ABSREF(*"R[-1C[-1]"*,D4) returns C3 because C3 is one row up from and one column to the left of D4.

You can apply this function to external references as well. For instance, ABSREF(*"R[-1]C[-1]"*,Budget!D4) returns Budget!C3.

You also can apply this function to a range of cells. For example, ABSREF(*"R[-1]C[2]:R[3]C[3]"*,D4:G2) returns F3:G7. The relative references are applied to the upper leftmost cell in the range, which is D4 for both the beginning and end of the range address returned.

ACTIVE.CELL( )

This function returns a reference to the active cell as an external reference. For instance, if Z10 is the active cell in a document called Projections, ACTIVE.CELL( ) returns Projections!Z10.

CALLER( )

This function returns the reference of the cell that called the active macro. You may want a macro to take different actions, depending on the routine that called the macro. The cell address that this function returns enables you to pinpoint the location in the calling macro at the time the call is executed. If the macro is called with Run or the Option-Command-key sequence, CALLER returns #REF!.

DEREF(ref)

DEREF returns the value of the cells in the argument *ref*. This function is convenient because sometimes you want to refer to a cell's address and other times to the value the cell contains. For example, in SET.NAME(*"Address"*,B3), Address refers to B3, the cell address.

If *ref* is one cell, DEREF returns a single value. If *ref* is a range of cells, the function returns an array of values. If you use the SET.NAME function with DEREF, the statement returns the contents of the cell. For example, if B3 contains the value 22 and the statement SET.NAME("Contents",DEREF(B3)) is executed, then "Contents" refers to the value 22.

DOCUMENTS( )

This function returns an array of text values containing the names of all documents currently open. The names are arranged in alphabetical order. They can be selected with the INDEX function and used in functions that accept document names as arguments.

GET.FORMULA(ref)

This function returns the contents of the upper left cell of *ref* as the contents would appear in the formula bar. The contents are in text form; references are in R1C1 format. If the cell contains a value rather than a formula, the function returns a value. For example, if A3 contains the formula A1+A2, GET.FORMULA(!A3) returns "=R[-2]C+R[-1]C". If, on the other hand, A3 contains 678, the formula returns 678. This macro command and the one that follows are used primarily in automated applications in which you may want to take different actions depending on operator input or actions taken up to this point.

GET.NAME(name)

This function provides the definition of *name* as it would appear in the Define Name "Refers to" box. The *name* argument, which must be in text form, can be an external reference to a name defined in a worksheet or macro sheet. References in the *name* argument must be in R1C1 format.

LINKS(document)

This function displays the file names for all external worksheet references in the form of a text array. For *document*, you should specify the name in text form. If *document* is omitted, the active document is used. When no external references exist, #N/A is returned. For example, if you want to open all the linked files for a worksheet named Annual, you use OPEN.LINKS(LINKS("Annual")). OPEN.LINKS opens the specified files, and LINKS displays all the document names contained in external references in Annual.

OFFSET(ref,row-offset,column-offset)

This function generates a new reference of the same size and shape as the argument *ref*. The location is shifted from the original by the *row-offset* and *column-offset* arguments, which must be numbers. If *row-offset* or *column-offset* is zero, the new reference begins in the same row or column as the argument *ref*. If *row-offset* or *column-offset* is a positive number, the reference is shifted down or to the right. If *row-offset* or *column-offset* is a negative number, the reference is shifted up or to the left. If either *offset* argument causes the new reference to go beyond the edge of the worksheet, #REF! is returned. For example, OFFSET(B2,3,2) returns D5, and OFFSET(B2:D4,-1,-1) returns A1:C3.

RELREF(ref-1,ref-2)

This function provides a relative text reference in R1C1 format for *ref-1*. This reference is relative to the starting location of *ref-2* (upper left cell of *ref-2*). For instance, RELREF(B1,C2) returns "R[-1][C-1]".

SELECTION( )

This function provides an external cell reference to the cells selected. For example, if the document in the active window is Budget, and cells B2:B10 are selected, the function returns Budget!B2:B10.

WINDOWS( )

This function generates an array of text values that includes all the windows on the screen. The active window is listed first, followed by the other windows, according to their level numbers.

Index

More Computer Knowledge

LOTUS SOFTWARE TITLES

1-2-3 Business Formula Handbook	19.95
1-2-3 for Business	18.95
1-2-3 Financial Macros	19.95
1-2-3 Macro Library	19.95
1-2-3 Tips, Tricks, and Traps	19.95
Using 1-2-3, 2nd Edition	19.95
Using 1-2-3 Workbook and Disk	29.95
Using Symphony	23.95
Symphony: Advanced Topics	19.95
Symphony Macros and the Command Language	22.95
Symphony Tips, Tricks, and Traps	21.95

IBM TITLES

IBM PC Expansion & Software Guide	29.95
IBM's Personal Computer, 2nd Edition	17.95
Networking IBM PCs: A Practical Guide	18.95
Using PC DOS	21.95
PC DOS Workbook	14.95

APPLICATIONS SOFTWARE TITLES

dBASE III Plus Application	19.95
dBASE III Advanced Programming	22.95
dBASE III Handbook	19.95
Multiplan Models for Business	15.95
R:base 5000 User's Guide	19.95
Using AppleWorks	16.95
Using Dollars and Sense	14.95
Using Enable	17.95
Using Excel	19.95
Excel Macro Library	19.95
Using Javelin	19.95
Using Paradox	19.95
Using Reflex	19.95
Using Smart	22.95

Que Order Line: **1-800-428-5331**
All prices subject to change without notice.

Books from Que

WORD-PROCESSING TITLES

Improve Your Writing with Word Processing 12.95
Using DisplayWrite 18.95
Using Microsoft Word 16.95
Using MultiMate 18.95
Using the PFS Family: FILE, WRITE, GRAPH, REPORT 14.95
Using WordPerfect 18.95
Using WordStar 2000 . . . . 17.95

COMPUTER SYSTEMS TITLES

Apple Favorite Programs Explained 12.95
Commodore Favorite Programs Explained 12.95
Introducing the Apple IIc: Applications and Programming . 12.95
MS-DOS User's Guide 19.95
The HP Touchscreen 19.95
The HP 110 Portable: Power to Go! 16.95
Using NetWare 24.95

PROGRAMMING AND TECHNICAL TITLES

Amiga Programming Guide 18.95
Advanced C: Techniques and Applications 21.95
Common C Functions 17.95
C Programmer's Library 21.95
C Programming Guide, 2nd Edition 19.95
CP/M Programmer's Encyclopedia 19.95
C Self-Study Guide 16.95
Turbo Pascal for BASIC Programmers 14.95
Turbo Pascal Program Library 16.95
Understanding UNIX: A Conceptual Guide 19.95
Understanding XENIX: A Conceptual Guide 19.95

Que Order Line: **1-800-428-5331**
All prices subject to change without notice.

Polish Your Apple Techniques
with Computer Books from Que

Using Excel
by Mary V. Campbell

A comprehensive reference, *Using Excel* offers a thorough examination of Microsoft's powerful spreadsheet for the Macintosh 512K. The author provides plenty of examples and screen shots to help you understand and use all of Excel's capabilities, including advanced features such as data management, graphics, macros, and arrays. This book's practical, hands-on approach will have you using Excel productively sooner than you ever expected.

Using AppleWorks
by Arthur and Elaine Aaron

Using AppleWorks will help you with every stage of your program. You will learn how to set up Apple IIe or IIc, install AppleWorks, create files and file commands, enter and edit data, and configure and use your printer. This book shows the more advanced user how to use the individual functions of word processing, databases, and spreadsheets and how to integrate them in one report.

Whether your needs are for business, home, or school, *Using AppleWorks* is an excellent learning tool.

Introducing the Apple IIc: Applications and Programming
by Chris DeVoney

The IIc is the exciting portable computer from Apple. Designed to run the extensive selection of software available for the popular Apple IIe, this computer is a winner! *Introducing the Apple IIc* describes and explains the hardware components of the IIc, as well as available peripherals. The book also discusses the ProDOS and DOS 3.3 operating systems and programming languages. Several popular applications packages are described in detail with photographs of appropriate screens. If you want to understand the benefits and capabilites of the IIc, be sure to read this interesting book.

Using Dollars and Sense
by John Hannah

This applications-oriented book from Monogram addresses the questions most commonly asked of Monogram's support line for business applications. In the home and small business, *Using Dollars and Sense* will teach readers how to track their accounts, determine their net worth, and estimate their tax liability at any time of the year. Additional features include "hands-on hints" and actual examples of business applications representing different business styles.

Mail to: Que Corporation • P. O. Box 50507 • Indianapolis, IN 46250

Item	Title	Price	Quantity	Extension
198	Using Excel	$19.95		
181	Using AppleWorks	$16.95		
152	Introducing the Apple IIc: Applications and Programming	$12.95		
182	Using Dollars and Sense	$14.95		
		Book Subtotal		
	Shipping & Handling ($1.75 per item)			
	Indiana Residents Add 5% Sales Tax			
		GRAND TOTAL		

Method of Payment:

☐ Check   ☐ VISA   ☐ MasterCard   ☐ AMEX

Card Number _____ Exp. Date _____

Cardholder's Name _____

Ship to _____

Address _____

City _____ State _____ ZIP _____

If you can't wait, call **1-800-428-5331** and order TODAY.

All prices subject to change without notice.

REGISTER YOUR COPY OF
EXCEL MACRO LIBRARY

Register your copy of *Excel Macro Library* and receive information about Que's newest products. Complete this registration card and return it to Que Corporation, P.O. Box 50507, Indianapolis, IN 46250.

Name _____

Address _____

City _____ State _____ ZIP _____

Phone _____

Where did you buy your copy of *Excel Macro Library*?

_____

How do you plan to use the information in this book?

_____

_____

_____

What other kinds of publications about microcomputers would you be interested in? _____

_____

_____

THANK YOU!

_____

_____

_____

_____

Que Corporation
P. O. Box 50507
Indianapolis, IN 46250

Take the Fast Track!

EXCEL MACRO LIBRARY DISK   Only $79.95

The quickest route to using the macros presented in this book is the *Excel Macro Library* Disk. You will be up and running in no time at all with these tested, accurate, ready-to-use macros. Use them to instantly automate your worksheets, or modify them for complex custom-designed applications.

Available in the popular Macintosh format, the *Excel Macro Library* Disk is a convenience the busy user will treasure.

Order yours TODAY!

Mail to: Que Corporation • P. O. Box 50507 • Indianapolis, IN 46250

Please send _____ copy(ies) of the *Excel Macro Library* Disk in the Apple Macintosh format ($79.95).

Subtotal	$	_____
Shipping & Handling ($2.50 per item)	$	_____
Indiana Residents Add 5% Sales Tax	$	_____
TOTAL	$	_____

Check ☐   VISA ☐   MasterCard ☐   AMEX ☐

Card Number _____ Expiration Date _____

Cardholder's Name _____

Ship to _____

Address _____

City _____ State _____ ZIP _____

If you can't wait, call **1-800-428-5331** and order TODAY.

All prices subject to change without notice.

Que Corporation
P. O. Box 50507
Indianapolis, IN 46250